Michael Moore and the ~~Rhetoric of Documentary~~

MICHAEL MOORE

AND THE

RHETORIC OF DOCUMENTARY

Edited by Thomas W. Benson and Brian J. Snee

Southern Illinois University Press
Carbondale

Cover illustration: The sign reads "The Facts Don't Lie: Moore '04"

Library of Congress Cataloging-in-Publication Data
Michael Moore and the rhetoric of documentary / edited by Thomas
   W. Benson and Brian J. Snee.
   pages cm
Includes bibliographical references and index.
   ISBN 978-0-8093-3407-0 (pbk. : alk. paper)
   ISBN 0-8093-3407-0 (pbk. : alk. paper)
   ISBN 978-0-8093-3408-7 (ebook)
   ISBN 0-8093-3408-9 (ebook)
   1. Moore, Michael, 1954 April 23—Criticism and interpretation.
   2. Documentary films—Political aspects—History and criticism.
   3. Motion pictures—Political aspects—United States. I. Benson,
   Thomas W. editor. II. Snee, Brian J. editor.
PN1998.3.M665M525 2015
791.4302'33092—dc23   2014034578

The paper used in this publication meets the minimum requirements
   of American National Standard for Information Sciences—Perma-
   nence of Paper for Printed Library Materials, ANSI Z39.48-1992. ∞

Contents

Michael Moore and the Rhetoric of Documentary

1. Michael Moore and the Rhetoric of Documentary: Art, Argument, Affect

Thomas W. Benson and Brian J. Snee

[handwritten: Supportive evidence]

[handwritten: language designed to have a persuasive or impressive effect on its audience — way with words]

his book is a collection of original essays by scholars and critics who undertake a film-by-film critical analysis of the documentaries of Michael Moore. These close readings of the films illuminate the contributions of Moore to the art of rhetoric and to documentary, analyze the progressive political arguments of the films, and explore how Moore cultivates affect and sentiment not simply to arouse support but also to bring a radical perspective to life as thought and feeling.

Michael Moore has contributed to a renewal of documentary by responding to historical change and opportunity, as the earliest practitioners would have understood. John Grierson, a founder of the documentary idea, wrote in 1942, "The materials of citizenship today are different and the perspectives wider and more difficult, but we have, as ever, the duty of exploring them and of waking the heart and will with regard to them. That duty is what documentary is about."[1] Michael Moore's own adventure in "the materials of citizenship" and "waking the heart" introduced changes that over a quarter of a century have challenged the roots of documentary.

Brian Winston has argued that Michael Moore "liberates documentary" from the "burden Grierson laid on the documentary," while suggesting that Moore's films raise additional questions about their own fundamental value as political argument:

> The burden Grierson laid on the documentary was to pretend that his films were reports on the news pages, as it were, when in fact they were editorials for the established order. Moore liberates documentary from

this spurious position and admits it is a species of editorializing *in its essence*. Complaints that he is partial, biased, unfair and simple-minded (while all true) are completely irrelevant to the basic documentary value of his work. His ethical strength is that, however dubious his treatment of those he films can be on occasion . . . his audiences can be in no doubt whatsoever about his position. No pretended "fly-on-the-wall" he. Moore might have abandoned the sober Griersonian "public education" tone, but he is making documentaries nevertheless.[2]

[handwritten margin note: Know where he stands!]

We agree with Winston that Michael Moore is certainly making documentary films and that he can be "partial, biased, unfair, and simple-minded," and yet these two observations leave much to be discovered about Moore's contributions to documentary and to the political conversation. The present collection is our own exploration as scholars of rhetoric and media into the sorts of public rhetoric Michael Moore has created in a hugely successful career as a documentary filmmaker. In our account of Moore's reputation and the reception of his films, we rely heavily on responses to Moore in the popular press, not because we suppose they are the best arbiters of Moore's achievements in the art of documentary—that will take a long while to sort out, though film scholars in a variety of disciplines have made a good start—but because the popular press both reveals and constructs Moore's persona and reputation, both of which have a bearing on the rhetoric of the films. As a rhetorical matter, Moore achieves public status as the author of his works, though it is good to keep in mind from a historical perspective that film is a collaborative art, calling on the skills of many others in preparation, production, postproduction, circulation, and publicity.

Michael Moore was born in Flint, Michigan, on April 23, 1954, to middle-class parents, a General Motors assembly line worker and an office secretary. He was raised in the Catholic Church and educated in Catholic schools. After considering the priesthood, Moore turned his attention to politics and media. According to his biography in the *New York Times*, Moore "won a merit badge as an Eagle Scout by creating a slide show exposing environmentally unfriendly businesses in Flint, and in 1972, when 18-year-olds were granted the right to vote, he ran for a seat on the Flint school board, soon becoming one of the youngest people in the United States to win an election for public office."[3]

After a year at the University of Michigan's Flint campus, Moore dropped out of college. He eventually started an alternative newspaper, the *Flint Voice* (later the *Michigan Voice*). The muckraking publication provided Moore with a media outlet for his developing views on social, political, and economic issues, a mission that continues to define his career. In 1986, Moore closed the paper when he was hired to edit the national liberal magazine *Mother Jones*, whose offices were located in San Francisco. Moore lasted only four months before being fired. The details of the events that led to his sudden dismissal remain contested. Moore has long maintained, including in his film *Roger & Me*, that he was let go after putting an unemployed autoworker from Flint on the magazine's cover. Others tell a different story. Writer Paul Berman, whom *Mother Jones* had hired to write a piece on Nicaragua and the Sandinistas that Moore refused to print, later described Moore as "a very ideological guy and not a very well-educated guy."[4] Moore sued the publication for wrongful dismissal, eventually settling out of court for a small sum that he used as seed money for a documentary about General Motors and the city of Flint.

Roger & Me (1989) changed Michael Moore's life and career, and it led some journalists to claim that he had changed the face of documentary film. This is a claim that scholars of the long and distinguished history of documentary might justifiably resist, but it helps us see, from a rhetorical perspective, how rapidly Moore established an outsize public reputation. That reputation came to have a force of its own. Matt Labash of the *Weekly Standard* writes that "pre-*Roger*, social-conscience documentaries (is there any other kind?) tended to be low-sugar, high-fiber affairs. Whether the subject was striking miners, Great Plains soil erosion, or copulating manatees, these pictures were more medicinal than entertaining. *Roger* was different, and it became to documentaries what the New Journalism had been to feature writing. Moore infused the form with subjective vitality, inserting himself into his narrative to drive it with a novelist's ingenuity. What he delivered in *Roger* was a dark and devastatingly funny social satire—a tautly edited trove of snappy narration, vivid characters, and cruel ironies."[5] Labash's comments about the mainstream documentary are surely oversimplified, but they do reflect something of the public reputation of documentary at the time Moore upended expectations.

Moore's documentary was personal, political, funny, and rude. He was on-screen as his own witness and on the sound track as interpreter of the scenes in which he did not appear. He combined biographical and historical accounts with a stirring spirit of radical nostalgia for progressivism and the Social Democratic New Deal compact.

The commercial and critical success of *Roger & Me* initiated Michael Moore's transformation from failed magazine editor to a rich and famous documentary filmmaker. Moore has become a public figure whose name is regularly invoked in connection with politics and public policy, for his unapologetic progressive arguments and for the force of his political persona. His work is cited as a reference point in virtually any serious critical commentary on the current state of documentary, even in books and articles that are about other filmmakers. His political views have become place markers of political journalism and debate, both left and right. Conservatives disparage a position by saying that Michael Moore believes it. It may well be that the public reputation of Moore as a filmmaker obscures the work of many other worthy and influential—and perhaps better—filmmakers, who prepared the way for him and who will continue to make contributions to documentary after he has moved on. Still, his public reputation remains a touchstone in the popular press.

In October 2004, soon after the release of *Fahrenheit 9/11* and in the midst of his son's presidential reelection campaign, former president George H. W. Bush said in an interview that Michael Moore was a "total ass, slimeball" and that it was "outrageous, his lies about my family."[6] That a former president would use such crude language in public was peculiar. The incident was widely reported, adding to the sense that Moore, in eliciting such a remark, had become a destabilizing force, able to induce major political figures to enact something other than their usual self-portrayals. Precisely this effect is at the center of many of Moore's films, so even while President Bush disparaged Moore, he seemed to be enacting Moore's picture of him and other leaders. The Moore effect was taking place outside the Moore film, as an aftereffect and as a rhetorical frame. And it was news.

Michael Moore has captured the sort of celebrity that makes his name a vernacular sign, with sharply varying connotations depending on one's political views and commitments and on one's vision of the decorum of political debate and the burdens of documentary film. Moore is sufficiently famous that when his name is mentioned in news stories, it is not thought necessary to identify him; it is assumed that readers and viewers will know who he is. Thus, for example, when Pennsylvania congressman John Murtha, a longtime hawk, called in 2005 for the withdrawal of US troops from Iraq, the Bush administration accused him of being a "Michael Moore."

In 2009, Bill Moyers interviewed Wendell Potter, a retired health insurance executive. Potter said he had resigned his job to campaign against the industry partly because of Michael Moore's *Sicko*, which he had been assigned to undermine as part of a vast public relations and lobbying campaign.

> WENDELL POTTER: I thought that he hit the nail on the head with his movie. But the industry, from the moment that the industry learned that Michael Moore was taking on the health care industry, it was really concerned.
>
> BILL MOYERS: What were they afraid of?
>
> WENDELL POTTER: They were afraid that people would believe Michael Moore.[7]

In January 2010, the US Supreme Court issued a sharply controversial five–four decision in the case of *Citizens United v. Federal Election Commission*. The ruling, according to commentators on both sides of the issues, overthrew a century of restrictions on corporate spending to influence elections. Michael Moore became part of the narrative of *Citizens United*. The triggering events in the *Citizens United* case arose when the Federal Election Commission (FEC) declared that the film *Hillary: The Movie*, by conservative political activist David Bossie, could not be advertised on television or broadcast as a paid advertisement during the 2008 presidential primary season, as it constituted a direct election appeal by a corporation, in violation of the McCain-Feingold Act. In the lead in the *Washington Post* coverage of the *Citizens United* decision, Philip Rucker directly links this momentous case to Michael Moore, writing that David Bossie, "a Republican campaign operative" who in 2004 produced the film *Celsius 41.11* as an attempt to refute Moore's *Fahrenheit 9/11*, later made another film, attacking Hillary Clinton, which precipitated the *Citizens United* case. "And after it became clear that Bossie's longtime enemy Hillary Rodham Clinton would run for president, Citizens United released another flick: 'Hillary: The Movie.' Featuring a who's-who cast of right-wing commentators, the 2008 film takes viewers on a savaging journey through Clinton's scandals. The sole compliment about the then-senator comes from conservative firebrand Ann Coulter: 'Looks good in a pantsuit.'"[8]

From the perspective of this book about Michael Moore's films, it is interesting not only that Moore's work provoked a response that led to a radical change in US election laws, but also that when his role was described, it could be assumed that any reader would know exactly who he was without further exposition. The original motivator for this unusual level of public recognition was the body of documentary film work created by Michael Moore, though by now his persona and his work have extended far beyond the films themselves.

Moore's controversial movies have addressed a range of national issues, including presidential politics, foreign wars, school violence, media sensationalism, health care, and corporate greed. Moore's larger public reputation, perhaps influencing the reception of the films, depends as well on his other public activities as an author and activist. In addition to his documentary films, Moore has written several best-selling books, some as companions to his films and television series, others as freestanding advocacy of his politics. Moore's first book, *Downsize This! Random Threats from an Unarmed American*, was published by Crown Publishers in 1996. The book was an extension of Moore's economic critique of corporate capitalism articulated in *Roger & Me*. The book tour that followed its publication was documented in Moore's second film, *The Big One* (1998). The *San Francisco Chronicle* printed a review of the book that forecast the power Moore was beginning to accumulate, noting, "Moore's subtitle is 'Random Threats From an Unarmed American,' but it's not true: This book, like his films, is a lethal weapon."[9] The *New York Times* offered a similarly positive review but questioned whether Moore's on-screen persona could survive the celebrity status that the author and filmmaker was beginning to achieve: "Mr. Moore may not be able to maintain his image (pro-union, plain folks, blue collar, never went to college) much longer. Once a man has negotiated, among other things, a $4 million deal with Warner Brothers (involving 'Roger and Me'), there's no going back to Flint, Mich. But he still seems fighting mad at corporations and governments on behalf of women, blacks, Holocaust survivors and the working class."[10]

Following *Downsize This!* was another book, *Stupid White Men* (2002), which tested Moore's ability to criticize American leaders and institutions during a period of heightened patriotism. Moore finished writing the book before the attacks of September 11, 2001, but publication was set for the fall. Moore's publisher, HarperCollins, feared that the book would be rejected by even liberal Americans in the post-9/11 climate of national unity. The book's subtitle—"*. . . And Other Sorry Excuses for the State of the Nation!*"—set the tone. Rupert Murdoch's News Corporation, the parent company of HarperCollins, threatened to delay publication unless Moore rewrote much of the book. When Moore began to speak publicly about a possible delay as corporate censorship, he found an ally in Ann Sparanese, a librarian in Englewood, New Jersey. According to the *Library Journal*, "Michael Moore says she saved his book, *Stupid White Men*, which his publisher refused to release because it was critical of George W. Bush. The publisher disputes that this is the reason the book was finally distributed, but when Sparanese raised the alarm, librarians swamped the company with complaints and orders. Sparanese sees this as proof that librarians can fight back—and win—against the squashing of dissent."[11] *Stupid White Men* spent fifty consecutive weeks on the *New York Times* best-seller list, including eight weeks at number one.

Other books by Moore include a companion publication to *Fahrenheit 9/11*, a 2008 voting guide, and a collection of supportive letters that Moore received from military families after the release of *Fahrenheit 9/11*. On the book jacket of *Here Comes Trouble: Stories from My Life* (2011), Moore identifies himself as a filmmaker and author. More recently, he calls himself a "public figure."

Moore has made several attempts at television as a rhetorical vehicle, though never with great success. Despite the hopes of some of his supporters and some liberals who lamented the rise of right-wing talk radio, Moore never became the liberal answer to Rush Limbaugh, Fox News, and the editorial page of the *Wall Street Journal*—what Kathleen Hall Jamieson and Joseph N. Cappella called the "Echo Chamber."[12] Moore was a more independent voice, and he was up to something else. In 1994, *TV Nation*, directed and hosted by Moore, debuted on NBC in the United States and on the BBC2 in the United Kingdom. *TV Nation* was a mix of comedy and video journalism similar in style to *Roger & Me*. Moore later described the scene of his unorthodox pitch to NBC television executives, which somehow gained their support: "'It would be a cross between *60 Minutes* and Fidel Castro on laughing gas.' The suits sat up in their chairs, interested. 'The show would be the most liberal thing ever seen on TV. In fact, it would go beyond "liberals" because liberals are a bunch of wimps and haven't gotten us anything. This show would go boldly where no one has gone before.'"[13] To Moore's surprise, the show was picked up. It ran for two seasons in the United States, the first on NBC and the second on Fox. In all, seventeen episodes were broadcast. *TV Nation* struggled in the ratings, but someone in Washington, DC, was watching. On May 10, 1994, a bill was introduced in the US House of Representatives designating August 16 of that year as *TV Nation* Day.[14]

A similarly formatted comedy–news magazine program by Moore titled *The Awful Truth* debuted in 1999. This program also lasted only two seasons, on Bravo in the United States and on Channel 4 in the United Kingdom. At least one episode of the show later resurfaced in Moore's documentary work. In one episode, Moore staged a mock funeral outside the corporate headquarters of the health-care corporation Humana. The funeral was for a man—not yet dead—who had been denied a potentially lifesaving organ transplant because the procedure was not cost-efficient. Moore drew inspiration from this episode when he made his health-care film, *Sicko* (2007).[15] His most recent TV venture was *Michael Moore Live*, a six-part late-night series broadcast in 1999 on Channel 4 in the United Kingdom. The series never aired in the United States.

Moore spent much of the first decade of the twenty-first century trying his hand at political activism. He publicly supported Ralph Nader in the 2000 presidential election, is assumed to have made *Fahrenheit 9/11* primarily to defeat George W. Bush in the 2004 election, and chronicled his get-out-the-vote rallies before the 2008 election in his documentary *Slacker Uprising*. Moore also has worked closely in recent years with the progressive advocacy group and political action committee MoveOn.

The public's responses to Michael Moore and his films were already intense when *Fahrenheit 9/11* (2004) turned up the temperature on his partisan rhetoric in a way that changed how audiences view Moore as a filmmaker. His subsequent films seem to have been designed to agitate at least as much as investigate, a formula that has earned Moore millions of dollars, four of the top-grossing documentaries of all time, and a long list of enemies.

Roger & Me reinvented a genre that much of the public had all but forgotten. During the twentieth century, documentary film, with some notable exceptions, had often been relegated to remote outposts on the cultural landscape, such as art house theaters, public television stations, and college campuses. Moore's films helped revive attention to the documentary mainstream once again and helped create a market for his successors. Films by others, like *Super Size Me* (2004) and *An Inconvenient Truth* (2006), got onto theater screens and found a broad audience, possibly because of the visibility and profitability of *Roger & Me* and *Bowling for Columbine* (2002). Moore's commercial and financial success may have given producers, distributors, and exhibitors renewed confidence in nonfiction film as a marketable commodity. Furthermore, his work reminded audiences that documentary and entertainment are not exclusive categories.

The production and marketing of Moore's films contributed to the development of a new documentary practice. Though arguably he did not invent any single element in the new model, Moore did bring visibility and success to a model that spoke with a personal voice about a contemporary social issue. The productions are usually shot in videotape with a single camera, and they use stock footage from news and other sources to lend authenticity and scope. Some of the films find their way into theaters, having been adopted by distributors, but they also have a long second life, first through videotape and DVD sales and rentals, and more recently through Internet sales and streaming video. Moore's films were part of a larger wave of political documentaries that found large audiences and new ways to challenge or hitchhike on the political economy of an increasingly consolidated media system.[16]

Moore helped put documentary film back at the center of political debate, acting as filmmaker, participant, and reflexive interrogator of his own method. His films found an audience in large part because they were unlike what audiences had come to expect from the genre, and yet they still gained force from the implied sense that documentary is based on the real. Bill Nichols notes that documentary films are increasingly shot in what he calls a "participatory mode," in which the filmmaker appears on screen and is part of the narrative.[17] Moore did not invent the mode, but he exploited it in fresh ways. The image of Moore in his baseball hat and windbreaker was central to the rhetoric and appeal of his early films. The frumpy Everyman asked embarrassing questions of a corrupt culture, and audiences seemed to love it. That Everyman has been replaced by a rich and sometimes caustic political activist, but even that image is at the center of the rhetoric of his more recent films. Michael Renov has explored the phenomenon of self-reflexivity in documentary in *The Subject of Documentary*. Like Nichols, Renov acknowledges the popularity of documentary films in which the director appears as the star and the narrative centers on the making of the film.[18] This, too, was not invented by Moore, but he popularized it and gave it a new flavor. Moore thus re-created documentary as a genre in which the *auteur* could work both behind and in front of the camera, in contrast to the typical (but not universal) invisibility of the author in the preceding generation of direct cinema and *cinéma vérité*, in documentary by artists such as

Frederick Wiseman, Richard Leacock, Donn Pennebaker, Robert Drew, Al and Susan Raymond, Joan Churchill, and the Maysles brothers.[19] At the same time, Moore's own work owes much to the work of these and other predecessors, not least to the prestige and artistic merit of nearly a century of documentary film and photography, including Robert Flaherty, John Grierson, the New Deal documentarians, Charlotte Zwerin, Barbara Kopple, Les Blank, Connie Field, and Julie Reichert, as well as to his contemporaries, such as Robert Greenwald, Ken Burns, Werner Herzog, Alex Gibney, and Laura Poitras.

The reflexivity of Moore's films is highly controlled and delimited. Moore's presence in his films gives them a seeming directness, as if the spectator is directly observing the process of filmmaking, which has nothing to hide. On the other hand, Moore is being followed by a camera operator and sound recordist, he and his crew are working to present a carefully planned scenario, and Moore and his collaborators are able to edit the results of his encounters and add voice-over and other materials. The reflexivity is an effect, an appearance—it is not an absolute condition, nor could it be. Hence the reflexivity effect itself becomes a potential source of mystification.

Moore's *Bowling for Columbine* won the Academy Award for Best Documentary and brought in $4 million at the box office. The film, an investigation of gun violence in the United States, derives its name from a massacre by students at a high school in Colorado. Accepting the Oscar at the awards ceremony on March 23, 2003, five days after the US invasion of Iraq, Moore set off something of a scandal when he said:

> Whoa. On behalf of our producers Kathleen Glynn and Michael Donovan from Canada, I'd like to thank the Academy for this. I have invited my fellow documentary nominees on the stage with us, and we would like to—they're here in solidarity with me because we like nonfiction.
>
> We like nonfiction and we live in fictitious times. We live in the time where we have fictitious election results that elect a fictitious president. We live in a time where we have a man sending us to war for fictitious reasons.
>
> Whether it's the fiction of duct tape or fiction of orange alerts we are against this war, Mr. Bush. Shame on you, Mr. Bush, shame on you. And any time you got the Pope and the Dixie Chicks against you, your time is up. Thank you very much.[20]

As Moore spoke, members of the audience cheered or booed him, and his brief speech was eventually ended by the withdrawal of the microphone into the floor and a wave of music from the orchestra.[21] Now, years later, Michael Moore is a member of the board of governors of the Motion Picture Academy of Arts and Sciences.

In 2004, Moore's *Fahrenheit 9/11* agitated audiences, and it changed the rules of how such films are distributed and consumed. Moore's assault on the Bush administration, the Iraq War, and conservative politics marks the beginning of the "new political documentary."[22] *Fahrenheit 9/11* may be the most controversial nonfiction film ever made; it was highly polarizing in a sharply partisan age, and it attracted the heated attention of politicians, commentators, and the public. Moore's film was strategically released during the 2004 presidential campaign in an apparent attempt to influence the election. Some earlier political documentaries were released well after an election to offer a behind-the-scenes look at what voters could not see during the campaign. *Fahrenheit 9/11* purported to offer a revealing and directly critical look at candidate Bush before audiences went to the polls. This now common technique was unusual in 2004, and although Moore's effort to thwart Bush's reelection failed, he contributed to making the documentary film a staple of the preelection campaign cycle.

Fahrenheit 9/11 mobilized liberal voters and galvanized conservatives, including right-leaning documentary filmmakers. Because documentaries can now be produced in digital format and quickly, by making extensive use of preexisting footage and online editing software, Moore's film drew respondents in kind. Several films were released straight to DVD in the wake of *Fahrenheit 9/11*—some offering unprecedented point-by-point refutations of Moore's claims. These films also emerged before the 2004 election. *Fahren*HYPE *9/11* and *Celsius 41.11* are among the films called into existence solely as rebuttals to *Fahrenheit 9/11*. Debates have long been a standard part of campaign seasons, but point-counterpoint cinematic debate was new and largely owed to the work of Michael Moore.[23]

Critics and scholars have been divided about Moore's films but increasingly agree that he has brought something new and influential to documentary rhetoric. Robert Brent Toplin's *Michael Moore's "Fahrenheit 9/11": How One Film Divided a Nation*, a work that brings the perspective of an academic historian to the film, raises important questions about the potential of the film to contribute to documentary rhetoric, and to the larger American conversation more generally, asserting that "the question is not whether *Fahrenheit 9/11* delivered *the* truth to audiences but whether the movie communicated *a* truth," a question that he answers affirmatively and in detail.[24] Toplin writes that Moore's film, while certainly partisan, is squarely in the tradition of documentary film and writing, and that Moore raised legitimate issues having to do with the 2000 election and the Bush administration's initiation and conduct of the war in Iraq, employing information and argument that have largely been vindicated. Moore's film, he says, "demonstrated the potential of a feature-length documentary film to engage the American people in lively discussions about important political matters."[25]

Roger Rapoport's investigative biography, claiming that Moore's is "the media's longest coming of age story," argues that "finding someone to blame for your difficulties remains his unique artistic achievement." And yet, writes Rapoport, "Beneath his meek, mild-mannered garb, his super-reporter powers were formidable. He was patient with his subjects, deferential, a good listener. Sitting down for a talk with Michael Moore was a little like taking a seat in a confessional—with cameras. When Moore returned to the editing room to look at the day's rushes, he mentally sorted his interviewees into two categories: those who'd been honest with him and those who wished they hadn't." Rapoport joins some other critics who claim that Moore misrepresents the cases he reports. Moore's *Roger & Me* is based on the premise that Moore is trying to find and interview Roger Smith, CEO of General Motors, and that Smith, surrounded by secrecy and power, avoids him while bringing ruin to Flint, Michigan. But Moore's colleague Jim Musselman testified to Rapoport that Moore had interviewed Smith on film and deliberately left the interviews out of the film. Musselman told Rapoport, "It wasn't about the issues it was about him. He's got to be the underdog, the victim. It's always the world against Michael." About the missing interviews, he told Rapoport that Moore "had talked to Smith three times. He asked him questions at the GM annual meeting in 1986, filmed an interview with the GM Chairman at the 1987 annual meeting . . . and again at the Waldorf in January 1988. All three interviews were missing" from the film.[26]

Major film scholars have celebrated Moore as a filmmaker, at the same time worrying whether film is enough in an age of political turmoil. Writing in 2007, documentary scholar Bill Nichols celebrates Moore's film work but worries that without follow-through it may come to nothing. He observes that the work of Moore and other progressive filmmakers remains "disconnected from the American populace except in their capacity as a (significant) theatrical experience. It is not the primary task of such films to build a Left movement in America; that responsibility lies elsewhere. Until that responsibility is taken up, however, the triumph of the political documentary will remain a great achievement and well worth celebrating but not the political victory that will turn the tide of recent events from their catastrophic direction."[27] In a highly celebratory review of *Sicko* in 2007, Ernest Callenbach, the founding and longtime editor of *Film Quarterly*, notes that "in some ways it begins to look as if Michael Moore in his very different way is a wild child of the greatest documentarian of our age, Frederick Wiseman.... But where Wiseman was oblique and understated, here comes Moore, lumbering and low-class, slapping his films together with a fierce and shameless humor, impatient, openly disrespectful of what used to be called The Power."[28]

Other scholars place Moore's career, and his films, in the larger context of cultural and political action. In *The New Blue Media*, Theodore Hamm includes Michael Moore as part of a movement of liberal media innovators, including MoveOn, Jon Stewart, *Daily Kos*, and others, that, he argues, "have succeeded in transforming the style and, to a lesser extent, the substance of progressive politics."[29] *Michael Moore: Filmmaker, Newsmaker and Cultural Icon*, edited by Matthew H. Bernstein, is a collection of original and previously published essays examining what Bernstein calls the "Michael Moore phenomenon," with chapters on some of Moore's films, television programs, books, news appearances, lectures, and other forms of political activity.[30] The book makes the case that part of Moore's influence, if any, arises from his emergence as a celebrity and a cultural figure and that the effects of any one element of his activities have come to depend on his existence as a cultural "phenomenon." It also offers an excellent sample of the best previously published writings on Moore's films.

Although recent years have witnessed the beginning of serious academic inquiry into the work of Michael Moore as a cultural and political phenomenon, as yet there has been no book-length critical scholarship devoted to close readings of all Moore's documentary films as rhetoric. *Michael Moore and the Rhetoric of Documentary* offers such a film-by-film critical analysis, with a group of accomplished and established rhetorical scholars and critics who have made significant contributions to the study of mass media and film examining production, rhetorical structure and appeals, and reception of the films.

The project has been deliberately constructed as an anthology of essays, rather than laying out a single thesis or argument, but all the chapters focus on the way documentary film is put to the use of public argument. Each film is the focus of a separate chapter focusing especially on detailed critical, rhetorical analysis of the documentaries. The authors comment on context, genre, antecedents and counterparts, accuracy, and relevant theoretical matters. Broadly speaking, the authors seek to identify the sorts of experiences the films invite, examine the responses they appear to evoke, and trace in some detail how the films work to invite these responses, an approach that is at the core of rhetorical criticism.

In every chapter, the primary focus is on the film itself. The authors examine the films primarily as modes of public argument and political art. Whatever argument or affect a film embodies and provokes is enacted in and through a documentary film. The primary audience for this book may come to this work from an interest in rhetorical studies. And yet we also hope to offer something useful to our colleagues who are interested primarily in film rather than rhetoric. Though we have offered a sketch of the documentary context in this introduction and aspire to make a contribution to studies of the rhetoric of documentary, we have not attempted a comprehensive film studies analysis. We offer this work in an interdisciplinary spirit and with gratitude to our colleagues in film studies who have supported our work so generously.

Holding the films together, and often providing a focal experience for the viewer, is Michael Moore, the filmmaker. From an analytical perspective, it is worth remembering that the "Michael Moore" of the films and their reputation is itself a performance and a collective construct. Michael Moore performs "Michael Moore" in the films as a narrator and interviewer, and as the author of the films he is a collective "Michael Moore," the product of a changing team of talented writers, editors, technicians, camera operators, and others. The rhetorical effect of a Michael Moore film suggests very strongly the authorship and identity of "Michael Moore." We by no means claim that this effect is a mistake or a deception, but it is an effect rather than an infallible guide to the processes of production and the actuality of shared contributions that bring about that effect. The Moore persona, as a rhetorical construction and as a representative for the viewer, displays a peculiarly American aspiration to a politics of moral purity coupled with a refusal to be humiliated into a slavish false belief in the pretensions of the powerful.

We are grateful to have secured the collaboration of a group of leading rhetorical scholars whose work bridges rhetorical history, theory, and criticism more generally, and who have also made distinguished contributions to the study of film, media, and popular culture.[31] They bring a variety of approaches to this first study of Michael Moore's contributions to the rhetoric of documentary.

In chapter 2, Jennifer L. Borda examines Moore's first film, *Roger & Me* (1989), which established Michael Moore as a filmmaker and an agitator.[32] The film chronicles Moore's childhood in Flint, Michigan; the economic devastation suffered in his hometown after the closing of several General Motors plants; and his pursuit of an on-screen interview with General Motors chairman Roger Smith. Several techniques used in the film are now regarded as part of Moore's signature filmmaking process, including his visible and sometimes cartoonish presence, his quest for an interview with an elusive authority figure, his progressive outlook on politics, and his construction of himself as a voice of the unrepresented. In 2013, *Roger & Me* was added to the National Film Registry by the National Film Preservation Board and the Library of Congress.

Borda notes the incongruities in the film's structure and appeal and the variety of critical responses. She identifies *Roger & Me* as a revival of the traditional American jeremiad, with a prophetic voice seeking redemption by reclaiming ancient values—in this case, the values of the American dream, which themselves are a precarious balance of the moral and the material. Borda argues for a critical analysis that acknowledges the film's refusal to adopt fully the generic conventions of traditional documentary or political satire, gaining much of its power from its mixing of familiar genres. And yet, she argues, perhaps the potential effect of the film is weakened by its contradictions. The satire, combined with a moral jeremiad on the one hand and nostalgia for an American Dream of industrial prosperity on the other, undermines the call to a new political consciousness, especially in the context of the strongly contradictory critical responses to the film.

Christine Harold examines *The Big One* (1998) in chapter 3. Moore followed his mediocre debut as a fiction film director (*Canadian Bacon*, 1995) with this documentary about the tour to promote his book *Downsize This!* As with *Roger & Me*, *The Big One* was largely autobiographical, including attempts to interview several heads of American corporations (only Nike CEO Phil Knight agreed to appear on camera) and Moore's championing of the underdog—in this case, the exploited labor in Nike's

Indonesian sweatshops. By returning to the formula that had proven successful in *Roger & Me*, Moore established a persona that continues to shape audience expectations of and responses to his films, and thus greatly influences the rhetorical appeals that he has available to him as a social and political critic. Harold shows how Moore reshapes the rhetoric of downsized and exploited workers, creating a moral drama in which their situations result from decisions and actions of human beings, not the inevitable hidden hand of a free market. Harold argues that the film brilliantly succeeds in capturing the spirit and the human experience of the new capitalism, the self-satisfaction of the corporate winners, and the suffering of the displaced and downsized workers, but that it fails in its analysis of what is driving that experience—new patterns of consumption in a global economy, a rogue financial industry, and the regimes of multinational capitalism.

In chapter 4, Brian L. Ott and Susan A. Sci analyze the Oscar-winning *Bowling for Columbine* (2002), Moore's most controversial film before *Fahrenheit 9/11*. Released five years after the modestly received *The Big One*, *Bowling for Columbine* is a meditation on school violence, gun culture, media sensationalism, video games, song lyrics, and nearly a dozen other issues that Moore connects in web of causal relationships. The film was enormously successful and controversial, and it began Moore's transition from David to Goliath, from the average guy from Michigan to a powerful social critic and activist with an unparalleled platform from which to speak. Perhaps because Moore was becoming more famous, the film generated both admiration and backlash; some accused him of exploiting the Columbine shootings and of harassing an aging Charlton Heston, who was suffering from Alzheimer's disease when Moore interviewed him at his home.

Ott and Sci write that the film's implicit message about the connection of gun violence to a media cultivation of racialized white panic is established not so much through argument as through the creation of a series of affective states, powerful moods that function ideologically and politically. Moore begins the film by establishing a mood of irony and curiosity, then moves to the terror and sublimity of the massacre in Littleton, Colorado. He evokes fear and loathing in his depiction of the culture of American media, especially the news media. When Moore then visits Canada to ask how it can have so many guns but so little gun violence, he invites the viewer to an experience of cool rationalism. The film ends with an evocation of what Ott and Sci identify as mourning and melancholia; it ends with a designed refusal to offer catharsis, comfort, or resolution. It thus refuses to provide a solution or to offer a role for active political agency. Even so, write Ott and Sci, the grief to which Moore leads his audience, and in which he leaves them, may cultivate a shared sense of inclusion and caring.

Thomas Rosteck and Thomas S. Frentz examine *Fahrenheit 9/11* (2004) in chapter 5, concentrating on the pivotal role a grieving army mother plays in the narrative. *Fahrenheit 9/11* is one of the most controversial films ever made. Moore's attack on the Bush administration fundamentally changed Moore's image in the American imagination, as well as how documentary films are produced, distributed, and consumed. *Fahrenheit 9/11* initiated the era of the new political documentary and marks the beginning of Moore's career as a political activist first, documentary filmmaker second. It remains the most successful documentary film ever made, having earned nearly $120 million.[33]

Rosteck and Frentz observe that after the initial celebrity of *Fahrenheit 9/11*, the film came to be strongly criticized by the media and by academic critics. But they note that parts of the film, at least, seem to linger in the imagination and in the shared political conscience of the country. The key scenes in the film, according to Rosteck and Frentz, are the four in which Lila Lipscomb appears, at first proudly defending the invasions of Afghanistan and Iraq and celebrating the role of her son, who is serving in the military. After her son is killed, Lipscomb comes to see the war as a fraud, and the grief she shares with Moore, the authors argue, comes to stand as the key representative example of the film. The particularizing and universalizing of Lila Lipscomb provide the film with a sense of grounded authenticity, and through this process of representation, it appeals to the viewer's judgment of the Bush administration's war policies. This is not a matter of "argument," in the normal discursive sense, but an achievement of the rhetoric of documentary. Rosteck and Frentz trace in detail how the particular and universal work of the Lipscomb scenes is brought about in the film. Lipscomb's conversion, as constructed by the rhetorical and aesthetic resources of documentary film, provides the willing viewer with a model of personal transformation and political action.

Edward Schiappa, Daniel Ladislau Horvath, and Peter B. Gregg discuss *Sicko* (2007) in chapter 6. Although Moore had stated after President Bush's reelection that his next film would be *Fahrenheit 9/11 ½*, he instead produced and directed a film about heath care in the United States. *Sicko* attacks the health-care and pharmaceutical industries, among other villains, for putting profit before the well-being of patients. The most controversial segment of the film involves Moore taking a 9/11 rescue worker to Cuba to receive treatments he was denied in the United States. The US government even began an investigation to determine whether Moore had violated the law by traveling to Cuba to shoot part of the film.

Schiappa and his colleagues trace the panic induced in the health-care industry by announcements that the film was in the works, the highly positive journalistic responses to *Sicko*, and the sometimes flawed "fact checking" of the film in politics and the press. But, they find, "the same elements that account for its punch may limit its efficacy as a political instrument." The core of Moore's rhetoric, they say, is less in the argument of the film than in its affect, its appeal to anger, fear, and hope that is built into its stylistic grammar, which is traced in detail. In *Sicko*, Moore does without the ambush interviews that were used with such effect in *Roger & Me*, but he still employs the logic those interviews implied—the logic of the "impossible conversation" with the corporation and the industry. Moore creates "blue collar irony" by juxtaposing the advertising of health-care insurers with case studies of those denied the benefits for which they have paid. Schiappa and his coauthors celebrate the cultivation of affect as a legitimate, even essential, element of rhetoric and persuasion. But, they ask, does the arousal of affect stimulate social action? In a study of attitude change in a sample group, the authors find what they call a "nontrivial shift of opinion," which is as much, they suggest, as a single film could hope to accomplish.

Slacker Uprising (2008), a get-out-the-vote film for the presidential election season, is a reediting of Moore's film, *Captain Mike across America*, which was received so poorly at the 2007 Toronto Film Festival that Moore reworked much of the film, including the title. Perhaps the most significant consequence of its initial reception was Moore's decision not to release it in theaters but to make the film available for free online. This marked a second phase in the era of the new political documentary, one in which films are distributed free online because their primary purpose is political and not financial. In chapter 7, Davis W. Houck and Joseph Delbert Davenport report that *Slacker Uprising* was met with bad reviews, and that it deserved them. They argue that the film is self-defeating and contradictory, celebrating deliberative engagement as a democratic value but foreclosing any sense of actual deliberation, calling the "slackers" to action but disrespecting them by offering a campaign of personality over policy, failing to achieve minimal narrative or thematic coherence, and undermining itself with a ramshackle structure.

Finally, Kendall R. Phillips examines *Capitalism: A Love Story* (2009) in chapter 8. Just as *Sicko* had anticipated the ongoing battle to reform health care, *Capitalism* went into production before the collapse of Wall Street and the US economy. Once the economy began to struggle, Moore changed the focus of the film to include the dramatic current events. Once again Moore pits himself against the rich and powerful—in this case, Wall Street corporations and their highly paid executives. *Capitalism* brings Moore's career back to where it began, investigating the imbalance between Wall Street and Main Street, between the minority with both wealth and power and the majority with neither. Phillips writes that *Capitalism* is Moore's "most ambitious critique of the American political and cultural system." He finds some of the same incoherencies that critics have noted in Moore's other films but argues that the film nevertheless hangs together and achieves a continuous narrative momentum because of Moore's construction of a rhetoric of nostalgia, which draws the disparate elements of the film into a coherent experience. Phillips shows how Moore implicitly draws on nostalgia as a cultural-rhetorical resource, balancing progressive and radical longings with restorative and reactionary desires.

From the perspectives of the critics represented in this project, Michael Moore's films have made important contributions to the art of documentary film, introducing a spirit of brash populism and taking on major social and political issues with personalized interviews and exposition. The films have had a consistently strong argumentative perspective and analytical point of view. Some of the critics here speculate that the effect of Moore's films in spurring voters to action may be diminished by argumentative and analytical incoherence. Others demonstrate how Moore draws on familiar, though usually implicit, grooves of American response—nostalgia, the jeremiad, guilt and redemption—creating a variety of emotional states that provide coherence to the film experience, a coherence that may not be evident if the "argument" is simply abstracted from the rhetorical experience of the films themselves as films.

Some of the critics represented here press against Moore's films the consideration that they may be incoherent or incomplete. Surely, if art and literature (in this case the art of documentary film) suggest political sentiments and arguments, critics have a responsibility to ask whether the artist is making a fair case for the views suggested. At the same time, a rhetorical critic is interested not only in the coherence of the "text" but also in how, if at all, a viewer might form a coherent response to a film, what such a response would appear to be (a state of thoughts and feelings or perhaps some action), and what the filmmaker did to bring it about. Coherence is not just in the text, it is in the eye of the beholder, rendering rhetorical criticism always a somewhat hypothetical project.

The rhetorical critic and theorist Carroll C. Arnold once noted that Europeans looking at the American scene in the era of our bicentennial celebrations found our rhetoric incoherent. To these observers, we seemed to be mixing contraries. "Very many of these observers expressed perplexity at what seemed to them illogicality in Americans' historical and present public behaviors," Arnold writes. "The general record of American public discourse does, indeed, justify perplexity and a sense of contradiction in whoever seeks logical consistency or philosophical consistency in the American experience." He suggests that "within our *successful*, public problem solving three rather discordant themes seem indigenous and pervasive and that when public problem solving has failed, it has frequently been because the pertinent discourse became dominated by one or two but not all three of these themes." These three discordant but essential themes are "(1) transcendental or idealistic, (2) doctrinaire, and (3) pragmatically rational."[34] Arnold was writing about public deliberation and not about documentary film, so the tensions among these three themes may not apply to Moore's films, but perhaps his suggestion points to a way of finding an American logic in Moore's apparent incoherencies, of accounting for their appeal to audiences and the limits of that appeal.

Some of the critics represented here take another view, pointing out the scattered structure of a film and its risk of incoherence, and yet maintaining that the argumentative logic and the scattered structure are held together by deep and familiar patterns of feeling and political sentiment that pull the films together into a unified experience. It may be that the affect, the emotion, of these films both creates a sense of rhetorical coherence and constructs a pattern of political sentiment deeper and stronger than "argument." The interactions of thought and sentiment, idea and emotion, identification and division, argument and affect that the authors discover in these films perhaps brings a fresh perspective to an observation made by Lionel Trilling in his 1950 preface to *The Liberal Imagination*, in which he argues for the role of the literary artist and the critic in creating and "putting under some degree of pressure" liberal sentiments:

> Goethe says somewhere that there is no such thing as a liberal idea, that there are only liberal sentiments. This is true. Yet it is also true that certain sentiments consort only with certain ideas and not with others. What is more, sentiments become ideas by a natural and imperceptible process. "Our continued influxes of feeling," said Wordsworth, "are modified and directed by our thoughts, which are indeed the representatives of all our past feelings." And Charles Péguy said, *"Tout commence en mystique et finit en politique"*—everything begins in sentiment and assumption and finds its issue in political action and institutions. The converse is also true: just as sentiments become ideas, ideas eventually establish themselves as sentiments.[35]

Trilling—an erudite critic, impatient of sensationalism and sentimentality, a key figure of postwar intellectual and cultural liberalism—perhaps would have been impatient with or dismissive of Michael Moore, the sometimes clownish, sentimental, self-constructed popular advocate of our recent political scene. And yet Trilling might have understood and appreciated, at least as an act in the historical comedy, this surprising reappearance of "liberal sentiment." In his own way, Michael Moore may be seen as answering the recent call by philosopher Martha Nussbaum for attention by liberals to the legitimate function of political emotions. "All political principles," she writes, "the good as well as the bad, need emotional support to ensure their stability over time, and all decent societies need to guard against division and hierarchy by cultivating appropriate sentiments of sympathy and love."[36]

The critics represented here come to Michael Moore's films from a variety of political and theoretical perspectives, which is as it should be. Together they help us understand the art, argument, and affect of the documentary films of Michael Moore. Moore's films arouse strong feelings and call attention to big questions that are important to Americans but are often obscured in the ongoing cacophony of American political discourse. Moore has contributed to the renewal of documentary film as an important part of the American political debate, helping identify and intensify grievances, stimulate political hope, and shrug off a decorum that, he seems to imply, stifles radical persuasion and legitimate claims for social justice.

Notes

1. John Grierson, "The Documentary Idea," in *Nonfiction Film Theory and Criticism*, ed. Richard Meran Barsam (New York: E. P. Dutton, 1976), 86. Originally published as an essay in 1942.

2. Brian Winston, *Claiming the Real II: Documentary; Grierson and Beyond*, 2nd ed. (London: British Film Institute, 2008), 274–75.

3. Mark Deming, "Michael Moore: Full Biography," *New York Times*, accessed July 27, 2011, http://movies.nytimes.com/person/103383/Michael-Moore/biography.

4. Paul Mulshine, "A Stupid White Man and a Smart One," *Newark Star Ledger*, March 30, 2003.

5. Matt Labash, "Michael Moore, One-Trick Phony," *Weekly Standard*, June 8, 1998.

6. "Michael Moore Is a Slimeball," News24.com, October 14, 2004, http://www.news24.com/Content/World/Archives/USElections2004/1076/a0d9868a795f470dbb94a783694f8103/14–10–2004–10–26/Michael_Moore_is_a_slimeball (site discontinued).

7. Interview with former insurance industry insider Wendell Potter, *Bill Moyers Journal*, PBS, July 10, 2009, http://www.pbs.org/moyers/journal/07102009/transcript2.html.

8. Philip Rucker, "*Citizens United* Used *Hillary: The Movie* to Take On McCain-Feingold," *Washington Post*, January 22, 2010.

9. Patricia Holt, "Moore Banging on Corporate Doors Again," *San Francisco Chronicle*, September 2, 1996, http://www.dogeatdogfilms.com/dtsfchrn.html.

10. Anita Gates, "How the Other Half Lives," *New York Times*, December 29, 1996, accessed July 27, 2011, http://www.nytimes.com/1996/12/29/books/how-the-other-half-lives.html?src=pm.

11. "Small and Large Acts of Resistance—Ann Sparanese," *Library Journal*, March 15, 2003, accessed July 28, 2011, http://www.libraryjournal.com/article/CA281662.html.

12. Kathleen Hall Jamieson and Joseph N. Cappella, *Echo Chamber: Rush Limbaugh and the Conservative Media Establishment* (New York: Oxford University Press, 2008).

13. Michael Moore and Kathleen Glynn, *Adventures in a TV Nation: The Stories behind America's Most Outrageous TV Show* (New York: Harper Paperbacks, 1998), http://dogeatdog.michaelmoore.com/books/atvnchapt1.html.

14. To Designate August 16, 1994, as "*TV Nation* Day," H.J. Res. 365, 103rd Cong. (1994), http://thomas.loc.gov/cgi-bin/query/z?c103:H.J.RES.365:.

15. Daniel Fierman, "Ready for Moore?," *Entertainment Weekly*, May 25, 2007, http://www.ew.com/ew/article/0,,20040352,00.html.

16. See Thomas W. Benson and Brian J. Snee, eds., *The Rhetoric of the New Political Documentary* (Carbondale: Southern Illinois University Press, 2008). Descriptions of the political economy of the new documentary may be found especially in the chapters by Benson and Snee, "New Political Documentary: Rhetoric, Propaganda, and the Civic Prospect," 1–13; Susan Mackey-Kallis, "Talking Heads Rock the House: Robert Greenwald's *Uncovered: The War on Iraq*," 153–72; and Ronald V. Bettig and Jeanne Lynn Hall, "Outfoxing the Myth of the Liberal Media," 173–201.

17. Bill Nichols, *Representing Reality: Issues and Concepts in Documentary* (Bloomington: Indiana University Press, 1992), 32–75.

18. Michael Renov, *The Subject of Documentary* (Minneapolis: University of Minnesota Press, 2004).

19. See, for example, Thomas W. Benson and Carolyn Anderson, *Reality Fictions: The Films of Frederick Wiseman*, 2nd ed. (Carbondale: Southern Illinois University Press, 2002); P. J. O'Connell, *Robert Drew and the Development of Cinema Verite in America* (Carbondale: Southern Illinois University Press, 1992); Jonathan B. Vogels, *The Direct Cinema of David and Albert Maysles* (Carbondale: Southern Illinois University Press, 2005).

20. Michael Moore, Oscar awards ceremony, March 23, 2003, transcribed from YouTube, https://www.youtube.com/watch?v=M7Is43K6lrg.

21. For descriptions of the event, see Robert Brent Toplin, *Michael Moore's "Fahrenheit 9/11": How One Film Divided a Nation* (Lawrence: University Press of Kansas, 2006), 1–2; Roger Rapoport, *Citizen Moore: The Life and Times of an American Iconoclast* (Berkeley, CA: RDR Books, 2007), 1–7.

22. See Benson and Snee, *Rhetoric of the New Political Documentary*.

23. For an analysis of the documentary responses to *Fahrenheit 9/11*, see Jennifer Borda, "Documentary Dialectics or Dogmatism? *Fahrenhype 9/11*, *Celsius 41.11*, and the New Politics of Documentary Film," in Benson and Snee, *Rhetoric of the New Political Documentary*, 54–77.

24. Toplin, *Michael Moore's "Fahrenheit 9/11*," 7.

25. Ibid., 146.

26. Rapoport, *Citizen Moore*, 274, 277, 4, 126–27.

27. Bill Nichols, "What Current Documentaries Do and Can't Do," *Velvet Light Trap* 60 (2007): 86.

28. Ernest Callenbach, "*Sicko*: Ernest Callenbach Applauds a Witty Documentary Broadside," review of *Sicko*, *Film Quarterly* 61, no. 2 (Winter 2007): 20.

29. Theodore Hamm, *The New Blue Media* (New York: New Press, 2008), xiii.

30. Matthew H. Bernstein, ed., *Michael Moore: Filmmaker, Newsmaker, Cultural Icon* (Ann Arbor: University of Michigan Press, 2010).

31. In the bibliography, we cite a generous sample of the film and media scholarship of the book's authors for readers who wish to pursue these modes of inquiry further.

32. See also Doyle Greene, *The American Worker on Film: A Critical History, 1909–1999* (Jefferson, NC: McFarland, 2010); Miles Orvell, "Documentary Film and the Power of Interrogation: *American Dream* and *Roger & Me*," in Bernstein, *Michael Moore*, 127–40.

33. For a contrasting rhetorical analysis of *Fahrenheit 9/11*, see Shawn J. Parry-Giles and Trevor Parry-Giles, "Virtual Realism and the Limits of Commodified Dissent in *Fahrenheit 9/11*," in Benson and Snee, *Rhetoric of the New Political Documentary*, 24–53. See also Richard R. Ness, "Prelude to Moore: A Comparison of Rhetorical Techniques in Frank Capra's *Why We Fight* Series and Michael Moore's *Fahrenheit 9/11*," in Bernstein, *Michael Moore*, 149–66; Charles Musser, "Truth and Rhetoric in Michael Moore's *Fahrenheit 9/11*," in Bernstein, *Michael Moore*, 167–201; David Tetzlaff, "Dystopia Now: *Fahrenheit 9/11*'s Red Pill," in Bernstein, *Michael Moore*, 202–21.

34. Carroll C. Arnold, "Reflections on American Public Discourse," *Central States Speech Journal* 28 (1977): 73, 74.

35. Lionel Trilling, preface to *The Liberal Imagination* (1950; repr., New York: New York Review of Books, 2008), xvi–xvii.

36. Martha Nussbaum, *Political Emotions: Why Love Matters for Justice* (Cambridge, MA: Belknap Press of Harvard University Press, 2013), 2–3.

2. Laughing through Our Tears: Rhetorical Tensions in *Roger & Me*

Jennifer L. Borda

O n March 5, 2011, during the height of the protests for union rights in Madison, Wisconsin, filmmaker Michael Moore made an impromptu appearance on the steps of the state capitol and issued this observation: "Contrary to what those in power would like you to believe so that you'll give up your pension, cut your wages, and settle for the life your great-grandparents had, America is not broke. Not by a long shot. The country is awash in wealth and cash. It's just that it's not in your hands. It has been transferred, in the greatest heist in history, from the workers and consumers to the banks and the portfolios of the uber-rich."[1]

Moore's speech lambasting the distribution of wealth, abuse of power, and ensuing class warfare plaguing America rearticulates the critique of neoliberalism he presented more than two decades ago in *Roger & Me*, the film that launched his career as a documentary filmmaker. (For the purposes of this discussion, neoliberalism is defined here as the foundation of today's free-market economy, which includes governmental policies that maximize the role of markets and profit-making and minimize the role of nonmarket institutions. As a result of such a philosophy, corporations have become the standards of our culture and corporate profits trump public service values.) The consequent themes of corporate indifference to the public good, the violation of workers' and citizens' rights, and the erosion of fundamental American democratic values have served as guideposts for Moore's career as a documentarian ever since. The media response to *Roger & Me* also established Moore's reputation as one of the most talked-about film directors—for better or for worse—in recent cinematic history. Beginning with that historic documentary, and continuing throughout his corpus of work, Moore has earned considerable critical acclaim from many inside the film industry, evoked consistent controversy and criticism within the public domain, and attracted an unprecedented level of press coverage for a documentary filmmaker.

In the months before the December 1989 theatrical release of *Roger & Me*, many of the nation's leading film critics compared Michael Moore to Jonathan Swift, Voltaire, Charlie Chaplin, H. L. Mencken, Sinclair Lewis, and Mark Twain. Having viewed the film on the festival circuit, these critics described it as "gutsy, populist, outraged, and outrageous"; "a David and Goliath revenge story, in which a plain-speaking nobody triumphs morally over an evil corporate giant"; "one of the most subversively comic political films in memory"; and "one of the funniest tragedies ever filmed, with a twin assault of surrealistic comedy and politically charged pathos."[2] An even louder chorus of popular press journalists and critics was more often disparaging of both Moore and the film in the months after its release, however. These critics chose different labels intended to malign Michael Moore and his efforts, such as radical, gonzo journalist, demagogue, propagandist, and political agitator. These same critics also downplayed *Roger & Me* as "a mock-u-mentary," "confrontational journalism," and sensationalist muckraking as they tried to make sense of it within the framework of a more conventional view of the documentary form, which some contended should uphold certain, perhaps outmoded, standards of nonfiction filmmaking.[3] As these polarized responses to Moore's inaugural film show, the filmmaker had become a lightning rod in the public sphere as likely to attract unabashed praise as outright indignation; such sentiments continued to be evoked in response to the subsequent films he has produced during the last two decades.[4]

It is no longer possible to think about *Roger & Me* without taking into account the immediate controversy surrounding the film and how those initial reviews and characterizations have since become a rhetorical force in shaping Moore's reputation and influence. Analysis of a sampling of representative reviews that appeared in widely read national publications also reveals how film critics' insights into *Roger & Me* may have reflected, or perhaps even shaped, the broader public response to the film. I begin with a rhetorical analysis of those debates by discerning the themes that emerged through film reviews published in a cross section of the popular press. When read in conversation with one another, film critics' response to and critiques of *Roger & Me* provide an interpretive framework for considering an array of complicated perspectives regarding the objectives of documentary film, the ethical responsibilities of documentary filmmakers, and the political efficacy of "documentary satire." The public debates that emerged between some of these critics also reveal how Moore's film was evaluated as a call to social and political action, deemed successful by some and a failure by others. When considered in toto, I argue that the very incongruence of these reviewers' experiences of the film also alludes to an underlying rhetorical contradiction within the film itself.

While scholars over the last two decades have analyzed *Roger & Me* using classical documentary film theory and a critical perspective that attends to the film's formal incongruities (for example, analyzing the film as a hybrid form of nonfiction film and political satire), my analysis builds on those critical insights and also addresses how such a generic hybrid functions rhetorically. I argue that *Roger & Me* is an example of a cinematic jeremiad, preached by a misunderstood modern-day prophet, that offers explicit opinions and arguments about the consequences of postindustrialization in Flint, Michigan. Through an analysis of the film's overarching structure, I demonstrate how Moore's comedic juxtaposition of the economically powerful and powerless in 1980s Flint were framed as conflicting visions of the economic climate and its social effects, which reflect Walter Fisher's moralistic and materialistic myths of the American Dream. I conclude that the contradictions of the secular jeremiad as a rhetorical form, and the contrasting myths of the American Dream presented in *Roger & Me*, constrain the film as a critique of the socioeconomic realities of global capitalism and create an unstable sense of how viewers should respond to it as a documentary call for social justice and political reform.

Michael Moore and the Critics

Roger & Me represented Michael Moore's foray into uncharted artistic territory, inspired by an abrupt end to a decade-long career working as an editor for several leftist publications. Having lost faith in the power of journalism to inspire social change, Moore imagined this film project as a means to convey his sense of America gone awry to a broader audience through a more personal and accessible medium. The film ostensibly charts Moore's unsuccessful mission to interview Roger Smith, chairman of General Motors, about how Smith could justify his Reaganomics-inspired decisions in light of their damaging impact on Flint, Michigan, the birth-place of GM. The film opens with a short autobiographical montage of Moore, encapsulating his memories of boyhood in Flint during the 1950s. As Moore represents this time and place in the film, it is the epitome of the promises of American industrialism, middle-class prosperity, and the American Dream. While Smith remains elusive over the course of Moore's journey, the filmmaker encounters and interviews a sampling of former GM factory workers (now unemployed), the Flint elite, a GM lobbyist, the city's ministers of tourism, and the busiest man in town, Fred Ross, the deputy sheriff in charge of evictions. Moore chronicles Flint's devastation over the decade of the 1980s, which the film attributes to the economic absurdity of mass layoffs by one of the world's richest corporations, city planners throwing good money after bad, and the entrepreneurial panacea endemic in the economic discourse of Reagan's America.

The early reviews of *Roger & Me* were full of admiration for the film's innovation, its political use of humor, and the ambition of its novice film-maker. Ed Kelleher regards the film as "great filmmaking—pure, simple, and true," writing that "watching Moore's portrait of greed, selfishness, absurdity and despair, you'll be laughing like mad one minute and fuming like mad the next."[5] Writing for the *Village Voice*'s New York Film Festival Consumer Guide, Alex Patterson asserts that Moore's "contrasting of se-rious misery and moronic hedonism may not be subtle, but it certainly is effective—and far funnier than it has any right to be."[6] According to Roger Ebert, "The genius of 'Roger & Me' is that it understands the image-ma-nipulating machinery of corporate public relations and fights back with the same cynicism and cleverness."[7] Peter Rainer of the *Los Angeles Times* extols the film as "a piece of cockeyed outrage," noting that "the black comedy arises naturally, inevitably from the seriousness of the situation" and that "Moore has a wicked gift for fulfilling audience expectation that many a veteran director might envy; he dispenses with statistics in favor of the 'found' humor that is seemingly all around him in Flint."[8] Stuart Klawans declares in a review for the *Nation*, "The real delight of *Roger and Me* comes from Michael Moore's personality—his dry, common-sense wit as a narrator, his shambling on-camera presence, his interest in the people he encounters as he knocks around Flint."[9] *Washington Post* film critic Hal Hinson notes that "Moore's slapstick reportage strikes the perfect balance between irony and sincerity; it's slyly deadpan and committed, democratic and kingly all at once."[10]

Many of these laudatory reviews were written as a result of the film's successful showings on the independent film festival and awards circuit, but before its nationwide release. By late 1989, *Roger & Me* had been honored as Best Documentary by the LA Film Critics, National Society of Film Critics, National Board of Review, and New York Film Critics Circle, where it also received a rarely seen standing ovation. The film also won the People's Choice Award at the Toronto Film Festival and the Most Popular Film Award at the Vancouver International Film Festival. Such a level of critical acclaim for an independent documentary film was unprecedented.[11] The initial praise stemmed from these early reviewers' general approach to the film as a counterpoint to the pervasive optimism of the Reagan-era view of America as a "shining city upon a hill." These critics applauded Moore's attempt to document instead what had gone wrong in the past decade and how the "progress" of Reaganomics had led to the postindustrial deterioration of the American working class, jeopardizing their claims to such optimism and the American Dream. Further, early critics recognized Moore's innovative use of black comedy as a means of injecting a notoriously staid art form—documentary—with an entertaining narrative. While these reviewers focused on the film's populist stance, political comedy, and reflexive style as a new and refreshing contribution to the documentary genre, other film critics found Moore's departure from that genre's established conventions problematic.

The tide began to turn against *Roger & Me* with the publication of Harlan Jacobson's now infamous interview with Michael Moore in *Film Comment* at the end of 1989. In that piece, Jacobson comments that the filmmaker is "glitteringly smart in his analysis and arrestingly right in essence" but argues that the film is compromised by Moore's having created "the impression of a direct sequence of events that didn't happen in Flint in the one-to-one causal fashion his documentary implies." Jacobson asserts that Moore's portrayal of events suggested a false chronology and was an act of deception perpetrated on the audience, rather than the director's artistic choice to present factual information in a more relatable narrative form for a national audience, as Moore had countered in the interview. According to Jacobson, "*Roger & Me* is too good to be true" and contains a number of "disquieting discrepancies" with regard to Moore's compression of events in the film, such as visits to the troubled city by the Reverend Robert Schuller and Ronald Reagan, the development of principal commercial projects commissioned by Flint city officials in hopes of invigorating tourism, and the timing of the GM layoffs, which ultimately downsized Flint's primary industry by more than 50 percent but actually occurred over the span of a decade. Specifically, Jacobson impugns Moore for "playing fast and loose with sequence—which viewers don't understand is happening," arguing that "we expect that what we are seeing there happened, in the way in which it happened, in the way in which we are told it happened."[12]

In essence, rather than address the film's subject as other reviewers had, Jacobson chose to critique the film's narrative style and Moore's artistic choices. Consequently, this widely read and referenced interview stirred up a media controversy that would serve to question Moore's credibility as a filmmaker and call into question the film's effectiveness as social critique. The controversy ignited by Jacobson's piece also laid the groundwork for a series of characterizations of Michael Moore that would undermine his reputation as both a journalist and documentarian, and work to discredit him as a political commentator, over the course of his high-profile directorial career.

In the wake of Jacobson's interview, many reviewers began to regard both *Roger & Me* and Michael Moore with a tone of preconceived incredulity. By January 1990, the articles questioning Moore as a filmmaker rivaled in number the celebratory reviews published just after the release of the film a few months before. Three major themes emerged from the onslaught of criticism published in the wake of Jacobson's interview: ad hominem attacks against Moore that malign him as an unethical propagandist who manipulates an unsuspecting audience; the film's use of facile humor, which makes too easy targets of both the elite and the working poor; and too much focus on Michael Moore himself and his mock mission to interview Roger Smith at the expense of a more complex political analysis of the economic system that enabled GM's actions and Flint's fate.

Pauline Kael published a scathing account of her own experience of *Roger & Me* in the *New Yorker*, stating, "The film I saw was shallow and facetious, a piece of gonzo demagoguery that made me feel cheap for laughing." Following Jacobson, Kael notes her own suspicion of the film, writing, "I had stopped believing what Moore was saying very early; he was just too glib," and claims that Moore "chases gags and improvises his own version of history." She concludes that Moore "comes on in a give-'em-hell style, but he breaks faith with the audience. The picture is like the work of a slick ad exec."[13] Similarly, Michael Sragow applauds Jacobson's interview in his review of the film for the *San Francisco Examiner*, writing that it is the best thing Jacobson had ever done and that he "doesn't let Moore bull his way through factual discrepancies." In Sragow's opinion, the film "is a movie you like less the more you think about it," because Moore "played propaganda tricks with chronology."[14] *Chicago Tribune* critic Dave Kehr similarly denounces the film by noting that it has rearranged the order of events it claims to be reporting on "in order to tighten their grip on an audience" and "to emotionally arouse [its] public, and in so doing, change minds and control opinions." Kehr compares Moore to German filmmaker Leni Riefenstahl, who made the 1935 pro-Nazi propaganda film *Triumph of the Will*, noting that both aggrandized the ideologies of their political parties through the form of propaganda, and concludes, "Left wing or right, that's a scary prospect."[15]

Entering into the debate, several film critics publicly responded to the negative commentary sparked by Jacobson's piece, characterizing criticisms of Moore's misrepresentation of facts as a fundamental misunderstanding of the nature of, and rhetorical strategies inherent in, the making of documentary film. For example, Carley Cohan remarks in *Cineaste*, "One wonders if Jacobson and Kael are holding Moore to standards set long ago in the golden age of voice-over documentary, during the newsreel boom of WWII. Clearly, Moore's loose lips belong to a post-Eisensteinian generation, where the bias of the observer is taken for granted."[16] Revisiting the film in the *Chicago Sun-Times*, Roger Ebert explicitly disputes Jacobson's charges, explaining, "There is no such thing as a truly objective, factual documentary"; rather, all documentaries "manipulate factual material in order to make a point, and they imply by their style and tone what kind of point they are making."[17]

In fact, *Roger & Me* may be best interpreted, as several scholars have, as representative of a wave of boundary-crossing documentaries appearing at the end of the Reagan decade, which also included Ross McElwee's *Sherman's March* (1985), Errol Morris's *The Thin Blue Line* (1988), and Barbara Kopple's *American Dream* (1990). Films such as these, which blur the boundaries between objectivity and subjectivity, as well as documentary and entertainment, also instigated a new wave of documentary theorizing that began to deconstruct such seemingly contradictory impulses. Film historians, feminist scholars, and rhetorical film scholars, in particular, have investigated and problematized the various forms through which documentary films mediate reality, as well as the ways in which various documentary modes and styles rhetorically invite viewers to consider particular perspectives on the world. For example, according to feminist documentary scholar Paula Rabinowitz, the documentaries produced during this period problematize standard conventions of documentary film and circulate "between the public and private, personal and political spheres by becoming simultaneously an aesthetic and archival object—part-fiction; part-truth." Arguing that these boundary crossings and exchanges are crucial to documentary as a political project, she also notes that what is at stake is "the status, meaning, interpretation, and perhaps even control of history and its narratives."[18] Film historian Erik Barnouw similarly classifies every aspect of documentary filmmaking as meaningful expressions that reveal motivations and attempt to change ideas. He notes that "it is in selecting and arranging their findings that [documentarians] express themselves; these choices are, in effect, their main comments. And whether they adopt the stance of observer, or chronicler, or painter, or whatever, they cannot escape their subjectivity. They present their version of the world."[19]

In an effort to understand the rhetorical influences of this new wave of documentary, scholars have argued that as a documentary work inspired to raise consciousness, *Roger & Me* resists strict adherence to fixed documentary modes. According to Matthew Bernstein, Moore's genre-mixing approach, motivated by a desire to counter audience "documentaphobia" and combined with his status as a novice filmmaker, was partly to blame for the "startling vehemence" of the critics' negative reactions to the film. Bernstein writes that "defining documentary is difficult," but he argues that the challenge is compounded in this case by the fact that Moore plays with the various modes of documentary representation and the expectations they invite.[20] Bernstein references four modes of representing, and conveying a perspective on, reality outlined by Bill Nichols, which Nichols argues serve as the dominant organizational patterns that structure most documentary films. In the expository mode, Nichols says, "the rhetoric of the commentator's argument serves as the textual dominant, moving the text forward in service of its persuasive needs. . . . Editing in the expository mode generally serves to establish and maintain rhetorical continuity more than spatial or temporal continuity."[21] Bernstein asserts that *Roger & Me* functions largely in the expository mode, and he notes, "Moore has a general thesis about why General Motors closed its manufacturing plants in and around Flint, Michigan, and he has a clear argument about its effects on the town. The film is rhetorically organized to support this thesis."[22] In this regard, *Roger & Me* may best be analyzed as an interpretation of truth and history rather than an objective and balanced presentation of reality.

Film scholar Miles Orvell also strives to understand the film's departures from conventional documentary form, asserting, "We expect 'truth' from documentary: we don't expect it in quite the same way from satire. 'Documentary satire' is almost, then, an oxymoron, unless we are willing to admit it is a strikingly original hybrid." He explains that Moore employs both the interactive and reflexive modes of documentary, and through this combination, he "sacrificed historical accuracy in order to achieve the unity of satirical fiction."[23] Roger Ebert defends Moore's creative choices along these same lines, writing that Moore "was taking the liberties that satirists and ironists have taken with material for generations, and he was making his point with sarcasm and deft timing." Ebert argues that what such irony affords viewers "is both more important and more rare than facts. It supplies poetry, a viewpoint, indignation, opinion, anger, and humor."[24]

Further, Bernstein argues that Moore also integrates the interactive mode into the film from the outset, which acknowledges the filmmaker's presence in, and contribution to, the narrative of the film. "One strategy for defending Moore's creative chronology," Bernstein explains, is that "Moore makes his point of view—and the very fact that he is presenting *his* own point of view—clear."[25] As Nichols explains it, the interactive mode also "introduces a sense of partialness, of *situated* presence and *local* knowledge that derives from the actual encounter of filmmaker and other," allowing for the possibilities of the filmmaker "serving as mentor, participant, prosecutor, or provocateur in relation to the social actors recruited."[26] Moore acts as all four, at times simultaneously, and these subjective interventions into the filmed "reality" provoked further concern on the part of the film's critics.

Even reviewers sympathetic to Moore's innovative blending of documentary modes and imposition of a narrative form found his employment of the tragicomic style and treatment of his subjects somewhat troubling. For example, in his review in the *New York Times*, Richard Bernstein seeks to understand how Moore challenges the limits of traditional documentary genre, and he asserts that the film invites a complicated viewing experience. He explains, "What Mr. Moore's detractors are saying, in a sense, is that the very qualities that made the film successful—the elements of irreverence, satire, ridicule—are the very ones that make it misleading, since satire inevitably depends on a certain partiality and exaggeration, the creation of a villain, an artistic deformation of the real world."[27] Sragow similarly rebukes Moore for turning "everyone into a political caricature, including himself," which ultimately "reduces the corporate prosecutors, their victims, and all the people caught in between, into a fool's parade."[28] In a review for the film journal *Cineaste*, Gary Crowdus argues that "the critical hullabaloo engendered by the *Film Comment* interview has unfortunately served to deflect attention from more significant shortcomings of *Roger & Me*. . . . A more troubling aspect . . . is that for Moore, as a self-styled comedian, everyone in Flint becomes fair game. While corporate honchos like Roger Smith and others in similar positions of wealth and power are legitimate targets of Moore's lampooning sensibility, his scattershot satirical approach too often also includes those who are victims of the economic crisis."[29] Kehr regards this aspect of the film as an indictment of Moore's self-serving motivations, suggesting that "when real life tragedy is used as a basis for movie comedy, some consideration of responsibility has to enter the equation. Roger Smith has used the people of Flint for his own ends, but so, in a way that's different mainly in degree, has Michael Moore."[30]

While Bernstein argues that it was the film's blending of expository and interactive modes that led to the "unwitting alienation of even those viewers who applaud his film's politics," Orvell explains that Moore's use of documentary satire "eschews the tradition of observational documentary and opts instead for a more complex rhetoric," namely, the hybridization of Nichol's interactive and reflexive modes.[31] The rhetorical complexity of the reflexive mode allows viewers to see and hear the filmmaker engage in metacommentary about the act of making a film. According to Nichols, the filmmaker using the reflexive mode is "speaking to us less about the historical world itself, as in the expository and poetic or interactive and diaristic modes, than about the process of representation itself." Nichols contends that the reflexive text poses the question of how to represent people *not as an issue for the filmmaker,* but rather *for the viewer,* "by emphasizing the degree to which people, or social actors, appear before us as signifiers, as functions of the text itself," and in which every representation is "a constructed image rather than a slice of reality." Using *Roger & Me* as a representative example, Nichols illuminates some of the potential failures of the reflexive mode for viewers, including that "when the filmmaker moves to center stage . . . the risk is that other characters will fall into the narrative slots reserved for donors, helpers, and villains." Nichols argues that while "Michael Moore overtly, if also ironically, embraces the role of hero and champion," he also "renders others as helpless, indifferent, or ignorant," reducing them to "victims or dupes."[32]

It is relatively simplistic to dismiss much of the backlash against the film advanced by film critics as their failure or refusal to critically engage with this newly emerging mode of documentary and its challenges to balanced and objective truth telling. Some critics and scholars recognized and applauded the film as something in between documentary "truth" and a purely editorialized work of satire. Others, however, were merely unwilling to engage with Moore in his self-conscious, and somewhat contradictory, merger of historical narrative, comedy, and irony intended to call into question documentary conventions, expectations, and effects. This kind of engagement with the film and the filmmaker require work on the part of a sophisticated spectator, as well as entry into an emotional relationship with the filmmaker that accepts his interpretation of the world, and this was a rhetorical dynamic in which some critics were unwilling participants.

Perhaps more significantly, though, some critics argued that Moore's ironic tale did not accomplish the level of social critique to which *both* political satire and documentary film typically aspire. Rainer writes of Moore, "Outrage brings out the political cartoonist in him, and he is content to leave the drawings sketchy," but "the way these issues are skimped and glossed carries its own element of condescension toward the audience."[33] Orvell concludes that "Moore's neglect of the macro-economic issue in his film may be a more serious problem finally than the worries about chronology, although to address it would have blunted his criticism of General Motors."[34] Indeed, Moore's reflexive construction of the "quest narrative" elevates his own status to "hero and champion" in the film, thus subordinating the relative representation of the other social actors.[35] Moreover, these creative choices also resulted in a relatively surface analysis of the economic ills of global corporate domination, of which GM is only a representative example, in favor of establishing a clear structural resolution involving a hero's (Moore's) failed quest to sufficiently expose a despicable villain (Smith). Through its innovative blending of genres and employment of the reflexive mode, the film succeeds in depicting an entertaining and melodramatic narrative of the powerful versus the powerless, yet it is less successful as an invocation to greater critical assessment of economic injustice, and warning of impending consequences, for a post-Reagan-era America.

While identifying the film as a complex hybrid of competing modes and genres partly explains critics' and viewers' difficulties with the film, it does not fully account for why the film provoked such strong negative reactions and the failure for so many to connect with the film's messages. Read in aggregate, I argue that the reviews of the film found in the popular press allude to a rhetorical problem with how the film failed to create a sense of identification for viewers, a rhetorical strategy necessary to then advocate for social change. The conversation that emerged through the critical reception of the film provides a template for interpreting how *Roger & Me* not only invites, but requires, a complex viewing experience from its audience. That is, while Moore deems GM responsible for the plight of his community, and offers a biting commentary to that extent, he fails to fully elucidate the link between free-market economics and the rise of corporate domination. Further, Moore overlooks how quickly these political initiatives had begun to harden into American ideologies, as well as the dire consequences for American citizens, particularly the working class. While Moore wants to argue for a corporate philosophy more committed to social justice and economic security for American citizens, he offers no viable solution for moving Americans closer to that vision at the end of the twentieth century. The framework of prophetic rhetoric and the contradictions of the secular jeremiad form, which solicits community redemption through a reaffirmation of the values of the American Dream, more fully explain these varied responses by revealing a series of rhetorical tensions in *Roger & Me* that made it difficult for the film to invite identification with a wide audience.

Documentary and the Jeremiad Prophet

Rhetorical, political, and historical scholars have long studied the jeremiad form in its various incarnations as a rhetorical response to crisis and threat. According to Andrew Murphy, the term *jeremiad* "refers us back not only to Jeremiah, but to the long line of prophetic critics who, driven by a sense of crisis and deep anxiety about their community's health, interpreted Israel's violation of its covenant with God as a story of decline that threatened God's punishment."[36] The American version has been traced back to New England Puritans during the early colonial period. The American

Puritans transformed this inherited pattern for their own purposes and, according to Kurt Ritter, developed the theme of sin-repentance-reform through a rigid organizational pattern that applied religious doctrine to secular, even political, affairs and was delivered by "a minister who spoke as a scolding prophet—a voice in the wilderness—but who was at the same time a part of the community."[37]

In the contemporary version of the jeremiad, the civil religion of the American Dream and the principles of our founding documents, the US Constitution and Declaration of Independence, replace biblical doctrine and have become reminders of American's special destiny as humanity's "last, best hope."[38] As the modern American jeremiad has been adapted for political purposes, its framework has been transformed once again. According to Richard Johannesen, "The contemporary secular jeremiad depicts present societal ills or calamities as urgent, as requiring action, redemption and reform before it is too late, as representing the verge of impending doom, and as a sign of broken commitments to the fundamental principles of the American Dream."[39] Scholars also have examined the rhetorical potential of the jeremiad to ritualistically respond to social crisis and identified four characteristic features of the form: jeremiads define the present through the values, principles, and traditions of the past; propose political policies that measure up to past ideals; promote cultural cohesion; and provide a powerful impetus to action and reform.[40] Jeremiad speakers function as society's prophets, not in the biblical sense of Jeremiah, but rather as marginal figures in the contemporary public sphere who expose the threatening cataclysm of American social, economic, and political experiments to an often dubious audience. These crises frequently are couched in the secular prophet's vision of the American Dream, which serves as a premise for the return of the community to traditional American values.

Following this framework, *Roger & Me* qualifies as jeremiad rhetoric, and Michael Moore serves as a jeremiad prophet similar to fellow radical Americans and rhetorical prophets Eugene Debs and Mary Harris "Mother" Jones, both legendary Progressive Era socialist agitators.[41] According to James Darsey, "Every radical vision challenges the society to which it is presented. Visionaries tend to be stringent in their demands on us, and the extraordinary nature of what they claim to see makes them alien."[42] Yet, while Debs and Jones were fiercely critical of the impact of industrialism on the modern worker, in *Roger & Me*, Moore upholds industrial America as a nostalgic past relative to the impending crisis of neoliberalism and a postindustrial economy. Despite the difference in historical context and perceived socioeconomic evils, Debs, Jones, and Moore share a commitment to the fate of the worker in the face of material power, whether that of the Carnegies and Rockefellers or General Motors.

Moore's prophetic role is established in the opening scenes of *Roger & Me*. Accompanied by a montage of black-and-white family snapshots and grainy home movie footage, Moore introduces himself in voice-over as "kind of a strange child," saying, "I crawled backwards until I was two, but had Kennedy's Inaugural memorized by the time I was six." Moore explains that his entire family worked for General Motors, while he aspired to escape a life on the assembly line, as did his heroes, the members of Grand Funk Railroad, radio announcer Casey Kasem, and game show host Bob Eubanks, all of whom left the factories of Flint behind to seek out greener pastures. Moore remarks, "I figured if Bob Eubanks could make it out of here, so could I." He explains how after editing his own newspaper, the *Michigan Voice*, in Flint for a decade, he seized the opportunity to start a new life in San Francisco as the editor of a muckraking magazine (*Mother Jones*). However, after just a three-month sojourn to "the other side of the world from Flint," the owner of the magazine declared Moore and California a "mismatch," and Moore returned. The subtext of this opening montage is that Moore is a little "different" from the other members of his Flint community, and having left for a brief period to live in a more cosmopolitan city that did not even carry "non-dairy creamer," he returned with a view of Flint's economic crisis from the perspective of an insider/outsider. As Darsey notes, "The prophet is simultaneously insider and outsider . . . it might fairly be said that the prophet shares the ideals of his audience rather than the realities of its everyday life."[43]

Following Moore's introduction of himself, he describes his hometown of Flint as "the birthplace of General Motors, the largest corporation in the world," saying, "There were more auto factories and auto workers here than in any other city on Earth. . . . We enjoyed a prosperity that working people around the world had never seen before, and the city was grateful to the company." This statement is confirmed by a newsreel of the city's "birthday party" for the people of General Motors on its fiftieth anniversary in 1958. Thousands of people pack the streets and sidewalks to watch a parade featuring Zorro, Miss America, Pat Boone, the Elks Junior Drill Team, and Harlow Curtis, then president of GM, who delivered a keynote address titled "The Promise of the Future." Moore recalls, "This is Flint as I remember it, where every day was a great day."

However, Moore's nostalgic longing for the Flint of his boyhood is ruptured just days after his return from San Francisco when "the bad news hit." Interspersed between news clips and newspaper headlines, Moore encapsulates the devastating impact of free-market capitalism, globalization, and union busting on his hometown in just under two minutes. He explains, "I mean, maybe I got this wrong, but I thought companies lay off people when they've hit hard times, but GM was the richest company in the world and it was closing factories while it was making profits in the billions." Moore then describes Roger Smith's "brilliant plan" for GM as follows: "First, close 11 factories in the US. Then, open 11 in Mexico where you pay the workers 70 cents an hour. Then, use the money you've saved by building cars in Mexico and take over other companies, preferably high tech firms and weapons manufacturers. Next, tell the union you're broke and they happily agree to give back a couple billion dollars in wage cuts. You then take that money from the workers and eliminate their jobs by building more foreign factories."

The organizational structure of the film follows the basic elements of the jeremiad form in that it details contemporary decline (in this case, the socioeconomic crisis in Flint), contrasts the present state of Flint (as a microcosm for the country at large) with a nostalgic view of a more glorious past (the Flint of Moore's boyhood), and offers a warning of an indifference to, or outright embrace of, free-market ideologies. The jeremiad form by its very nature is beset by contradiction and rhetorical tensions, however. According to Ritter, "The jeremiad stands as a bridge between the past and the future, charting the course to future glory by calling for fidelity to old ideals."[44] Ritter also notes that, consequently, the jeremiad "thrives upon an inconsistency between the ideal and the real," while Andrew Murphy asserts that the jeremiad relies on a sense of nostalgia that "presents an idealized portrait of both the past and present," which functions as a "double distortion." [45] In both the jeremiad and *Roger & Me*, historical realities are revised through the mythic lens of the American Dream, and present ills are contrasted with sentimental, and often distorted, memories of an idyllic past. These tensions also contribute to the film's failure to achieve the two necessary features of the jeremiad: the promotion of cultural cohesion and a concerted call to political action in order to reverse current policies.

In *Roger & Me*, Moore's nostalgic view of the American Dream is largely established through his opening flashback to Flint in the first half of the twentieth century. He contends that after the historic Flint Sit-Down Strike of 1936–37 and the formation of the United Auto Workers union, the GM corporation and its employees enjoyed a mutually beneficial relationship based on commitment and respect. Moore includes brief newsreel footage of the strike, which concludes with the following statement by a GM representative: "The GM employee has made great advances and it is our wish that he continue to prosper. Most of our employees, even those who at times caused problems, are conscientious and hardworking men and women; men and women to whose imagination, ingenuity, energy, and dedication our country owes its industrial leadership in the world." Rainer notes, "Moore tells us that these movies show Flint as he remembers it, and, judging from the honeyed tone in his voice-overs for this section, he must really revel in those days. He accepts the boosterism of boomtown Flint as a populist artifact. It's a mythology he chooses to believe in."[46] Here Moore employs two conflicting conventions of documentary, narrative voice-over and newsreel footage, to present the viewer with a glimpse into Flint's past. This sets up an initial contradiction in the film between Moore's own reflexive memory of, and nostalgia for, such an idyllic past and the evocation of historical truth offered through the perceived "objectivity" of newsreel footage within the expository mode.

The remainder of the film calls attention to our present condition in terms of the tragic economic failures taking place in Flint and offers these as a warning of impending economic crisis for the rest of the country. In contrast to the American Dream of Flint's mythic past, Moore shows viewers the American nightmare of late-1980s Flint, in which boarded-up businesses line the downtown streets, abandoned houses pepper the surrounding neighborhoods, and rats outnumber the population by more than fifty thousand. The contrast between the heyday of 1950s Flint and the present serves as a reminder of what this community, built on the foundation of an industrial workforce, has lost in a postindustrial economy. Throughout the film, Moore includes interviews with unemployed GM workers who perceive the layoffs as a violation of a social contract between the corporation and the community, which they believed had provided the possibilities of the American Dream for members of the working class. When Moore asks some GM employees what they would say to Roger Smith in light of the recent wave of layoffs, one woman admonishes, "I'd tell Roger Smith to get off of his big bucks and start giving some of it back to the workers. I'm sick of these fat cats!" Another comments, "He can't look an autoworker in the eye because he should be feeling guilty."

In a poignant scene that depicts the sense of great despair felt for a dream that seems just out of reach now for many in Flint, Deputy Ross is shown giving an eviction notice to a young man who went to the same high school as Michael Moore. Clearly distraught, the man comments, "I feel sorry for the people who have kids right now, what are they going to grow up to? What are they looking forward to? Out there [pointing to the GM factory], it's nothing. They got a bleak future." When Moore asks where he will stay that night, the man answers regretfully, as his voice begins to crack, "The thing is, I don't wanna stay with somebody. I want a chance to have something of my own, which doesn't look like it's going to happen, ever. Not in this town."

A rhetorical contradiction within the film, and with the contemporary secular jeremiad as a rhetorical form, is that present failings are measured against an idealized past founded on a universal, and mythic, notion of the American Dream that never really existed in the first place. Johannesen notes that in the jeremiad, "the past values, ideals, principles, and achievements that now collectively constitute the American Dream serve as the grounding for arguments and appeals, although interpretations of those elements often are controversial."[47] While Moore implicitly argues that GM owes something to its workers, without whom the corporations would not have succeeded, this perception is based on a vision of the American Dream already challenged and redefined in the decades following the political and cultural unrest of the 1960s.

Walter Fisher outlines the antithetical nature of Americans' competing visions of the Dream, each of which pervades political discourse and "has its own rhetorical power and potential for destruction." Fisher maintains that the moralistic myth, which is what Moore upholds, "is well expressed in the basic tenets of the Declaration of Independence: that 'all men are created equal,' men 'are endowed by their Creator with certain inalienable rights,' 'among these are life, liberty and the pursuit of Happiness.'" This version of the American Dream works to "sustain the continuing endeavors to invest all public institutions with guarantees that all men will be treated equally and, in addition, serve to inspire cooperative efforts to benefit those who are less fortunate than others." In contrast, the materialistic myth "undergirds competition as the way of determining personal worth, the free enterprise system, and the notion of freedom, defined as the freedom from controls, regulations, or constraints that hinder the individual's striving for ascendency in the social-economic hierarchy or society."[48]

Moore's contrasting of "the haves" and "the have nots" in Flint portrays the discrepancy between the apathy of the Flint elite and the desperation of the unemployed GM workers, further exposed through the leitmotif of Fred Ross's series of evictions, with regard to the current economic climate. This juxtaposition both dramatizes the present social ills of Moore's jeremiad and demonstrates the discordance between the two visions of the American Dream. For example, Moore interviews a group of "the more fortunate at Flint" at an annual Great Gatsby party held at the home of one of GM's founding families. One attendee comments, "Things are tough here for the people that are laid off [but] there still are people working and I don't think it's as bad as people believe." Asked what advice he would offer to those who are having a rough go of it, one man responds, "Get up in the morning and go do something. Start yourself, get your own motor going. There's things to do out there." In the next scene, at the site of another eviction, Deputy Ross comments, "Out here, I've put out some good people. You have a lot of people in this town that is paying $800–$900 a month house notes. That's a lot of money to try and pay on unemployment."

Later in the film, Moore interviews a group of well-to-do, elderly women at a golf course. One comments, "I really don't know the answer, I feel sorry for people. But, you can't help them. I mean, you have such a good welfare program and, so, they just don't want to work. I don't think so, I really don't know. I absolutely don't know." Another offers, "I think everybody should try to, um, uh, find another job or do something else in training or something like that." When Moore asks, "Do you think a lot of people are just being lazy?" She responds, "I think some of them, a lot them, they take the easy way out, I think." This scene is followed by Deputy Ross evicting yet another unemployed family. Ross observes, "A lot of these people bought school clothes and then didn't pay the rent. The system has got to change because if they didn't have enough money to pay the rent and buy the clothes, they're in trouble anyway."

These conflicting views of what is happening in Flint, and whether the problem lies with unmotivated people or a broken system, reveal the dichotomous meanings and actions called forth by competing visions of the American Dream, and the ideologies that inform those visions. Fisher notes that the materialist myth "promises that if one employs one's energies and talents to the fullest, one will reap the rewards of status, wealth, and power." Those who are unaffected by the economic crisis in Flint uphold these ideals. Moore and Deputy Ross represent a counterpoint to the elite view of the economic situation by advocating the moralistic myth, which "advocates the natural rights and values of tolerance, charity, compassion, and true regard for the dignity and worth of each and every individual."[49]

The social and political incongruities of the materialistic and moralistic visions of the American Dream are further illustrated when the entrepreneurial self-help slogans proffered by the elite are juxtaposed with their material effects on working-class people's lives. To illustrate this irony, Moore includes a montage of interviews with Anita Bryant and Pat Boone, both GM-sponsored celebrities from the 1950s brought back in the 1980s to "provide entertainment and escape during Flint's hard times." Bryant offers this advice to the unemployed:

The opportunities are still in Flint, Michigan and they are still in America so just take one day at a time. . . . Go forward and be positive about life, don't be regretful or guilty about the past, don't fret or worry about the future. You have today, it's a new day, a new opportunity for you to look about you and look at the positive within yourself and within your community. . . . So, we live in a free society, today is a new day, it's an opportunity to do something for yourself, um, uh, if nothing else thank God for the sunshine, and for the fact that you're not starving to death, and go out and do something with your hands. I don't know.

In response to Moore's question, "Who is to blame for what's happened in Flint?" Pat Boone says:

I don't think it's anybody's fault. In a free society, in a capitalistic democratic society, things just do change, there's shifts, trends. I'm sure General Motors doesn't have any desire to either close down a plant or put people out of work. The key becomes the attitude, and folks wind up saying, "hey, you know, it was the best thing that ever happened to me is when my job at the plant phased out, 'cause I was only gonna go so far at the plant and now I've got my own business," whatever it is.

These two vignettes highlight the discrepancy in the Reagan-era political discourse emphasizing an elusive sense of progress and renewal embodied in the "entrepreneurial spirit" most often espoused by the upper class, many of whom had profited from the sweeping tax cuts of that period. These former members of the Flint community are safely distanced from the brutal realities of the supply-side economics that led to the dissolution of the working class.

One of the most memorable, and most remarked about, scenes in *Roger & Me* serves as a disturbing meditation on the incompatibility of the entrepreneurial panacea offered by the GM mouthpieces and the reality of this option for the working class in Flint. The scene features a woman who runs a business that sells bunnies as "pets or meat." She explains to Moore, "I'm on social security and the only other income I have is my rabbits for groceries and bills, and my dogs, I also raise Doberman pinschers. 'Cause sometimes I only make $10–$15 a week, but that's better than nothin', at least I can go out and buy $10, $15 worth of groceries, because you only get paid once a month from social security, and that's not very much!" Later in the film, Moore revisits the woman, whose operation had been shut down by the city's health inspector. She tells Moore that her next business venture is to make rabbit fur coats, as she illegally slaughters and skins a rabbit on film. While she's snipping the rabbit pelt from its motionless body, she explains, "I was brought up to learn to survive like if you were out in the wilderness." This sequence in the film, along with others featuring unemployed GM workers turning to Amway sales, the fast-food industry, and plasma donation, illustrate how the materialistic myth of the American Dream manifests striking problems when enacted in real-life situations. Fisher writes, "The myth is not believed by those who have tried to live by it and found in practice that it is flawed by favoritism and corruption."[50]

When viewed through Moore's imposed apposition, the chasm between the economic and social classes in Flint is striking. However, while the successful jeremiad, according to Ritter, "provides a source of renewal of cultural unity in the midst of political conflict," *Roger & Me* uses comedic juxtaposition to draw a sharp distinction between those he regards as the victims of the economic system and those who have been its benefactors, which further accentuates the political incompatibility between them.[51] Consequently, the organizing structure of *Roger & Me* reflects both the irreconcilability of the jeremiad's appeals to the values of a mythic American

Dream (which, in this case, only further elucidates the incongruous visions of that Dream produced through political discourse) and the consequent challenges for social cohesion necessary to enable redemption and reform on the part of the community. Hugh Duncan notes that "social tensions become unbearable, not when there are great differences between ranks or conditions of life (as in differences between generations), but when there are no common social symbols through which superior and inferior can communicate."[52] The film's depiction of such social tensions successfully illuminates the widening gap between the social classes in terms of personal wealth, while it also highlights the influence of their political ideologies on their interpretations of the larger economic situation in Flint and the responsibilities of market (versus social) citizenship.

One possibility for the difficulty some critics and viewers experienced with the film, then, is that Moore's blending of the seriousness of the documentary jeremiad with the comedic incongruities of political satire result in a distanced critique of both visions of the American Dream. Duncan notes that satirical comedy may have the potential to "re-create our social bonds even as we recognize our differences," in that it allows us to laugh through our tears. However, he also cautions that satire does not allow us to laugh through our fears, also arguing that "we cannot laugh at what we secretly or unconsciously fear, and we cannot think well about fears we cannot submit to group discourse."[53] The problem with Moore's portrayal is that the audience comes to fear both extremes, the rich who are getting richer and the poor who are becoming poorer, and is not invited to identify with either group. The viewing public and the film's critics are left unable to participate in the constitution of shared symbols and feel disconnected from the members of the Flint community. The audience also fails to experience a sense of cultural cohesion or united purpose, which is imperative for completing the jeremiad's call for reform.

While Moore seeks to reveal the disparities between the industrial rich and the working poor in bold relief, he ultimately draws caricatures of both sides and creates spectacles of many of the film's subjects. *Village Voice* film critic J. Hoberman observes, "The Toronto Film Festival audience with whom I saw the movie loved the spectacle of American kooks and American degeneration."[54] Sragow comments in his critique of the film, "Moore's cynicism about corporate America is justifiable; his cynicism about people is appalling. I can't think of a single moment of empathy in the movie.... Moore takes aim at the capitalist pigs, but his blunt sensibility

whacks everybody."[55] The consequence is that while viewers are invited
to mock those benefiting from the system, they also do not empathize
with those who have been left out. Viewers are offered a perspective that
invites them to laugh at the failures of others, while distancing themselves
from the class warfare that becomes the subject of the film's critique. A.
Cheree Carlson notes that "the comic frame requires the careful creation
of identification among all actors required to alter a social order."[56] Yet,
while the incongruities in *Roger & Me* may provide comic relief for some
members of the audience, these contradictions make it difficult for viewers
to see themselves in the story, and thus it becomes impossible to fulfill the
rhetorical mission of the jeremiad, which is to "promote social cohesion—a
sense of community, shared effort and sacrifice, and national unity."[57]

The rhetorical implications of the moralistic myth of the American
Dream favored by Moore in the film also complicate the film's ability to
reinforce a sense of community. Obviously, viewers predisposed to the
materialist vision of the American Dream would have a difficult time
accepting the premise of the film. However, as Fisher points out, the rhetorical weakness of moralistic values is that their appeals are predicated on
the arousal of guilt for what we *are* in relation to what we *should be*. "Put
another way: in order to be moved to moralistic appeals, one must condemn himself in some way or other." Further, Fisher explains, "moralistic
values are also weakened by their association with movements to produce
fundamental social and political change. . . . Because of this association,
moralistic values not only engender feelings of guilt, they also tend to
arouse fear and feelings of threat."[58] To condemn an audience to guilt is
standard jeremiad practice and may implore audience members to rise
up and heed ideals greater than themselves. But fear and threat have the
opposite effect, alienating the audience and leaving them feeling powerless, because if they are feeling defensive, they are less likely to make the
connection among the subjects in the film, their own actions, and their
joint responsibilities for salvation.[59]

Further, while feelings of guilt also may be constitutive of prophetic
rhetoric, since "the prophet is an accuser and judge" and "is called into being
when the law has been violated, a critical time,"[60] Moore presents himself
as an uneasy prophet in the film and therefore fails to show his audience
the road to redemption. Although the underlying plotline of the film is
Moore's quixotic pursuit of Smith from Grosse Pointe to GM headquarters
in Detroit to a stockholders meeting in New York City to try to persuade

him to come to Flint, we know Moore will never fulfill this mission. By portraying himself as a hapless and impotent "everyman" observer of Flint's calamities in the film, Moore fails to live up to the promise of the jeremiad prophet able to interpret the meaning of the chaos around him and restore boundaries and order. Darsey writes that the prophet "reminds the audience of the transcendental side of its culture that makes it larger than our individual wants and needs and aspirations and challenges us toward the achievement of that ideal."[61] Yet, as Rosenbaum points out, "On some level, we were being invited to laugh at our own defeat as human beings, our incapacity to affect Roger Smith's conscience any more than Michael Moore could. . . . I suspect he wants us to laugh at his own impotence and our own as a way of goading us into action; but if that's the case, he doesn't even begin to show us what form that action could take."[62]

Viewers, then, are left with an ineffective jeremiad with no proposed solution, uncertainty about how to address the problems of the present, and uneasiness about the future.

Michael Moore's Vision and the Failed Jeremiad

Through his breakout film, *Roger & Me*, Michael Moore formulated one of the first political critiques of a pervasive neoliberalism that would eventually result, in the opinion of many, in the collapse of democratic political life in America.[63] The rise of neoliberalism began in the Reagan-Thatcher era, the period in which *Roger & Me* takes place, but it has continued throughout two decades and multiple political administrations. Moore viewed his film as a warning to Americans about the aftermath of a "violent economic system, designed to keep a few people rich and the rest poor."[64] He saw the dangers of globalization more than a decade before the World Trade Organization protests in Seattle and almost two decades before journalists and scholars engaged in the serious treatment of antiglobalization movements, as well as the critique of neoliberalism.[65] Despite Moore's remarkably apt prophecy of the national economic and social decline that resulted from the next two decades of free markets, deindustrialization, and unregulated corporate domination, *Roger & Me* seems to be remembered more for its generic challenge to the conventions of both documentary film and satiric fiction, and its failure to live up to the political standards of either, rather than as a warning siren regarding the impending crisis of global capitalism. While a few of the reviewers interpreted the film as a warning of impending economic doom for the country at large, others were more frustrated by the contradictions inherent in both Moore's satirical documentary and the secular jeremiad as a prophetic form.

According to John Murphy, "In times of crisis, [the jeremiad] functions to shape responses to the difficulties that reaffirm the viability and nobility of the American experiment. . . . By looking to the past through the jeremiad, Americans limit the kinds of choices they can make about the future."[66] *Roger & Me* suffers from such limitations wrought by a form that offers political solutions for the present (and future) by looking back to a nostalgic past that existed only in our distorted collective memory rather than in any historical reality. Similarly, Andrew Murphy argues that "the critic—the Jeremiah—constructs a past that serves as a limiting or *constraining* condition on the present, a sort of empirical checklist to hold up in order to assess the propriety of certain features of contemporary life."[67] Moore's response to the threat of corporate warfare on the middle and working class is to hark back to an ideal America in which corporations and workers shared a relationship of mutual respect. However, even this view is flawed, because the heyday of workers, unions, and corporations that Moore recalls has been glorified through its remembered successes (such as the Flint Sit-Down Strike), its failures now forgotten. In fact, workers and corporations have always been in a state of struggle within the context of a profit-driven national economy that upholds the creation of private wealth over the maintenance of social citizenship and the values of the community. Constrained to this imagined checklist against which to measure our present failings, Moore's jeremiad is unable to imagine a new identity for workers in a postindustrial era, which is necessary in order to encourage "political engagement with the realities of twenty-first century global dynamics."[68]

The film also may have failed to resonate with a wide range of audiences as a social and political call to action because of the incompatibility of the jeremiad and political satire as rhetorical forms for documentary film. While many viewers found Moore's overarching political arguments persuasive, the film lost ground by not reconciling its formal attributes as satiric comedy with the necessities of documentary film as an agent of change. Carl Plantinga notes of *Roger & Me* that using an ironic structure has implications, writing, "Hayden White implies that ironic history—as a narrative structure—is disabling and impotent, that it engenders belief in the 'madness' of civilization and dissolves optimism about the possibility of positive political action."[69] Further, Duncan asserts that "where there are great gaps between classes or conditions of life, irony fails," since "the only social certainty offered by the ironist is the certainty of open and free discussion as a means to truth," which "creates and sustains social bonds."[70] The ironic mode of *Roger & Me* did not foster such discussion and the re-creation of social bonds, but rather further divided its audience away from the absurdity of both those who are powerful and those who have become powerless in the current economic climate. The film does not attempt to invite audiences to question their own ideologies or to examine the consequences of emerging political views on the material conditions of the working poor, but merely underscores the vast incompatibility between the social classes in terms of villains versus victims.

This is where the hybrid form of "documentary satire" fails as a rhetorical form, because irony invites us to laugh through our social differences, while documentary strives to politically motivate us to unite toward social justice. Anna Misiak observes that while Moore approaches his films with the aim of awakening the political consciousness of the public, "the satirist-ironic mood is another bow toward the audience to make their reception more enjoyable. The laughter is generated not only to ridicule, but also to produce catharsis. We can laugh at the characters, but then the difficult feelings of uneasiness and shame come, which certainly provoke more profound reflections."[71] Yet, I would argue that the rhetorical experience of *Roger & Me*, while entertaining, does not so clearly resolve the tensions between ridicule and political catharsis. While the film allows audiences into the documentary jeremiad frame in order to witness the illnesses within our society, its satiric edge does not provide the impetus for collective redemption and reform necessary to cure them.

Notes

1. Michael Moore, "America Is NOT Broke," *MichaelMoore.com*, March 5, 2011, http://www.michaelmoore.com/words/mike-friends-blog/america-is-not-broke.

2. J. Hoberman, review of *Roger & Me*, *Village Voice*, October 3, 1989, http://cinefiles.bampfa.berkeley.edu/cinefiles/DocDetail?docId=45719; Hal Hinson, review of *Roger & Me*, *Washington Post*, January 12, 1990, http://www.washingtonpost.com/wp-srv/style/longterm/movies/videos/rogermerhinson_a0a906.htm; Richard Bernstein, "'Roger & Me': Redefining the Limits," review of *Roger & Me*, *New York Times*, February 1, 1990, C20; Alex Patterson, "Putting a Face on the Enemy," review of *Roger & Me*, *Village Voice*, September 26, 1989, 68.

3. See Michael Sragow, "Roger and the Demagogue," review of *Roger & Me*, *San Francisco Examiner*, January 12, 1990, C1, C7–C8; David Armstrong, "Everyman Makes Waves," review of *Roger & Me*, *San Francisco Examiner*, January 12, 1990, C9.

4. For a discussion of similar debates that emerged around the release of *Fahrenheit 9/11* in 2004, see the special report by Maarten Pereboom and John E. O'Connor, "Michael Moore: Cinematic Historian or Propagandist? A Historians Film Committee Panel Presented at the 2005 American Historical Association Meeting," *Film & History* 35, no. 2 (2005): 7–16.

5. Ed Kelleher, review of *Roger & Me*, *Film Journal International*, January 1990, http://cinefiles.bampfa.berkeley.edu/cinefiles/DocDetail?docId=45740.

6. Patterson, "Putting a Face on the Enemy," 68.

7. Roger Ebert, review of *Roger & Me*, Dog Eat Dog Films, December 1989, accessed February 2, 2011, http://dogeatdog.michaelmoore.com/ebert.html.

8. Peter Rainer, "Film Maker Michael Moore Takes on Roger Smith and His Giant Corporation in Cutting Satire," review of *Roger & Me*, *Los Angeles Times*, December 20, 1989, reprinted at Dog Eat Dog Films, http://dogeatdog.michaelmoore.com/rainer.html, accessed February 2, 2011.

9. Stuart Klawans, review of *Roger & Me*, *Nation*, January 1, 2009, http://www.thenation.com/article/roger-and-me.

10. Hinson, review of *Roger & Me*.

11. Notably, *Roger & Me* landed on the top-ten lists of more than seventy film critics for 1989, earned over $80,000 in its opening weekend (during a limited run on only four screens nationwide), and grossed more than $5.5 million at the box office by the end of February 1990. *Roger & Me* still ranks number twenty on the list of top-grossing documentary films in history, while four of Moore's subsequent films, *Bowling for Columbine*, *Fahrenheit 9/11*, *Sicko*, and *Capitalism: A Love Story*, populate the top-ten list.

12. Harlan Jacobson, "Michael & Me," *Film Comment*, 25, no. 6 (1989): 16–18, 22.

13. Pauline Kael, "Melodrama/Cartoon/Mess," review of *Roger & Me*, *New Yorker*, January 8, 1990, 90, 91, 93.

14. Sragow, "Roger and the Demagogue," C1, C7–C8.

15. David Kehr, "'Roger & Me' Treads on Shaky Ground with Filmmaking Style," review of *Roger & Me*, *Chicago Tribune*, January 12, 1990.

16. Carley Cohan and Gary Crowdus, "Reflections on *Roger & Me*, Michael Moore, and His Critics," *Cineaste* 17, no. 4 (1990): 26.

17. Roger Ebert, "Attacks on 'Roger & Me' Completely Miss Point of Film," *Roger Ebert's Journal*, *Chicago Sun Tribune*, February 11, 1990, http://rogerebert.suntimes.com/apps/pbcs.dll/article?AID=/19900211/COMMENTARY/22010306.

18. Paula Rabinowitz, *They Must Be Represented: The Politics of Documentary* (New York: Verso, 1994), 6–7. See also Paula Rabinowitz, "Sentimental Contracts: Dreams and Documents of American Labor," in *Feminism and Documentary*, ed. Diane Waldman and Janet Walker (Minneapolis: University of Minnesota Press, 1999), 43–63; Lucy Fischer, "Documentary Film and the Discourse of Historical/Hysterical Narrative," in *Documenting the Documentary: Close Readings of Documentary Film and Video*, ed. Barry Keith Grant and Jeannette Sloniowski (Detroit: Wayne State University Press, 1998), 333–43; and Linda Williams, "Mirrors without Memories: Truth, History, and the New Documentary," *Film Quarterly* 46, no. 3 (1993): 9–21.

19. Eric Barnouw, *Documentary: A History of the Non-Fiction Film*. 3rd ed. (New York: Oxford University Press, 1993), 344–48.

20. Matthew Bernstein, "Documentaphobia and Mixed Modes: Michael Moore's *Roger & Me*," in *Documenting the Documentary: Close Readings of Documentary Film and Video*, ed. Barry Keith Grant and Jeanette Sloniowski (Detroit: Wayne State University Press, 1998), 397–415.

21. Bill Nichols, *Representing Reality: Issues and Concepts in Documentary* (Bloomington: Indiana University Press, 1991), 35.

22. Bernstein, "Documentaphobia," 402.

23. Miles Orvell, *After the Machine: Visual Arts and the Erasing of Cultural Boundaries* (Jackson: University Press of Mississippi, 1995), 125, 122.

24. Ebert, "Attacks on 'Roger & Me.'"

25. Bernstein, "Documentaphobia," 405.

26. Nichols, *Representing Reality*, 44.

27. Bernstein, "Roger & Me," C20.

28. Sragow, "Roger and the Demagogue," C8.

29. Cohan and Crowdus, "Reflections on *Roger & Me*," 29.

30. Kehr, "'Roger & Me' Treads on Shaky Ground."

31. Bernstein, "Documentaphobia," 412; Orvell, *After the Machine*, 114.

32. Nichols, *Representing Reality*, 56–57, 71.

33. Rainer, "Film Maker Michael Moore."

34. Orvell, *After the Machine*, 127.

35. See Nichols, *Representing Reality*, 71–72.

36. Andrew R. Murphy, "Longing, Nostalgia, and Golden Age Politics: The American Jeremiad and the Power of the Past," *Perspectives on Politics* 7, no. 1 (2009): 126.

37. Kurt W. Ritter, "American Political Rhetoric and the Jeremiad Tradition: Presidential Nomination Acceptance Addresses, 1960–1976," *Central States Speech Journal* 13 (1980): 157.

38. See Sacvan Bercovitch, *The American Jeremiad* (Madison: University of Wisconsin Press, 1978); Ritter, "American Political Rhetoric"; Richard L. Johannesen, "Ronald Reagan's Economic Jeremiad," *Central States Speech Journal* 37, no. 2 (1986): 79–89.

39. Johannesen, "Ronald Reagan's Economic Jeremiad," 81.

40. See Ernest G. Bormann, "Fetching Good out of Evil: A Rhetorical Use of Calamity," *Quarterly Journal of Speech* 63 (1977): 130–39; Ritter, "American Political Rhetoric," 158–167; Johannesen, "Ronald Reagan's Economic Jeremiad," 80–82.

41. See James Darsey, "The Legend of Eugene Debs: Prophetic *Ethos* as Radical Argument," *Quarterly Journal of Speech* 74 (1988): 434–52; Mari Boor Tonn, "The Rhetorical Personae of Mary Harris 'Mother' Jones: Industrial Labor's Maternal Prophet" (PhD diss., University of Kansas, 1987).

42. Darsey, "Legend of Eugene Debs," 435.

43. James Darsey, *The Prophetic Tradition and Radical Rhetoric in America* (New York: New York University Press, 1997), 202.

44. Ritter, "American Political Rhetoric," 164.

45. Ibid., 168; Murphy, "Longing, Nostalgia, and Golden Age Politics," 128.

46. Rainer, "Film Maker Michael Moore."

47. Johannesen, "Ronald Reagan's Economic Jeremiad," 80.

48. Walter R. Fisher, "Reaffirmation and Subversion of the American Dream," *Quarterly Journal of Speech* 59 (1973): 161–62.

49. Ibid., 161.

50. Ibid.

51. Ritter, "American Political Rhetoric," 171.

52. Hugh Dalziel Duncan, *Communication and Social Order* (New York: Oxford University Press, 1962), 413.

53. Ibid., 388–89.

54. Hoberman, review of *Roger & Me.*

55. Sragow, "Roger and the Demagogue," C8.

56. A. Cheree Carlson, "Limitations on the Comic Frame: Some Witty American Women of the Nineteenth Century," *Quarterly Journal of Speech* 74 (1988): 319.

57. Johannesen, "Ronald Reagan's Economic Jeremiad," 81.

58. Fisher, "Reaffirmation and Subversion," 162.

59. Mark S. Jendrysik makes a similar argument about the usefulness of the modern jeremiad in political discourse. He asserts that in order to avoid alienating too large an audience, contemporary jeremiad works direct their criticism at easy targets and "since she is not personally accused, the reader cannot easily see a connection between her own actions and the salvation of America." See Jendrysik, "The Modern Jeremiad: Bloom, Bennett, and Bork on American Decline," *Journal of Popular Culture* 36, no. 2 (November 2002): 361–83.

60. Darsey, *Prophetic Tradition*, 24.

61. Ibid., 202.

62. Jonathan Rosenbaum, "Nihilism for the Masses [ROGER & ME]," on Rosenbaum's website, February 2, 1990, http://www.jonathanrosenbaum.net/1990/02/nihilism-for-the-masses/.

63. See, for example, Noam Chomsky, *Profit over People: Neoliberalism and Global Order* (New York: Seven Stories Press, 1999); Naomi Klein, *Shock Doctrine: The Rise of Disaster Capitalism* (New York: Picador, 2007).

64. Quoted in Patterson, "Putting a Face on the Enemy."

65. See David Harvey, *A Brief History of Neoliberalism* (New York: Oxford University Press, 2007); Chris Harman, "Theorizing Neoliberalism," *International Socialism* 117 (Winter 2008), http://www.isj.org.uk/index.php4?id=399&issue=117; and Stanley Fish, "Neoliberalism and Higher Education," *Opinionator* (blog), *New York Times*, March 8, 2009, http://opinionator.blogs.nytimes.com/2009/03/08/neoliberalism-and-higher-education/.

66. John M. Murphy, "'A Time of Shame and Sorrow': Robert F. Kennedy and the American Jeremiad," *Quarterly Journal of Speech* 76 (1990): 412.

67. Murphy, "Longing, Nostalgia, and Golden Age Politics," 131.

68. Ibid.

69. Carl Plantinga, *Rhetoric and Representation in Nonfiction Film* (New York: Cambridge University Press, 1997), 94. See also Hayden White, *Metahistory: The Historical Imagination in Nineteenth-Century Europe* (Baltimore: Johns Hopkins University Press, 1973), 37.

70. Duncan, *Communication and Social Order*, 381.

71. Anna Misiak, "Not a Stupid White Man: The Democratic Context of Michael Moore's Documentaries," *Journal of Popular Film and Television* 33, no. 3 (2005): 165.

3. *The Big One* That Got Away

Christine Harold

ichael Moore's second full-length documentary, *The Big One* (1998), is one part stand-up routine, one part road movie, one part rabble-rousing. As a stand-up comic, Moore holds his own. The film is peppered, *Seinfeld*-style, with Moore onstage, microphone in hand, taking witty jabs at corporate America, finely honed by his months on the road promoting his 1996 book, *Downsize This!*[1] Moore wonders suspiciously with one audience, for example, about *Forbes* magazine editor and conservative presidential candidate Steve Forbes, as he seems to have "come from nowhere." "Didya ever notice that when he was on TV his eyes never blinked?" Moore says with a chuckle, as the screen cuts to Forbes on *Nightline*, eyes wide open. Moore tells the audience he was so puzzled by it that he called New York Hospital and asked an eyes, ears, nose, and throat specialist why Forbes never seems to blink. Moore tells the doctor, "I'm watching him on TV and he hasn't blinked in two minutes!" The doctor's response? "Well, *that's not human* . . . ," Moore's throaty voice echoes forebodingly through the auditorium. The audience erupts in laughter. "*Not human* . . . ," Moore repeats, speculating aloud that Forbes may be a "freak, *X-Files* brother from another planet." More laughter.

Moore's now famous persona—unrelenting champion of the little guy or obnoxious jerk, depending on your perspective—is much more prominent here than in *Roger & Me*, in which he largely remained behind the camera, letting the heartbroken, hapless citizens of Flint tell their own stories. In *The Big One*, Moore is clearly the star of the show, a choice he seems to have made ambivalently. As the film opens, the on-screen credits are accompanied by the sound of an audience cheering wildly while Moore interjects, "Thank you, thank you very much . . ." Moore's image—plaid shirt, jeans, perennial baseball hat—emerges on a dark stage under a glaring spotlight as he launches into a story about prank $100 donations he made to the presidential candidates in the name of nonexistent groups such as "Pedophiles for Free Trade" (Perot) and "Abortionists for Buchanan." The scene serves as a structural frame, alerting viewers that they will be joining Moore on his book tour, but it also establishes Moore's status as a celebrity storyteller who can command large, cheering audiences.

The film's posters play with Moore's newfound movie stardom and draw on the action hero theme. In one, outfitted in a black suit and tie and black Ray-Ban sunglasses, Moore is armed with a huge microphone, which he holds like a machine gun across his chest. "Protecting the Earth from the scum of Corporate America," reads the tagline. The poster invokes the popular 1997 film *Men in Black*, in which Tommy Lee Jones and Will Smith are "protecting the Earth from the scum of the Universe." In a second poster, Moore, with a microphone in one hand, stiff-arms with the other a giant wingtip-shod foot, single-handedly protecting the city behind him from a giant corporate invader. The tagline reads, "It's a BIG Country . . . and Only One Man Can Save It!" If the Moore of *Roger & Me* was an everyman with a movie camera, he is now working-class action hero, taking the fight to the greedy suits, the less-than-human "alien" invaders like Steve Forbes. For the most part, Moore's role as best-selling author on a national book tour is played with a wink and a nudge, but the film has its self-indulgent moments. As *Los Angeles Times* critic Kenneth Turan puts it, "His seat-of-the-pants approach is reflected in the final film, whose ramshackle structure seems to include anything of interest Moore ran into."[2]

As road movie, *The Big One* hits all the familiar notes. Moore and his team visit forty-seven cities in fifty days. Willie Nelson's "On the Road Again" and Johnny Cash's "I've Been Everywhere" ramble over montages of Moore and his beleaguered crew in the tour van, in airplanes, idling in any number of fast-food drive-throughs. At each stop, Moore meets with workers who either have lost their jobs or are making ends meet by burning the candle at both ends. One young mother having lunch in an Iowa diner called the Hearty Platter tells Moore that she works a day shift at one job and night shift at another, seeing her two little girls only on Sunday afternoons "'cause Fairway [grocery store]'s not open."

"That'd be like being divorced, only seeing your kids on the weekend," Moore notes sympathetically. "Yeah, but I'm not divorced," the woman responds sadly, "I'm married. I got a husband. But I still don't getta see 'em, because of the way it is in America, around the world. It's just not fair." Depressed, Moore and his crew pile back into their tour van and head for McDonald's as the Yayhoos' southern-fried cover of "Highway Junkie" extradiagetically resumes.

As the team leaves the heartland, the ambling film picks up its pace and speeds viewers through several cities, identified in large white letters across the screen and punctuated by Queen's underdog anthem, "We Will Rock You": "CLEVELAND," "NEW YORK," "BOSTON," "TORONTO," "LOS ANGELES," "SAN FRANCISCO." Interspersed in the montage are clips of stunts and demonstrations by Moore and assorted local citizens, such as a small group of angry HMO customers shouting, "We want to see the Kaiser!" as they pound on the doors of Kaiser Permanente's Oakland, California, headquarters. This extended montage culminates in the climax and most noteworthy segment of the film, a surprise interview with Nike CEO Phil Knight.

The Big One is very much a film of its time. It captures the hubris and havoc endemic to the years leading up to the turn of the new century. Although few would likely consider the film to be among Moore's artistic best, as an artifact attesting to the rise of global capitalism and its all-too-human fallout, it warrants our critical attention. But if *The Big One* testifies to the damage done by the apparent mandate of large corporations to remain competitive at all costs, it also illustrates the challenges facing those attempting a critical response.

Capitalism at a Crossroads

> Today, if your company is like GM, it's in deep trouble
> —Kevin Kelly, *New Rules for the New Economy*

In their titanic analysis of contemporary global economics, *The New Spirit of Capitalism*, French sociologists Luc Boltanski and Eve Chiapello describe a shift in the structure of capitalism that has occurred over the last three decades. They chart the political and cultural changes as capitalism moves away from a bureaucratic organizational model to one valuing flexible global networks and workers who are adaptable enough to navigate them. Downsizing and redistributing labor forces have been key tools as corporations transition from rigid nationalistic hierarchies to flexible global networks. Ironically, for Boltanski and Chiapello, the management rhetoric championing this sleeker, more "efficient" mode of capital has justified the shift in part by appropriating the language and imagery of 1960s artistic critiques of capitalism. In this new, flexible spirit of capitalism, flexible work is offered as a rejoinder to New Left arguments that the "organization man" of yesteryear was homogenized, oppressed, and alienated from authentic life.[3] Indeed, if the business advice literature of the nineties and today is to be believed, the clock-watching "man in the gray flannel suit" has been forever usurped by a goateed, tech-savvy freelancer who rebels against conformity and "thrives on chaos."[4] This romantic aesthetic has tended to gloss over the effects that the reorganization of capital has had on US workers, especially those dependent on a traditional industrial infrastructure in which manufacturing jobs were reliable and plentiful.

Moore's first two films, *Roger & Me* (1989) and *The Big One*, chronicle the impacts of this shift on the ground and what they have meant for working-class Americans struggling to survive amid the recent corporate mandate to scrupulously shave costs wherever possible in an effort to become lighter, sleeker, and more competitive. By today's business standards, an industrial landscape populated by monoliths like GM appears prehistoric and bloated. In their effort to radically streamline their operations, global corporations have increasingly moved heavy industrial jobs overseas and to Mexico and have relied on temporary, project-based workers in their corporate offices. Service jobs are being increasingly outsourced as well, such as to call centers in India, thanks to modern digital communications technology and other factors. By imbuing these changes with a rhetoric celebrating worker autonomy and initiative, this new spirit of capitalism appears to address New Left grievances that commercial culture oppressed the creative spirit and offered only inauthentic pleasures through the scintillating promises of consumer culture. However, although profits still flow upward, the new "freedoms" and responsibilities granted to US workers in the new economy have tended to place the burdens and risks of financial growth squarely on *workers'* shoulders, as they are forced to navigate an ever-changing, Darwinian work environment in which only the most flexible and adaptable survive.

In *The Cultural Work of Corporations*, Megan Brown analyzes the dominant rhetorical themes of some of the top-selling business self-help books of the late 1980s and 1990s, the era when Michael Moore first arrived on the national scene.[5] Business advice at the time purported to help anxious American workers survive the perils of the "new economy"—an economy in which job security for the "company man" was rapidly becoming a thing of the past. Analyzing biz lit best-sellers with titles like *Swim with the Sharks without Being Eaten Alive* and *Who Moved My Cheese?*, Brown observes that the overall rhetorical framework is a newfangled Social Darwinism in which "flexibility" and "adaptability" are the keys to survival. But unlike actual natural selection, these success manuals suggest that survival is a matter of choice for individual actors. That is, failure is an effect of one's own inability to sufficiently adapt to the changing marketplace. In saying this, these books perpetuate an unfortunate trend toward alleviating corporations of responsibility by displacing blame and expanding the cognitive distance between the accumulation of wealth and the labor that produces it.

Brown writes that sociologist Ulrich Beck "shows how corporate emphasis on flexibility in an increasingly global marketplace works to disguise 'a redistribution of risks away from the state and the economy toward the individual.' Simply put, flexibility can really signify job insecurity—'discursively "sweetened" . . . by the rhetoric of independent entrepreneurial individualism.' In this way, the individual employee, never the employer or the economy, is to blame when downsizing occurs. Anyone who becomes part of the mass in a mass layoff did not train and adapt diligently enough."[6] Whereas once capitalism alienated workers through the homogenization and repetition of labor, it has so radically moved away from factory-style alienation that workers are now tasked with keeping pace in an ever-changing workplace and blamed if they are discarded.

The reason capitalism was able to so successfully co-opt the revolutionary rhetoric of the 1960s as it evolved into its sleeker, more flexible form was that it focused only on one version of the left's critique, what Boltanski and Chiapello call the "artistic critique." To the artistic critics' attacks that capitalism is alienating and oppressive to the spirit, the market could readily respond. Want more flexibility? Easy: projects, not jobs. Need meaningful experience? Come, join our brand tribe. But the artistic critique that animated much of the 1960s is only half the story. What has been neglected in recent critiques of capitalism, say Boltanski and Chiapello,

is what they describe as the *social critique* of the 1960s. Unlike the grievances of the artistic critique, which could be addressed at an aesthetic and
emotional level, the social critique denounces inequality and poverty on
the one hand and egoism on the other. For the social critic, the "source
of indignation" is not *alienation*, but good, old-fashioned *exploitation*.
The authors acknowledge that social critique is showing a "hesitant and
modest" new lease on life, but in order to really take hold of the cultural
imagination, it must problematize the current tendency to blame or pity
workers through a rhetorical frame of inclusion and exclusion. Instead,
social critics must "establish a link between [the worker's] lot and that of
the better-off, particularly those who occupy privileged social positions.
Such an operation would make it possible to flesh out the responsibility
of the latter, and constitute a better guarantee for the most deprived, than
mere appeals to 'big-heartedness.'"[7]

Indeed, Boltanski and Chiapello advocate doing something very much
like Moore does in *The Big One*: foreground exploitation—not as an unfortunate side effect of the drive to expand profit, but as a crucial contributor
to it. This is Moore's modus operandi. He visually and discursively makes
explicit the links between those who benefit from the production of wealth
and those who actually produce it. A rhetoric of exclusion always portrays
the excluded as being *without*—"without a voice, without a home, without
papers, without work, without rights, and so on"[8]—even by those who are
fighting on their behalf. What is lost in this framework, and what Moore
is attempting to reinvigorate, is the positive features that have histori-
cally been attached to working-class struggles through the figure of what
Boltanski and Chiapello call the "man of the people—courage, candor,
generosity, solidarity."[9]

In *The Big One*, Moore sits down to discuss *Downsize This!* with Studs
Terkel, one of the American left's most beloved "men of the people." The
scene opens with a smiling Terkel, host of a long-standing radio show,
earnestly singing along to the traditional labor song "We're Gonna Roll
the Union On" before introducing Moore to his listeners. The mutual
admiration between the two is readily apparent. Terkel asks Moore,
"Hearing this passage from this old labor song, what thought comes to
your mind?" Moore replies that it makes him think of the great 1936–37
Sit-Down Strike of Flint and his uncle Laverne, who was a part of it. "I
think about how all of us gained from that and all the other labor actions
that came after that: the standard of living, health care, social security,

child labor . . . all these things came as a result of the struggle that those people participated in." He adds, "And if they could see what's going on now," punctuated with a contemptuous snort.

Terkel then holds up a copy of Moore's book, opened to the first page. "What Is Terrorism?" it asks, above two nearly identical pictures, each of a demolished building. One, the caption indicates, is Oklahoma City in 1995. The other is Flint, Michigan, in 1996, following GM's closing of its factories there. When Terkel asks him to explain, Moore acknowledges that the actions of Timothy McVeigh in Oklahoma City were obviously terrorism. However, he adds soberly:

> What do you call it, Studs, when you politely remove the people from the building first and then blow it up? But in the ensuing years the people who used to work in that building, because their livelihood has been stripped from them . . . a number of them will die. They'll die from suicide. They'll die from spousal abuse. They'll die from drugs and alcoholism, and all the social problems that surround people when they become unemployed. Those people are just as dead as the people in Oklahoma City, but we don't call the actions of the company terrorism, do we? And we don't call the company a murderer. But I do consider this an act of economic terrorism, when at a time you're making a *record profit* you would throw people out of work, *just so you can make a little bit more.*

Here Moore makes his case in the starkest possible terms. The devastation wrought on Flint and cities like it across the country is a direct result of the greed of individual actors. And this devastation is not incidental to the pursuit of profit—it is a mechanism for *producing* profit. By juxtaposing the "courage, candor, generosity, [and] solidarity" of his uncle and his comrades with the "terrorist" actions of GM and its ilk, Moore frames the issue of globalization in terms of exploitation, rather than merely exclusion. Hence, the answer is not for the market to simply expand its tent to include the "weak" and the "voiceless," but for workers to raise their collective voice and exercise their formidable power to force a fundamental restructuring of the economic system. Boltanski and Chiapello argue, "To relate exclusion to exploitation, we must, as a minimum, be in a position to found a principle of solidarity between the good fortune of the strong (great men) and the misery of the weak (little people). If, on the one side, we have highly prosperous strong people and, on the other, little people in a miserable state, but there is no link between them and they move in completely different worlds, then the idea of exploitation has no meaning. They must at least share a common world."[10]

Although Moore may not conceive it in just these terms, his films all attempt to do precisely this work—to bust the myth that the huge inequities of wealth under global capital are the logical effects of a faceless system or the natural outcome of a well-functioning meritocracy. By dragging privilege kicking and screaming onto the same plane as misery, he aims to demonstrate the intimacy of their association. When at his best, Moore's conversations—with downsized workers and with the various middle managers who buffer their bosses from Moore's antics—bridge the gaps of time and space that befuddle many of us trying to make sense of how value and profit are grown in the current economy.

If *The Big One* can be said to have a central theme, it is precisely to make the locus of blame explicit and personal. For Moore, it is not the workers at the bottom of the industrial food chain, nor is it the disembodied logic of an economic system run amok, but it is the choices of individual actors—the evasive CEOs he vainly pursues—who are causing global misery by refusing to restrain their own greed.

We see this theme play out early in the film, when Moore visits Johnson Controls, an automotive parts supplier that had just announced it was closing its Milwaukee facility and moving all jobs to Mexico. In an archetypically Moore moment, Moore and his camera crew walk into the company's corporate lobby with a huge check made out to the Johnson Controls CEO for 80 cents. As Moore explains to the confused spokeswoman, the paltry sum is "to pay the first Mexican worker for the first hour of work . . . this is what you'll be paying Mexicans down there, 80 cents an hour . . . just to help out, 'cause this is just, you know, I guess you've hit hard times here," he tells her, feigning concern. In her attempt to justify the plant closing to Moore, the spokeswoman explains that although the company has not done poorly, it simply must remain competitive:

SPOKESWOMAN: No, we haven't hit hard times.
MOORE: Well, you've only made a half a billion dollars in the last three
    years in profits.
SPOKESWOMAN: Our company is reasonably successful and we're
    committed to continuing to be successful.

MOORE: Then why would you leave Milwaukee if you're successful?
SPOKESWOMAN: Because we need to remain competitive in our businesses.
MOORE: You mean you want to be more successful.
SPOKESWOMAN: We need to continue to be successful, that's right.

In the subsequent segment, Moore talks with a Johnson Controls employee as he is leaving the plant for the last time. Having worked at the company for twenty years, he is unsure what he will do. As they talk, footage of a nearby security patrol car idling in the parking lot is spliced with that of Moore and the disheartened worker, a visual reminder that the workers were no longer welcome at the plant. The employee tells Moore that Johnson Controls was the last of the major manufacturers in Milwaukee, and now that it's closing, the prospects for work in the city are not good. Moore then takes the man to Manpower, a temporary employment agency that happens to have its headquarters in Milwaukee. As the two pull up to the offices, in what will be a vain attempt to secure the man a job, Moore crystallizes the volatile spirit of the new capitalism: "Manpower, a company that guarantees you a job for a day, was now the number one employer in the country."

In another scene, Moore visits a PayDay candy bar plant in Centralia, Illinois, on the day that Leaf, International, the company that owned PayDay, informed its workers, via videotape no less, that the plant was shutting down and they would all be losing their jobs. After a discussion with the outraged workers in a crowd outside the plant, Moore seeks some face time with the manager in charge. He is allowed in, albeit without his cameraman (who follows anyway and films surreptitiously from down the hall):

MOORE: What is the message to the American worker, if they come here and work hard, and do well, and because of their hard work, the *company* does well, their reward is . . . unemployment.
MANAGER: Well, if this place would have done better, and would have made more profit, we would've had a quicker [unintelligible].
MOORE: You mean, you're saying if they had made a bigger profit here, the move would've been even quicker to get out of here?
MANAGER: You're right.
MOORE: If the workers had done a *worse* job, if the candy bar hadn't done as well, there might still be a candy bar plant here?

MANAGER: Sure.
MOORE: That's insane!

In this exchange, Moore reiterates the central theme of the film: that companies are downsizing not out of necessity, but out of greed. It is a cultural logic anticipated by Oliver Stone's *Wall Street* (1987), in which Gordon Gekko (Michael Douglas) tells a roomful of shareholders, "Greed, for lack of a better word, is *good*. Greed is right. Greed works. Greed clarifies, cuts through, and captures the essence of the evolutionary spirit." Gekko suggests that the era of big, bloated bureaucracies is over. Gekko, in Stone's telling, represents the new guard, the new competitive spirit of capitalism, however cutthroat that may be. As Megan Brown puts it, "Gekko is a mouthpiece for an up-and-coming approach to business practices—an advocate of making companies 'lighter,' more intense, more efficient and above all more focused on creating value for shareholders than worrying about in-house development."[11]

Exploitation and a Critical Denouement: Mike versus Nike

In *The Big One*'s climactic sequence, Moore scores an unlikely interview with Nike CEO Phil Knight while visiting Portland, Oregon, the last stop on Moore's tour and home of the largest shoe manufacturer in the world. Since the early 1990s, human rights groups have criticized Nike for contracting with overseas factories, primarily in Southeast Asia, that use child labor, employ coercive labor practices, and have unsafe working conditions. In *Downsize This!*, Moore ranks Knight number three in his satirical collection of Corporate Crook trading cards, and apparently, Knight's wife gave her husband a copy of the book for their wedding anniversary, with his photo prominently circled. In an attempt to repair the company's public image, a Nike PR representative invites Moore, live on a call-in radio show, to come to the Beaverton, Oregon, headquarters and chat with Knight. Moore readily accepts.

Before transitioning to his interview with Knight, Moore offers some background on the controversies surrounding the sportswear giant's use of "sweatshop" labor. Opening with an image of the Portland skyline, the film cuts to a banner depicting Nike's slogan, "Just Do It." As the camera pans down, we see rows of young women standing at sewing machines. Many, ironically, are barefoot in the sweltering shoe factory. Moore tells his audience in a voiceover, "Nike makes most of their shoes in Indonesia, using teenage girls, and paying them less than 40 cents an hour." The film cuts to footage of Indonesian soldiers in military fatigues jogging in formation, batons in hand, then quickly cuts to a scattering crowd of Indonesian civilians, arms raised in surrender, as soldiers in riot gear chase them from a city street, apparently dispersing a political protest. Moore continues over the footage, "The company has the backing of Indonesia's brutal military regime, which has committed genocide in East Timor." As the film cuts back to young Indonesian women placing inserts into sneakers, Moore says soberly, "Nike makes no shoes in America."

Viewers are then taken from a sweatshop in Indonesia to a demonstration in Portland, with protesters holding placards reading "Stop Corporate Greed" and "Jobs with Justice" and chanting, "Phil Knight can kiss my butt!" "When I arrived in Portland," Moore says, "I found the local citizens pretty upset about the situation." It is then revealed that Moore is a speaker at the rally, as a police officer approaches the stage. "Uh oh," says Moore into the microphone, "Nike has sent in the Portland police." As the clearly embarrassed officer approaches, Moore throws up his hands in submission. "Officer, I wear a size 11 and a half 'E,'" he says. "Thank you."

In this short succession of images—an Indonesian shoe factory, soldiers intimidating demonstrators, Americans protesting corporate power in a West Coast city—Moore visually maps some of the key nodes in the vast global network that the industrial supply chain has become. Everything is related, Moore tells us. The young girls who make our sneakers, the equally young soldiers maintaining "order" in Jakarta, angry workers and protesters in Portland, and even Moore himself are subject to a powerful system that feels increasingly remote and unaccountable. Indeed, a governing trope of Moore's films is that the individuals who presumably control that system are forever secreted behind closed doors, buffered by private security guards and armies of PR managers. But then Moore is invited to Nike.

In the subsequent scene, Moore enters a glass door of a tall, gleaming building emblazoned with a bright red Nike swoosh. The corporate avenger has finally gained access to the halls of power. "I couldn't believe the chairman of Nike was granting me a visit," he muses. Moore is greeted by a casual and amiable Knight; his hands are shoved in the pockets of his jeans, and he smiles charmingly as he greets Moore at the door to his office suite. It seems Knight is determined to portray himself as the antithesis of Roger Smith, the stiff, gray-haired CEO of General Motors whom Moore doggedly sought in *Roger & Me*. It is clear Knight is eager to defuse tensions by welcoming Moore onto his home turf, but he seems unaware of what he's getting himself into. Jay Carr of the *Boston Globe* describes Knight's hubris well, suggesting that he "trips over his own ego and faces Moore on camera, apparently thinking he can charm his way into some positive spin."[12] Garry Trudeau, who also lambasted Nike's labor practices in his *Doonesbury* comic strip, wondered in a *Time* editorial, "What was Phil Knight thinking when he agreed to appear in [*The Big One*]? If he actually trusted the populist filmmaker to intervene as Knight went postal on camera and started pumping round after round into his own foot, then Nike's founder is even more out of touch than legend has it."[13] Nonetheless, as Moore and Knight shake hands and Moore thanks him for the invitation, Knight replies, "Not at all, it should be fun."

Although his smile rarely wavers, Knight does not appear to be having fun for long. Moore promptly offers the CEO a gift of two airline tickets, one for each of them, to Indonesia. "You show me those factories, you explain this to me . . ." Knight demurs and says he couldn't possibly. "Now c'mon, sit back down, we gotta negotiate this deal . . . ," he says with a chuckle, gesturing to a chair opposite him. But Moore persists. When Knight explains that he believes trade is a way out of oppression for Indonesians, Moore retorts, "That's a separate discussion from an *American* company going into Indonesia and working with a regime that killed *200,000 people*. That's almost a form of *genocide*. I *know* that's got to bother you. I don't know you personally, but I *know* you've got a conscience." Knight appears pained for a moment and seems unsure how to respond. He says weakly that he doesn't approve of such things and attempts to draw a comparison to China's Cultural Revolution. Moore cuts him off: "How much is enough? How much is enough? If you are a billionaire, wouldn't it be okay to be a half a billionaire? Wouldn't it be okay for your company to make a little less money if it meant providing some jobs here in this country?"

Knight responds that his goal is not money, but to make Nike the best company it can be. Like the low-level corporate spokespeople Moore encounters throughout the film, Knight says his goal is essentially to remain competitive. To do so, he suggests, he must go with the workers who are most adaptable. "I simply have a basic belief," he says, "having been burned on it once. . . . Americans do *not* want to make shoes. They *don't* want to make shoes." Moore interjects emphatically, "That's not true!" and tries to negotiate a deal with Knight to bring a Nike plant to Flint if Moore can find five hundred workers willing to make shoes. "They may *say* they want to make shoes," Knight responds, "but I think they *don't want those jobs*."

For Knight, it is American workers' refusal to adapt, their refusal to be flexible that makes them the wrong kind of workers for large manufacturing projects. In a portion of the interview that was not included in the film but is available on Moore's website, Knight tells Moore that Nike did make shoes in the United States from 1975 to 1982, but it became too expensive when Maine, where one of the plants was located, passed a workers' rights law that resulted, according to Knight, in "several hundred cases of carpal tunnel syndrome that happened overnight." When Moore asks Knight to acknowledge that carpal tunnel syndrome is a real condition, Knight says yes, it is, but he suspects many workers were filing false claims. "I mean, basically it's like whiplash of the wrist," he says as he shrugs dismissively.

Months after Moore's interview with Knight, before *The Big One* was released, Moore was invited to meet with Lee Weinstein, the director of public relations for Nike. As Moore recounts the story in several interviews, he sits down at a swank New York restaurant for breakfast with Weinstein, who immediately tells Moore, "We have the tape," referring to a bootlegged copy of *The Big One*. According to Moore, Weinstein asked him, "What would it take for you to remove two scenes from the film?" "I was really stunned," says Moore. "I didn't know what he meant and I didn't want to know what he meant. So I just cut him off and said 'I'm not cutting anything out of the film.' It made me horribly nervous. Once you start dealing, you're going down the wrong road." The two scenes Nike executives wanted removed were Knight's comment that he was not bothered by fourteen-year-olds working in Indonesian shoe factories and his sarcastic characterization of employees as "those poor little Indonesian workers," which Nike representatives said failed to accurately show Knight's respect for the people who make Nike products.

Moore refused to reedit the film, but he did offer a deal of sorts. He would not cut any scenes from the film, but he was willing to *add* one. If Knight would agree to open a facility of any kind in Flint, where workers were paid a living wage, then Moore would gladly document it and include it in the film. Nike never did open a factory in Flint, but less than a year after *The Big One* was released, Knight announced that Nike would raise the minimum age for workers to sixteen in its sports equipment factories and to eighteen in its shoe factories, where toxic fumes are more prevalent. Although he defended Nike's record, in a May 1998 speech Knight acknowledged, "The Nike product has become synonymous with slave wages, forced overtime and arbitrary abuse. . . . I truly believe that the American consumer does not want to buy products made in abusive conditions."[14] Today, although it has ratcheted up its oversight of foreign factories, Nike is still routinely criticized for its abusive labor practices.

Despite Knight's eventual, albeit partial, capitulation to pressure from Moore and other human rights activists, the tenor of his comments about workers in Nike's short-lived US plants is telling. His insistence that American workers do not want to make Nike products and in fact squandered their opportunity to do so by complaining and filing false workers' compensation claims exposes an assumption that dominates the "new spirit" of capitalism: that the kind of workers who can expect to succeed in the new economy will be those who, like Knight himself, don a winning smile and "go with the flow." Knight's easygoing demeanor and disarming shrugs cast, by contrast, the complaints and challenges of US workers as a failure not of corporate policies, but of workers' *attitudes*.

Many observers of contemporary business culture have noted the growing mandate to display a positive attitude in the workplace. Sociologist Richard Sennett, in *The Culture of the New Capitalism*, for example, argues that the flexibility endemic to this new era of capitalism requires a peculiar sort of worker—one who demonstrates an ability to navigate endlessly new work environments by letting go easily of previous relationships and skill sets: "This trait of personality resembles more the consumer ever avid for new things, discarding old if perfectly serviceable goods, rather than the owner who jealously guards what he or she already possesses."[15] Those who fail to go with the flow risk being labeled problematic. Barbara Ehrenreich denounces the trend fervently in *Bright-Sided: How the Relentless Promotion of Positive Thinking Has Undermined America*. She writes, "The flip side of positivity is . . . a harsh insistence on personal responsibility: if your business fails or your job is eliminated, it must be because you didn't try hard enough, didn't believe firmly enough in the inevitability of your success. . . . the promoters of positive thinking have increasingly emphasized this negative judgment: to be disappointed, resentful, or downcast is to be a 'victim' and a 'whiner.'"[16]

The irony of the positivity trend emerging in an age when record numbers of American workers have lost their jobs is not lost on Moore.[17] As he sardonically documents in *Roger & Me*, amid the devastation wrought on Flint by the GM plant closings, its mayor commissioned TV evangelist Robert Schuller to address Flint citizens for a fee of $20,000. "Turn your hurt into a halo," Schuller encouraged his desperate audience. "Just because you've got problems is *no excuse to be unhappy.*"

The Limits of "Big" Critique

As a cinematic element, the climactic interview with Phil Knight serves as a narrative linchpin, effectively bringing Moore's frustrations, the exploitation of labor in America and elsewhere, and corporate hunger for maximum profitability into a single notable confluence. But it also introduces something else, something that upsets the power of the narrative. Watching the interview, listening to Knight's vague and even at times confused responses, one realizes that the decisions Phil Knight is being asked to defend are not necessarily his own. One begins to wonder what degree of knowledge or even oversight someone like Phil Knight has over factories in Indonesia and the complicated social, technological, legal configurations that structure the lives of workers there. Maybe Phil Knight has that knowledge; maybe he has or had that level of control. Perhaps, had Moore been more persuasive, Knight could have declared a massive reorganization of Nike's factory infrastructure, enacting changes by executive fiat. Perhaps then the plant in Flint would have been built, and perhaps not just there, but in other places where American workers found themselves abandoned by the corporate giants who have taken their manufacturing elsewhere in order to "stay competitive."

This strikes me as unlikely. I am not convinced, watching Moore's climactic interview, that Knight has or had that sort of power. Maybe at some point a Knight-like figure did possess that sort of authority over his company, but by the time of "greed is good," with truly multinational corporate structures and thriving international capital flows, with the dot-com bubble beginning to swell and the growing speculative economy of the financial services industry on the horizon, the idea of persuading the big CEO of some big MNC to single-handedly enact corporate change seems to miss the spirit of the moment, however rhetorically inspiring it may be.

The concern here is not one of motivation, but of definition—the capacity of *The Big One* to properly delimit the forces that are responsible for the exploitation Moore rightly identifies. As he tells a lively audience at one of his many speaking events, Moore is sometimes confronted on airplanes by boozy captain-of-industry types who recognize him from *Roger & Me*. "Whatya got against profit?" Moore imitates a gravelly indignation. He continues relaying the (undoubtedly embellished) story: "Whatya got against profit? A company's got a responsibility to its shareholders. That's our system. The shareholders!" Moore returns to his own voice now: "That's not our system," he says with a chuckle. "Our system is a *democracy*. I've read the US Constitution. The word 'shareholder' does not appear once in that document!" Moore shakes his finger in defiance as the audience erupts in applause and laughter. He continues by saying that, as a democracy, "we can pass any law we want." We don't have to let shareholders and profit write the laws of the land. Indeed, corporations, despite their hubris, cannot do just *anything* in the name of profit, he reminds his audience, because "if it was just about profit, then why doesn't General Motors just sell crack?"

Moore here solidifies a mode of critique for which he is now famous—documenting his unsuccessful attempts to have the powerful defend their actions, in juxtaposition to the heartbreaking stories of everyday citizens who have been left behind by the system, contrasting the corporate stakeholders with the much larger throng of the American people. This formula, which proved so powerful in the more focused *Roger & Me*, is less so in this film. Because it is essentially a road movie, *The Big One* attempts to apply the themes of Moore's first film to American industry writ large, and it loses some of its expository value in the process. As a populist discourse or even a form of civic republicanism, Moore's efforts to juxtapose the uneven distribution of responsibility for capitalism's more problematic excesses can be lauded. Moore proclaiming the reality of "our system" being a democracy before an assembled crowd bridges a certain gap between the audience at the event and the audience of the film, presumably sympathetic to the plight of the workers depicted in *The Big One* and far more able to identify with the worker than with the corporate bigwig.

But if this style of critique has made Moore famous, it has also made him infamous to some of those who would champion the same cause, for Moore's approach lacks the sort of nuance and specificity needed to properly map the terrain of struggle. Moore's objection to the intoxicated captain of industry is, for all its bombastic appeal, an elision, a second ship passing by noisily in the night. The problem has to do with the nature of "our." For the corporate man, "our" refers to his and others' corporation, a public and private entity conjured by a complicated legal charter, constituted by shares and shareholders, executives and labor, and that makes decisions based on all manner of metrics and rationales tied to one central variable: profit margin. For Moore, "our" refers to the people, the American people, who are democratic, ruled by and for themselves. In an ideal world, that rule might include significant regulation and oversight that would curb the worst abuses of the corporate charter, but to suggest that shareholders are trumped by democracy, that corporations are governed by the people, is either rhetorical posturing or naïveté.

On the one hand, then, *The Big One* is a documentary critical of the excesses of 1990s capitalism, grounding that critique in concerns over exploitation rather than alienation. In this sense, it succeeds, both for pursuing a valuable critical toolset and for shining a high-powered spotlight on a particular moment in the evolution of American and global capitalism. On the other hand, the critique offered in *The Big One* remains too simple, too totalizing to truly challenge the structures that undergird the capitalism that Moore finds so problematic. In this sense, *The Big One* fails, as it is a film that may be more affectively successful than it is critically effective.

The Myth of the Big One

In contrast to the specificity and detail that made *Roger & Me* so powerful, in *The Big One* Moore paints in the broadest of brush strokes. As a film to be enjoyed, this is undoubtedly its weakness, but as a portrait of the general spirit of the new capitalism, it succeeds. Albeit sometimes clumsily, *The Big One* captures a particular moment of transition in the character of global capital, and for that it is worth our attention. Beyond identifying the implications of the massive outsourcing of production that began in the mid-1980s, Moore's film rehearses one set of responses to the trend.

At the end of the film, Moore reports that a group of Borders employees featured earlier in the film, covertly contacting him at a book signing in Iowa, had voted to unionize. A circle of Borders workers cheer in the parking lot as one falls to his knees, grabbing his head in what seems to be a combination of exhaustion and exhilaration. Viewers are then taken to suburban Philadelphia, where Borders employees had just voted to unionize as well. Two employees hug and jump up and down. Another shows his "Proud to Be Union" T-shirt and tells Moore and his crew with a smile, "There you go, it swells my chest to full size!" One of the elated workers says to another, "I'm gonna run over to Acme and let someone over there know!" He and a friend run, whooping, across the street to tell the baggers at a nearby grocery store their good news. "It kinda gave me a good feeling," says Moore, "them realizing that everyone's sorta in the same boat, and if things are gonna get better, it's gonna happen right here."

The film then cuts to Moore before yet another live audience, juxtaposing one final time the collective potential of the "little people" with the despotic rule of "the Man." Lest the monolithic character of the "Big One" be lost on audiences, Moore ends the film by putting a fine point on it: "Now we're at a point in our history where we have one candidate, one party, one company. . . . I like to say, one evil empire down, one to go."

What is most disheartening when watching the film nearly fifteen years later is the nostalgia for a particular kind of agency that Moore exhibits. For him, capitalism is just complicated enough to provide one large, integrated system, but not complex enough to provide a myriad of systems that function together monolithically as they do today. Moore heroically, and tragically, holds to the belief that there are actors with sufficient agency to effectively influence the way capitalism operates. Labor unions, omnipotent CEOs, righteous muckrakers—these are the figures of an era of capitalism that has largely transformed into something else. These figures still have agency, to be sure, but the larger system, or systems, in which they exert their influence is much more complicated than anything like *The Big One* could have foreseen.

Indeed, the title of Moore's second documentary film is telling. Throughout the film, it seems that the "Big One" simultaneously refers to the United States, corporate America, Nike, or whichever captain of industry Moore is attempting to confront with his camera. But today, looking back, it seems clear that the "Big One" that got away from all of us was capitalism itself. If *The Big One* feels like a relic of its time now, it is because even in 1998, its moment had already passed. It is a film about the geographies of production in an era when patterns of consumption had already come to dominate the global economy. It is a film about workers uniting against labor exploitation when the financial services industry was already producing the amorphous legal and accounting sleights of hand that would eventually trigger a worldwide financial crisis some ten years later. It is a film about the alleged power of people to change capitalism for the better without any realistic engagement with the legal regimes of incorporation, shareholder stakes, international currency, environmental regulations, trade flows, labor flows, technological change, and more—all those things that forever complicate the decision-making structure of multinational corporations.

Neither the complicated policies of international capital nor the speculative world of credit default swaps could ever be effectively challenged through collective bargaining or persuading the Phil Knights of the world to make more humane decisions. Indeed, Knight's impotence in the face of shareholders is crystal clear in the film, albeit unspoken. Although they benefit greatly from it, the reality behind *The Big One* is that the "Big One" of capitalism has gotten away from the capitalists as much as it has from the workers. This does not mean that it cannot be changed, radically, and for the better. But this change will likely not look like the David and Goliath scenario Moore offers us in *The Big One*. Instead, we must realize that the myth of the "Big One" may do more to distract from potential solutions than it does to inform them.

Notes

1. Michael Moore, *Downsize This! Random Threats from an Unarmed American* (New York: HarperCollins, 1996).

2. Kenneth Turan, "Moore Fun and Commentary in 'Big One,'" *Los Angeles Times*, April 10, 1998.

3. Luc Boltanski and Eve Chiapello, *The New Spirit of Capitalism*, trans. Gregory Elliott (New York: Verso, 2007).

4. I borrow this phrase from Tom Peters's best-seller *Thriving on Chaos: Handbook for a Management Revolution* (New York: HarperCollins, 1988), a defining book of the new spirit of capitalism.

5. Megan Brown, *The Cultural Work of Corporations* (New York: Palgrave Macmillan, 2009).

6. Ibid., 85.

7. Boltanski and Chiapello, *New Spirit of Capitalism*, 353.

8. Ibid., 349.

9. Ibid.

10. Ibid., 360.

11. Brown, *Cultural Work of Corporations*, 90.

12. Jay Carr, "Michael Moore on the Attack Again," *Boston Globe*, April 10, 1998.

13. Garry Trudeau, "Sneakers in Tinseltown," *Time*, April 20, 1998.

14. John Cushman, "Nike Pledges to End Child Labor and Apply U.S. Rules Abroad," *New York Times*, May 13, 1998.

15. Richard Sennett, *The Culture of the New Capitalism* (New Haven, CT: Yale University Press, 2006), 5.

16. Barbara Ehrenreich, *Bright-Sided: How Positive Thinking Is Undermining America* (New York: Picador, 2010), 8–9.

17. According to *New York Times* economics reporter Louis Uchitelle in *The Disposable American: Layoffs and Their Consequences* (New York: Vintage, 2007), 30 million full-time American workers lost their jobs between 1981 and 2003.

4. The Many Moods of Michael Moore: Aesthetics and Affect in *Bowling for Columbine*

Brian L. Ott and Susan A. Sci

The aesthetic dimension of politics is largely unacknowledged within our own experience.   —Robert Hariman, *Political Style: The Artistry of Power*

The aesthetic is not outside of politics. . . . But it makes its way by indirection and by infusing all questions with affect.
                              —George Levine, *Aesthetics and Ideology*

An aesthetic rhetoric counts on, attends to, and takes into account the body and its senses.   —John Poulakos and Steve Whitson, "Rhetoric Denuded and Redressed: Figs and Figures"

ichael Moore's Oscar-winning 2002 documentary film, *Bowling for Columbine*, is a moving and multifaceted meditation on the character of gun violence in the United States. Combining an array of visual media that, as one author describes it, includes "1950s television stock footage, digital cartoons, archival war footage, cowboy movie snippets, vintage toy ads and bizarre promotional videos,"[1] Moore spins a tale that has been characterized as being at once "humorous and horrifying."[2] Like Moore's other documentaries, *Bowling for Columbine* conveys a decidedly partisan message that urges a particular understanding of its central theme. The implicit, albeit fragmented and nonlinear, argument in the film is that the news media's nightly and highly racialized fearmongering has created a culture of white suburban panic[3]—one that accounts for recent school shootings such as the tragedy at Columbine High School on April 20, 1999, which was the deadliest school shooting in US history for more than a decade. After killing a teacher and twelve students, and wounding twenty-one others, eighteen-year-old Eric Harris and seventeen-year-old Dylan Klebold turned their guns on themselves, taking their own lives. During the sixteen-minute shooting spree, the pair fired more than nine hundred rounds of ammunition.[4] Based on a rhetorical analysis of the film, Brian Snee contends that Moore's message is facilitated by blending expository and participatory styles of documentary. But the film's message was lost on many viewers, who, according to Snee, lacked the sophistication to understand its modes of representation.[5]

Though Snee makes a convincing case for his structural(ist) reading of the film as a hybridized documentary form, he does not directly address the question that animates this chapter and fuels our own interest in the film: What, given (or in spite of) its complex and confusing structure,[6] is the appeal of *Bowling for Columbine*? The film, after all, was a striking critical and commercial success. In addition to winning the 2003 Academy Award for Best Documentary Feature, *Bowling for Columbine* was the first documentary selected for competition at the Cannes Film Festival in forty-six years, where it received the 55th Anniversary Prize and a thirteen-minute standing ovation.[7] Other awards followed, as did audiences. Despite its limited box office release (only eight screens the opening weekend), the film grossed over $10 million in the United States in its first two months, making it the "most commercially successful documentary" in history at the time.[8] Evidently, Moore's rumination on gun violence in the United States, while confusing, was also strangely compelling.[9]

Few filmmakers are as adept at moving audiences as Michael Moore. Central to the way Moore moves audiences is his ability to generate sensate experiences that resonate strongly with viewers. In the case of *Bowling for Columbine*, Moore managed to summon the unique cultural climate of the moment on film. "Decades from now," speculates reviewer Jonathan Curiel, "historians will look back at 'Bowling for Columbine' and say it captured the zeitgeist."[10] Indeed, we suggest that the film elicits emotional and psychical experiences homologous to those it represents.

Interestingly, and somewhat paradoxically, Moore accomplishes this feat by appropriating many of the very (aesthetic) strategies of the news media that lie at the heart of his critique.[11] The *rhetorical* appeal of those strategies, we maintain, operates more materially than symbolically. Though no film is exclusively material or symbolic in its rhetorical appeals, individual films can fall at different places along this continuum. *Bowling for Columbine* is, we contend, a film that heavily favors the material. Our central contention, then, is that *Bowling for Columbine*'s "argument" is activated affectively, that it is experienced sensually, felt viscerally. Specifically, we argue that the aesthetics of the film *move* the audience both temporally and emotionally through the argument by fostering five successive moods.

In support of this claim, we develop our thesis in three parts in this chapter. First, we briefly consider how cinema initiates a fully embodied sensate experience that in turn may function politically and ideologically. Second, we identify and analyze the five successive moods that move viewers through the film's argument. Third and finally, we discuss the implications of our analysis for films' evocation of cultural traumas.

Affect and the Cinematic Experience

Interest in the affective dimensions of rhetoric dates back to Aristotle, who devotes a considerable portion of his treatise on rhetoric to examining the role of *pathos* (appeals to emotion) in persuading audiences. George Kennedy elaborates: "These famous chapters [in Aristotle's *Rhetoric*] on the emotions, although reflecting some ideas of Plato found in *Phaedrus* and *Philebus* . . . , are the earliest systematic discussion of human psychology. . . . The primary rhetorical function of the account is apparently to provide a speaker with an ability to arouse these emotions in an audience and thus to facilitate the judgment sought."[12]

Despite rhetoric's long-standing concern with emotion and affect, the field of communication's "incentive to abandon or discipline affect was overdetermined" throughout much of the twentieth century.[13] Consequently, rhetorical analysis of twentieth-century communication technologies such as film and television focused disproportionately on symbolic inducement, discourse, meaning, and logical appeals.[14] Within this context, sophisticated critical vocabularies and tools (such as semiotics and psychoanalysis) for understanding the structural and discursive aspects of cinema developed rapidly, while similar vocabularies and tools for understanding the aesthetic, sensual, and erotic appeals of cinema languished.

This chapter is part of a broader ongoing project within the field of communication studies to (re)develop a vocabulary and set of critical tools for understanding and assessing the rhetorical affectivity of media, in particular cinema.[15] In his analysis of *V for Vendetta*, for instance, Brian Ott posits that cinema operates on three interconnected levels: representational, environmental, and experiential.[16] The first of these levels, the representational, entails symbolic (discursive) processes such as form, narrative, and identification. The environmental level, which is shaped by the technology or apparatus of cinema, entails factors such as spatiality and presence. The third level, and the one that concerns us most directly here, the experiential, refers to the material generation of sensations. Reflecting on documentaries in particular, Jane Gaines has observed that "films often make their appeal through the senses and to the senses, circumventing the intellect." One way that documentary films may appeal to the senses is through what Gaines calls "political mimesis," in which on-screen bodies generate an involuntary mimicry of sensation or emotion in spectators' bodies.[17]

Although political mimesis is not at work in *Bowling for Columbine*, there are other means by which films generally and documentaries in particular can appeal directly to the senses. For instance, the aesthetic dimensions of cinema may induce affective intensities in spectators. The connection between aesthetics and affect is an ancient one, and in fact, the Greek word *aisthetikos* (αἰσθητικός), which refers to the notion of sense perception or the faculty of feeling, derives from *aisthánomai* (αἰσθάνομαι), meaning to apprehend or to perceive through bodily senses.[18] The aesthetic dimension of cinema, including its "consonance, dissonance, harmonies of tone, light, colour, sound and rhythm"[19]—or of any other art form, for that matter—is experienced sensorily, as material sensations that act directly on the body. These sensations in turn produce affective states that range from feelings and moods to emotions and passions.[20]

Our interest in the aesthetic dimension of cinema and the particular affective states it elicits is motivated by the recognition that affect can be mobilized for social and political ends. Just as the signs and structural features of film can invite shared meanings, so too can the aesthetic elements (elements that do not directly signify) of film invoke shared affective states. Film, in other words, appeals to or enlists spectators in both a collective consciousness (common attitudes and beliefs) and a collective embodiedness (common sensations and feelings). Affect is political inasmuch as shared affective states (such as fear and uncertainty) invite a common orientation toward an object or event.[21] Ott suggests that these affective states function as "incipient attitudes, as energies, intensities, and sensations that function as the first step towards an evolving attitude,"[22] and attitudes, following Kenneth Burke, predispose us to act in certain ways.[23] Eliciting a shared affective state in spectators is a challenging affair whose difficulty increases proportionately to the specificity of affect being sought. Moore navigates this challenge, as we demonstrate in the following analysis, by fostering general moods rather than specific emotions.

Moore's Moods

"Moods," Charles Altieri writes, "are modes of feeling where the sense of subjectivity becomes diffuse and sensation merges into something close to atmosphere, something that seems to pervade an entire scene or situation."[24] Moods saturate cinematic spaces and texts, establishing unified and pervasive emotional qualities that spectators are invited to embody. By sensually engaging viewers, cinematic moods materially prepare them at a corporeal level—affectively priming them as part of the rhetorical experience of the film. Our conceptualization of cinematic mood functions similarly, then, to Aristotle's theory of pathos, which entails creating appropriate states of reception in audiences that positively orient them toward a rhetor's claims.[25] Recent studies in cognitive psychology lend scientific support for this ancient rhetorical technique. Gerald Clore and Stanley Colcombe find, for instance, that "mood influences evaluative judgments" when the mood is oriented toward the object of judgment.[26]

Cinematic moods, therefore, can be understood as affective predispositions, embodied invitations to feel the logic of a film. It is from *within* these moods that viewers take in the film and discern meaning from it. In other words, when spectators watch a film, they are asked to process its discursive elements through and in combination with particular affective states. Critics can analyze cinematic moods by identifying, examining, and critiquing the way films establish their emotional atmosphere via aesthetic dimensions in conjunction with structural and discursive elements. This type of analysis enables critics to better address how film mobilizes viewers' affective states politically by creating a collective embodied experience from which viewers are invited to have a specific visceral reaction to the ideological messages of a film. (Cinematic mood is a rhetorical invitation that spectators are always free to reject or may experience differently based on their particular beliefs and backgrounds.) In analyzing the cinematic moods of *Bowling for Columbine,* we are interested in both how the film fosters a particular sensual experience and how that sensual experience (of moods) affectively primes viewers, orienting them toward Moore's cultural and political stances (that is, the three hypotheses he put forth).

Moore uses a wide range of techniques to create and sustain the key moods in *Bowling for Columbine.* Although our analysis concentrates on the aesthetic elements of the film, we recognize that the film's structural and discursive elements contribute to the overall development of mood as well. Of particular importance in this regard is Moore himself, who serves as a surrogate for viewers at various points in the film. To this end, Moore's on-screen persona is meticulously constructed as "just a simple guy looking for answers to a few simple questions."[27] Moore's unassuming manner and appearance aid viewers in locating themselves in his *place,* thus allowing them to observe (in a seemingly objective, firsthand way) what he is observing. Viewers are not so much invited to *identify* with Moore (to empathize or align with him) as they are encouraged to experience a fully embodied sense of presence. Moore, or Moore's persona, then, is a vehicle for situating spectators *in* (rather than in front of) the film. The use of spatial language is intentional here, as we maintain that each of the key moods in the film is strongly correlated with a particular locale.

Irony and Curiosity in Flint

Bowling for Columbine opens with a grainy black-and-white promotional video for the National Rifle Association (NRA). A lone, mature white male in military uniform enticingly greets viewers, explaining that "the National Rifle Association has produced a film which you are sure to find of great interest." The calm, warm demeanor of this NRA representative as he urges, "Let's look at it," combined with the nostalgic appeal of the image, invites a sense of safety and security. This initial sense is at odds, however, with what will soon be revealed as Moore's purpose—repudiating guns and their tragic consequences—and his manner of doing so, bombarding viewers with violent and disturbing imagery. Thus, as the use of this contrived endorsement illustrates, Moore quickly establishes an ironic mood. Numerous critics have noted that the film owes much of its humor, as well as its title, to irony.[28] But critics have not considered the rhetorical consequentiality, especially as it relates to affect, of the film's extensive use of irony.

The ironic tenor of *Bowling for Columbine*'s opening sequence functions in two interconnected ways. First, framing the entire film in relation to a false endorsement highlights how the experience of irony is a posturing movement. As Brent Steele explains, "Irony's focus on pretence centres upon the *posture* . . . of a subject," creating a desire to find the "hidden defect" that exists in this context.[29] In other words, Moore's use of irony strategically realigns the audience's collective body in an emotional position of skepticism toward the NRA's support of guns before the film even begins. Second, the skepticism inherent in an ironic posture reflects what Berel Lang calls "an *ontology* of ambiguity" because of the relational disparity between the literal (the NRA's video endorsement) and the actual (the NRA's likely opposition to the film).[30] Affectively speaking, this irony initially provokes sensations of instability—feelings of uncertainty and doubt regarding what is seen and heard. We contend that Moore's use of irony, specifically the skeptical posture and sense of instability to which it appeals, creates and sustains a mood of curiosity.

From being inquisitive to feeling perplexed by apparent contradictions to experiencing something peculiar, a general atmosphere of curiosity pervades the early stages of Moore's investigation (scenes 2–7), which take place in and around his hometown of Flint, Michigan. These scenes act as Moore's own ruminations on the unspoken question, "What caused Columbine?"

Early in the film, Moore entertains the hypothesis that the culture of gun ownership in the United States is somehow responsible for this tragedy. Toward this end, he combines a diverse array of images with sardonic musical choices and voice-overs to provoke a sensate experience of (dis)ease that, while unnerving, rouses viewers' curiosity about what drives Americans to engage in violence. Through visual montage, Moore is able to concretize abstract ideas and transform "ideology into art."[31] For example, the film's opening montage, titled "Morning in America," intercuts imagery of the Washington Monument, American towns, rolling farmlands, ordinary Americans going about their daily business, the NATO bombing of Serbia, the Rocky Mountains, people bowling, and a bikini-clad blond woman with an automatic weapon, which fades into a close-up of the face of the Statue of Liberty before panning out. The implication of this visual juxtaposition is that gun violence and ownership are part and parcel of the American way of life, and indeed, the opening montage is overlaid with the patriotic "Battle Hymn of the Republic" and Moore's sarcastic claim that April 20, 1999, was "a typical day in the United States of America."

As he travels around the state of Michigan, Moore visits a number of everyday places, such as a bank and a barbershop, highlighting—often quite humorously—the ubiquity and ordinariness of guns in American society. Using clips of home movies from his childhood in which he plays with toy guns and narrating a story about the NRA marksmanship award he won in his youth, Moore suggests that he, too, grew up in a culture of guns. But even as these images "normalize" guns as commonplace, as does Chris Rock's comedic riff on bullets, Moore's interviews with several members of the Michigan militia, James Nichols (the brother of Terry Nichols, who was convicted of conspiring with Timothy McVeigh in the Oklahoma City bombing), and two teenage boys from Oscoda, where Columbine shooter Eric Harris spent part of his childhood, suggest the danger posed by the easy accessibility of guns to fanatical and fringe elements of society. Moore's story of US gun culture is a deeply conflictual one, then. It suggests that guns are, at once, banal and extraordinary, benign and malignant. Each time Moore appears to be narrowing in on an explanation, the film's ironic framing undermines it. Meanwhile, the sense of impending risk continues to rise.

Near the end of Moore's time in Michigan, he has a peculiar and unsettling exchange with James Nichols. Moore interviews Nichols in his home, seated at his kitchen table; the interaction is a strange hybrid of an evening chat, a rousing debate, and a zealot's soapbox. Aesthetically, the scene appears muted; the lack of clarity and sharpness supplies an almost dreamlike quality. The bland, neutral tones of the kitchen walls and cabinets contrast with the blue of Nichols's shirt and eyes. Already one of the most salient aspects of the image, Nichols's wide-eyed and unblinking stare makes the intensity of this maniacal expression only that much more pronounced. The already apprehensive atmosphere is reinforced by the reverse shot, which shows Moore stock-still, shoulders raised, face blank, looking visibly scared.

The sensation reaches a crescendo when Nichols takes Moore into his bedroom to prove he sleeps with a .44 Magnum under his pillow. Although the camera cannot join them, spectators can hear whispers as a gun is cocked, and the words "Nichols has cocked the gun and put it to his temple" appear in block letters at the bottom of the screen. In combination, the feelings of anxiety, the inability to clearly see what is happening, and the shocking discursive revelation lead to an inevitable conclusion—Nichols is an unstable man. Yet, cutting back to the interview, the scene is contrasted with Nichols conceding to Moore that there should be some limitations on the Second Amendment because, unlike him, "there's wackos out there." The general state of active curiosity fostered by the film's ironic sensibility has built to a fever pitch, concluding in a rapid montage of violent and startling images that begin scene 8, "Littleton."

Terror and Sublimity in Littleton

Moore's examination of gun culture in the United States, which fails to produce a satisfactory answer to the film's driving question, ends abruptly, and the camera cuts directly to a middle-class suburban neighborhood in Littleton, Colorado. The sudden and unexpected transition to Littleton invites viewers to wonder if there is something unique about that community that may have led to the shootings at Columbine. Moore quickly zeros in on an answer, floating his second major hypothesis of the film: that the general culture of violence in the United States is responsible for the tragedy. Initially, he investigates this idea through personal interviews with Denny Fennell, a local home security consultant, and Evan McCollum, a public relations officer at the Littleton Lockheed Martin facility, which viewers are informed through on-screen text is the "World's Largest Weapons Maker."

Though Moore is still in investigative mode, the general mood of the film has shifted radically. The ironic exploration of US gun culture that dominated the opening portion of the film has been replaced by a much weightier and more serious mood. A profound instance is when Fennell, in the midst of trying to explain what effects Columbine has had, almost breaks down in tears. Fennell is not able to retain his calm professional demeanor when he tries to describe what happened that day. First he's silent and looks away. But as Moore presses the subject, Fennell explains, "There's something overwhelming about that kind of, um, viciousness, that kind of predatory action, that kind of indiscriminate, um, killing" and from the tone of his voice, we know Fennell is choking back tears. His grief is palpable.

Another powerful example occurs following McCollum's claim about the US government that "we don't get irritated with somebody, and just 'cause we're mad at them—drop a bomb, shoot at them or fire a missile at them." Here the film cuts briefly to black before dissolving into a montage of gruesome and graphic images of US violence perpetrated around the world from 1953 to the present day. The horrific images, which are accompanied by Louis Armstrong's soulful "What a Wonderful World" and textual graphics indicating the year and nature of US involvement, unfold gradually and methodically. The slow, deliberate pacing allows spectators to soak up and internalize the horror of what they are seeing. The imagery is so ghastly—bloodied and dismembered bodies, mass graves, live shootings—that the music, though ironic, amplifies and intensifies rather than undermines the terror and disgust evoked by the images. In short, the way irony functions here has shifted from celebratory or humorous in the opening montage to condemnatory. Elaborating on this distinction, Bijana Scott explains that the celebratory is philosophical, revealing "the world in its moral ambiguity and man in his profound incompetence to judge others," and the condemnatory is political, exposing inconsistencies in an effort to invoke condemnation.[32]

Moore continues to develop his violence-begets-violence hypothesis in what is arguably the film's most powerful scene. The scene begins with a black screen emblazoned with large, white letters that read simply, "April 20, 1999." Before the film cuts away from this title frame, spectators hear the sound of rapid gunfire. The ensuing image alerts viewers that the sounds are coming not from the halls of Columbine, but from army helicopters. In a fast-paced montage that intercuts stock war footage, news coverage, and a statement from President Clinton, viewers are informed that the United States has just launched a strategic bombing campaign in Kosovo. The rapid pacing of the sequence elicits arousal, heightens anticipation of more violence, and propels the audience forward without time to reflect on the imagery, its meaning, or relation to what follows. Without warning, the heart-pounding montage is abruptly interrupted by a black screen that reads, "One Hour Later," and the voice of President Clinton announcing, "There has been a terrible shooting at a high school in Littleton, Colorado." For the next four minutes, spectators are immersed in a world of utter chaos. Audio recordings of Jefferson County 911 calls placed by terrified students, helpless teachers, and hysterical parents provide the "sound track" for the unspeakable images unfolding on-screen—images that include actual security video footage from the high school that morning. The scene closes with equally emotional images of students, crying and quivering as they recount the details of their ordeal.

The sensate experience of this scene exceeds all rationality and meaning. It ceases to signify, in part, because the scene does not merely depict terror and trauma, but works rhetorically to engender them. According to Roland Barthes, traumatic images, though rare, sublimate connotation. As he explains, "The traumatic photograph (fires, shipwrecks, catastrophes, violent deaths, all captured 'from life as lived') is the photograph about which there is nothing to say. . . . One could imagine a kind of law: the more direct the trauma, the more difficult is connotation."[33] It is difficult, if not impossible, then, to adequately capture in language the affective state it evokes. Indeed, so challenging is it to convey the emotional experience of this scene that one critic, in a remarkable instance of understatement, insipidly writes, "Harrowing surveillance camera footage taped during the deadly assault at Columbine, accompanied by recordings of frantic phone calls to police and radio stations, packs a wallop."[34] For spectators, a "wallop" hardly describes the utter terror the scene has invited them to feel.

Perhaps the best way to approach the sensory assault of this scene and the affective response it provokes is through reference to the sublime. The notion of the sublime has been variously theorized throughout history, but Edmund Burke's investigation of this concept is especially relevant to the case at hand. Burke writes, "Whatever is fitted in any sort to excite the ideas of pain and danger; that is to say, whatever is in any sort terrible, or is conversant about terrible objects, or operates in a manner analogous to terror, is a source of the *sublime*; that is, it is productive of the strongest emotion which the mind is capable of feeling."[35] He suggests in this passage (and Immanuel Kant later argues explicitly) that the sublime refers not to any particular quality possessed by an object, but to an effect on the imagination of a subject. That effect is to create a sweeping affective state, rather than an identifiable feeling or emotion, by mixing terror with awe, horror with fascination, and pain with pleasure. But the experience of sublimity created and fostered by scenes 8–10 cannot be sustained indefinitely; it must be directed and released. It finds such an emotional target, and is released as anger, in the opening shot of scene 11, which shows NRA president Charlton Heston, raising a rifle above his head and exclaiming, "From my cold, dead hands."[36]

Fear and Loathing in Los Angeles

The sense of contempt that is educed at the start of scene 11, "Heston at NRA Rally," dissipates in the coming scenes of the film without ever completely disappearing. It simmers just beneath the surface in the form of scorn and as part of a broader mood of cynicism and fear. This mood dominates the middle portion the film, spanning scenes 11–22 and advancing Moore's third and final hypothesis: that the (racialized) culture of fear in the United States is responsible for the tragedy at Columbine. By the time spectators are fully absorbed in this mood, the film will have fostered general feelings of distrust and disillusion toward the government, politicians, the news media, law enforcement, and corporate America. Of these targets, however, Moore settles on the news media as the primary perpetrator of fear and thus the "real" culprit. In the lead-up to this conclusion, Moore cynically rejects other possible culprits, such as entertainment media (including the animated sitcom *South Park*, singer Marilyn Manson, and violent films and video games), the breakdown of the family unit, poverty and unemployment, and the nation's violent past. Each of these appeals is executed chiefly through editing. Although the practices of film editing—shot selection and sequencing, pacing and duration, and combination and relation—are nonrepresentational, as they do not refer to or stand in for something else, they nevertheless have been shown to evoke emotional responses.[37]

Much of the editing in scenes 13–15, for instance, works rhetorically to elicit doubt or skepticism about what viewers are told in the media. In this segment of the film, Moore debunks the criticisms of Marilyn Manson, who was widely blamed in the news media as one cause of Columbine. To that end, Moore interviews Manson backstage at Ozzfest in Denver two years after the shootings. The style, pacing, and shot selection of the scene are central to Moore's construction of Manson as informed, intelligent, and likable—a perspective that directly contests the way the film, through the use of rapid montage of news images leading up to the interview, suggests he has been portrayed by the news media. Returning to an interactive mode of documentary, or *cinéma vérité* style, which appeals to authenticity,[38] the Manson interview accentuates the manufactured, fabricated, and thus misleading character of news media images. In contrast to the way news footage is edited in the film to appear shocking, highly stylized, and overproduced, the hand-held, naturalistic shots of Manson appear to be objective and unmediated. Manson is further constructed as rational and knowledgeable by intercutting his calm, steady voice in the interview with live shots of an angry, irrational protester speaking at the anti-Manson rally.

In scene 16, "We're #1," Moore levels his most devastating critique of the idea that violent entertainment may have contributed to Columbine. At the start of this scene, Moore rhetorically asks, Do they not listen to Marilyn Manson, watch violent movies, and play violent video games in other countries? Moore's queries are answered affirmatively by the montage of images that accompanies these questions, depicting such mediated violence. If media violence causes social violence, Moore reasons, then other countries would be equally violent—a conclusion he immediately disproves with a countdown of yearly gun deaths in Germany, France, Canada, the United Kingdom, Australia, Japan, and the United States. Each frame progressively displays a smaller number, from 381 in Germany to 39 in Japan, until arriving at the United States, where the downward trend is dramatically reversed and the number of gun deaths—11,127—zooms toward the audience until it fills the entire screen.[39] The zooming edit, building background music, and intensifying cadence of Moore's voice function to elicit a combination of fear, alarm, and anxiety.

The initial fear evoked by the interplay of sound, images, and editing in scene 16 continues to build and intensify in subsequent scenes. Following a hysterical (in both senses of the term: humorous and uncontrollably emotional) cartoon history of the United States narrated by a talking bullet, Moore plunges the audience into a state of near panic with a montage of televised news clips each warning of some imminent threat. Ironically, even as Moore describes the absurdity of some of these fears, the tempo and ominous music of the montage, which turns into the sound of an accelerating heartbeat, foster a sense of anxiety and tension that elicit fear. The scene climaxes with an image, lifted from a horror film, of a woman recoiling in fear. The next four scenes, which are shot predominantly in Los Angeles, refine Moore's hypothesis, suggesting that the fear peddled by the news media is also racist. This portion of the film is structured around a series of interviews with Barry Glassner, author of *The Culture of Fear*; Arthur Busch, Flint County prosecutor; and Dick Herlan, former producer of the television series *Cops* and executive producer of *World's Wildest Police Videos*. By intercutting statements made during these interviews with evidentiary editing and images, Moore connects a deep-seated loathing for African American men, rooted in racism, with the culture of fear in the United States. This claim is driven home by a humorous parody titled "Corporate Cops," which features Moore chasing down and arresting white executives.

Cool Rationalism in Canada

Having piqued viewers' curiosity about gun culture in the United States, terrorized them with sublime images from Columbine, and frightened them with clips from the evening news, *Bowling for Columbine* now offers viewers a temporary reprieve from this emotional onslaught by visiting Canada—a country viewers are told is "gun-loving, gun-toting, gun-crazy" but has little gun violence and even less fear. Scenes 23 and 24 favor a mood of cool rationalism and function as a brief interlude between the anxiety generated by the film thus far and the general malaise soon to follow. Like scene 14, with its Marilyn Manson interview, these two scenes are dominated by an interview format and use an interactive style of documentary. The implementation of this style is central to how these scenes appeal to viewers and promote a cool rationalism. Nichols explains that "interactive documentary stresses images of testimony or verbal exchange and images of demonstration. . . . Textual authority shifts toward the social actors recruited. . . . The mood introduces a sense of partialness, of *situated* presence and *local* knowledge that derives from the actual encounter of filmmaker and other."[40]

As Moore prompts Canadians of various ages to reflect on their culture, it is easy to overlook that these interviews have been edited to serve a larger argument within the film, that a culture of fear is unique to the United States. Although the interviews appear to objectively present ordinary Canadians testifying to their own experiences in Canada, the responses viewers see and hear have been selected, cut, sequenced, and reassembled to reflect a particular and homogenized viewpoint. In allowing viewers to witness both the questions and answers firsthand, however, the camera creates the impression of unfiltered dialogue and disguises the degree to which such exchanges serve a broader purpose. When a "specific agenda" is at play, though, Nichols notes that "the information extracted from the exchange may be placed within a larger frame of reference to which it contributes a distinct piece of factual information or affective overtone."[41] In the case of "Oh, Canada!" and "Unlocked Doors," the affective overtone is a cool, calming one. It is achieved not just by the content of the imagery, but also by the steady, even pacing of the editing, which stands in stark contrast to the rapid-fire montages that constitute earlier portions of the film.

The sequence explicitly reasons that Canada has less gun violence because, as Moore narrates, "Night after night, the Canadians [a]ren't being pumped full of fear." This serves to reinforce Moore's broader argument—that a culture of fear is responsible for violence in the United States—through contrast. But Moore offers only scant evidence of how US and Canadian cultures actually differ to support his argument of comparison and contrast. The force of Moore's argument relies not on data or support, but on the embodied emotional state of spectators. What Moore contrasts is not so much Canada with the United States, but the mood of cool rationalism with the mood of fear. Because the portion of the film involving Canada is cool, calm, and balanced in its mode of presentation, Moore's argument *feels* true. When viewers are told the US news media promotes a culture of fear, they experience fear, and when they are told Canada does not promote fear, they experience none. In other words, the sensory-emotive experience invited by the sound, images, and editing of film mirrors the film's argument.

Mourning and Melancholia in Michigan

"Mourning and Melancholia" in this subhead is borrowed from Freud's famous study of melancholia by the same name. We begin this portion of the analysis with this intertextual gesture because the distinction between mourning and melancholia is central to understanding not only the film's fifth and final mood, but also its unusual and seemingly misplaced final scenes.[42] For Freud, melancholia—the mood that we maintain dominates the remainder of the film—is a form of unspeakable loss and "pathological mourning,"[43] in which sorrow and suffering are combined with reflection and contemplation, and despair and depression are mixed with narcissism and mania.[44] Seen from another angle, melancholia is mourning gone awry. Unable to properly grieve loss (to relinquish an object, event, or ideal), the melancholic incorporates (introjects) this loss into the ego, "and the ego thus becomes a reminder of unresolved grief."[45] Once introjected, the lost object (of love) becomes paradoxically both lost and not lost (kept as a phantasm), giving rise to ambivalence and "the experience of an abysmal absence of meaning."[46]

The reflective component of melancholia is evident across scenes 25–27, the first three of the film's concluding sequence. Scene 25, "Little Kayla," opens with the Genesee County 911 call from a frantic teacher at Buell Elementary School telling the dispatcher that a little girl has been shot in her classroom. Unlike the earlier 911 calls from Columbine, which included images of the event as it unfolded, this call is accompanied only by a black screen. The call is followed immediately with an interview with Jimmie Hughes, the principal of Buell Elementary School, recollecting the events of that dreadful day. Although the difference in how the 911 calls are implemented may seem subtle, it is significant to the moods invoked. Scene 10, "Columbine," places viewers in the school at the moment of the shooting, allowing them to experience the horror firsthand. Scene 25, by contrast, situates the shooting in the past, inviting viewers to *reflect* on the tragedy. The temporal framing in the first instance elicits terror and sublimity, while in the latter it contributes to grief and melancholia. When Principal Hughes begins to break down in front of the camera, the audience feels her pain and sorrow. The mood of this scene differs dramatically from the terrifying (and terrorizing) mood evoked in relation to the shootings at Columbine.

The reflective aspect of melancholia is evident not only in the temporal framing of scene 25, but also in the way scenes 26 and 27 hark back to nearly all of the themes previously raised in the film. As Moore recounts the events leading up to "the youngest school shooting ever in the United States," he attempts through both imagery and narration to connect the dots among news media coverage of the shooting, poverty and welfare, Charlton Heston and the NRA, racism and fear, Lockheed Martin, and violence. Moore's tone—the actual timbre and rhythm of his voice—throughout this section is solemn and contemplative. The sheer gravity of Moore's voice in these scenes, which contrasts starkly with his ironic, playful tone early in the film, is significantly more important to the film's rhetorical appeal at this point than *what* he is actually saying, which entails a logic so tortured it borders on incoherence if not insanity. The somberness of Moore's voice is reinforced by the sound of a piano wistfully being played in the background. The film wallows in this reflective, melancholic mood as Moore seems unable to find a satisfactory answer to his driving question and to spin a narrative that transitions from grief to healing. This failure to move audiences temporally and emotionally beyond mourning—to provide any form of affective catharsis—accounts for the film's seemingly inexplicable final scenes.

More than an hour and a half into the film, Moore has made his "argument," such as it is, and one would expect the film to come to a close. But it does not and cannot, for there is no resolution and no sense of satisfaction. Thus begins scene 28, "Fear and Ammo," a fast-paced, rock-and-roll-pounding, adrenaline-pumping montage of classic George W. Bush fearmongering rhetoric intercut with images of the September 11, 2001, terrorist attacks and news media reports about a frightened public wildly arming itself to the hilt. As the film restages and subsequently reactivates a state of fear, it also unreflexively reverts to its original hypothesis and culprit, transitioning from the news media as the cause of social violence back to the easy accessibility of guns as the cause. The advantage, with regard to form, of this move is that it allows for the identification and punishment of a responsible party. In scenes 29 and 30, viewers learn that party is Kmart, where Eric and Dylan evidently had purchased the bullets they used at Columbine. Drawing on viewers' sympathies for two Columbine survivors who were injured during the shooting, Richard Castaldo and Mark Taylor, Moore confronts—with the boys in tow—executives at the Kmart headquarters in Troy, Michigan, with a request that the company stop selling bullets.

Had Kmart refused or even ignored Moore's request, he would have had his perfect scapegoat—an evil, uncaring, faceless corporation. But the following day, in front of both Moore's cameras and the press, whom Moore had invited, Lori McTavish, vice president of communications for Kmart, announces that the company will phase out the sale of all handgun ammunition within the next ninety days. With Kmart having completely thwarted Moore's efforts to generate a sense of catharsis through victimage, Moore must seek out a different villain to punish for society's collective sins. So in the film's final scene, he pays a visit to the home of then NRA president Charlton Heston, who agrees to sit down with him and talk on camera. As Moore's questions become increasingly aggressive and accusatory, a flustered Heston ends the interview by walking away. Pursuing him like an investigative journalist, Moore shows Heston a picture of six-year-old Buell Elementary School victim Kayla Rolland and invites him to comment. But Heston merely turns and continues on his way, prompting Moore to prop up the picture of Kayla on a stone column outside Heston's home.

Scene 31, "Charlton Heston," affords no more comfort or resolution than did the Kmart scene. Despite the undercurrent of racism in Heston's comments and his unwillingness to apologize for making NRA appearances in Denver and Flint shortly after the school shootings in each of these communities, Heston simply does not come off as an evil ogre who is in any way responsible for these tragedies. Indeed, Moore's attempts to embarrass this feeble, if misguided, old man just feel mean spirited and self-serving. The film ends at this point with a shot of Moore bowling. Hence, by the end of the two-hour-long emotional roller-coaster ride that is *Bowling for Columbine*, viewers possess no clearer understanding of what led to the tragedy at Columbine than when it began. What they do possess is an overwhelming sense of melancholia and malaise—a sinking feeling that they, too, are victims of a culture they do not understand and cannot change.

On Cultural Trauma in Film

The gruesome 1999 shootings at Columbine High School in Littleton, Colorado, function as the centerpiece of and narrative impetus for *Bowling for Columbine*.[47] Whether attributable to the loss of young lives, the pain of parental grief, or the shattered sense of safety, few acts of violence are as emotionally jarring as school shootings—Columbine being one of the most painful examples. As the biggest US news story of 1999, coverage of Columbine quickly overwhelmed the collective imaginary, fostering a "felt crisis"—a cultural trauma that provoked experiences of profound sadness, fear, and empathy in viewers.[48] As a cultural trauma, Columbine left "indelible marks upon [our] group consciousness," fundamentally called into question our collective sense of ourselves, and prompted serious social reflection—"a veritable searching of the collective soul."[49]

Michael Moore's documentary film *Bowling for Columbine* was one such collective soul searching—a broad-ranging social rumination on what would compel two white, middle-class, teenage boys to commit such a grisly act. Taking the term "rumination" seriously, we suggest that *Bowling for Columbine* can be understood as a cinematic experience that moves the audience through a series of hypotheses and successive moods as a means of working through the distress that Columbine, as a cultural trauma, initiated. Thus, in sequence, the film explores the following three hypotheses that address who or what in the United States is culturally to blame for Columbine: the culture of gun ownership; the general culture of violence; and the racialized culture of fear.

Within these broad hypotheses, Moore considers an array of possible culprits, ranging from fanatical gun owners who vigorously defend the right to bear arms and large corporations that manufacture weapons of mass destruction to governments that wage endless military campaigns to the news media, which stokes fear and anxiety in the interest of ratings and profit. Consequently, culpability evolves in the film, progressing from individuals to organizations to nations before finally narrowing in on the institution of journalism as the main perpetrator of social violence. Viewers are both told and directly experience that the news media—through its steady stream of stories about crime, murder, tragedy, and mayhem—produces a racialized culture of unmitigated fear that incites individuals to (re)act violently.

But like the conventions of the very news media he critiques, Moore explores these hypotheses in an *arresting* manner. Moore's use of rapid montage, graphic imagery, ironic music, personal interviews, and nonlinear editing generates sensate experiences that temporally and emotionally *move* the audience through a series of successive moods: irony and curiosity escalate into terror and sublimity, which evoke fear and loathing, only to be contrasted with cool rationalism, leading to a sense of mourning and melancholia. In guiding viewers through this sequence of moods, in inviting them to understand and process its central hypotheses regarding culpability from *within* these moods, *Bowling for Columbine* seizes not only viewers' attention but also their imagination. It does so by locating viewers in Moore's *place* (his positionality), by taking them on his personal journey of grief (through his moods and progressive claims of responsibility) prompted by the cultural trauma of Columbine.

In other words, Moore's own grief furnishes the affective undercurrent of *Bowling for Columbine*. At several key moments in the film, Moore's unconscious grieving process bubbles to the surface and becomes explicit. The most striking examples occur when the persons Moore is interviewing break down in tears, as these moments lay bare Moore's own emotional state. For instance, when Denny Fennell chokes up early in the film, Moore maintains his ironic and inquisitive tenor, as if still in denial about his own feelings of loss. Taking their cue from Moore, viewers are invited to adopt a similar ironic posture at that point in the film. Much later, however, when Jimmie Hughes breaks down, Moore empathizes with her, saying he understands, and indeed, he seems to genuinely share her pain. Between his initial struggle with loss, which takes the form of irony and curiosity, and his eventual sadness and pain, which takes the form of mourning and melancholia, Moore progresses (the audience) through the traditional stages of anger and bargaining. Following the terror and sublimity evoked by reliving the events at Columbine, the film transitions to a mood of fear and loathing, in which Moore angrily lashes out at an array of culprits, blaming them for the tragic loss. As his anger subsides, Moore begins the process of bargaining reflected by the mood of cool rationalism and his insistence that our culture does not have to be this way. As Moore relents in his plea for a world free of violence and (re)turns from his imaginary Canada-land, in which such a tragedy supposedly could not happen,[50] to the hard reality of the United States, he and the film surrender to a deep depression. But Moore and the film (and consequently the audience) never move beyond this melancholic stage to acceptance. Thus, at least within the context of the film, neither Moore nor the audience ever entirely escapes this cultural trauma, as a type of self-loathing lingers. The violent compulsions Moore identifies as the driving force behind this trauma continue to be deeply embedded within our collective US identity regardless of how much we protest. So neither growth nor healing can fully occur.

While *Bowling for Columbine* (re)enacts Moore's personal process of grieving the cultural trauma of Columbine, eliciting corresponding affective states in viewers, it leaves him as well as the audience largely untransformed and thus without political agency. The best evidence of this lack of personal transformation and subsequent political impotency comes in the final scenes in which Moore confronts Kmart and Charlton Heston. Moore's closing "victories" feel narratively and politically unsatisfying, emotionally empty, because they provide no prospect for a better tomorrow. There can be no prospect for social transformation, as there has been no personal transformation. Cinema, especially documentary, has tremendous potential for creating collective embodied experiences that address cultural trauma,[51] for films about cultural traumas can situate spectators as witnesses to the pain of others and engage them in sensate experiences of empathy and grief. By furnishing insight into the dynamics of collective identity and highlighting appropriate and inappropriate responses to traumas, cinema can symbolically and affectively foster ethical-political citizenship. *Bowling for Columbine* is disappointing, in our judgment, precisely because it fails to activate such processes; it represents a lost opportunity to harness the affective power of cultural trauma to empathize with others, reimagine ourselves, and connect loss to social conscience and civic responsibility.

Although based on immediate events, cultural trauma is necessarily a mediated construct that audiences experience vicariously through feelings of pain "evoked by empathy" and the fear of suffering similar tragedy.[52] Cultural trauma is a crisis of culture that (re)presents "a fundamental [symbolic] threat," Alexander says, yet simultaneously offers societies a means to reassess the ethical-political dimensions of their collective citizenship. "By allowing members of wider publics to participate in the pain of others," he elaborates, "cultural traumas broaden the realm of social understanding and sympathy, and they provide powerful avenues for new forms of social incorporation." Cultural trauma can ignite a process of political and cultural inclusion, and films about them can perform a similar function. By enabling affectively engaged spectators to (re)imagine who "we" are as a collective, cultural trauma can "redirect the course of political action" by establishing a moral obligation to help those in pain.[53] Consequently, prevention of similar traumatic events and the physical and emotional pain they cause is understood as a civic responsibility and becomes a priority on the collective's political agenda.

Finally, we feel compelled to note that not all tragic and unjust occurrences become cultural traumas, and thus not all those who suffer traumatic events are seen as "grievable" victims.[54] The extent to which a tragedy becomes a cultural trauma is determined not only by the number of casualties but also by what it means to us that *these* individuals are suffering. Alexander asserts that "only if the victims are represented in terms of valued qualities shared by the larger collective identity will the audience be able to participate in the experience of the originating trauma" and establish the ethical-political relation that collective grief and empathy create.[55] So, as Butler points out, the real question is, "What makes for a grievable life?"[56] For whom do we feel empathy and grief and recognize as deserving of our ethical-political obligation? As we hope we have shown, one way to address such questions is to examine the particular affective investments that film and other media invite us to make in some contexts and not others.

Appendix: Scene Titles from Bowling for Columbine (DVD)

1. Morning in America
2. North Country Bank
3. Mike's First Gun
4. Chris Rock
5. Michigan Militia
6. James Nichols
7. Oscoda Boys

8. Littleton
9. Wonderful World
10. Columbine
11. Heston at NRA Rally
12. South Park/Matt Stone
13. Scary Kids
14. Marilyn Manson
15. "Was It the Bowling?"
16. We're #1
17. A Brief History of America
18. Fear of Everything
19. Fear of Black Men
20. Suburban Guns
21. L.A. Cops
22. Corporate Cops
23. Oh, Canada!
24. Unlocked Doors
25. Little Kayla
26. The Other Victim
27. "Welfare to Work"
28. Fear and Ammo
29. Returning the Merchandise
30. K-Mart
31. Charlton Heston
32. Mike Bowling/Credits

Notes

1. Peter Wilshire, "Presentation and Representation in Michael Moore's *Bowling for Columbine*," *Australian Screen Education* 35 (Winter 2004): 92.

2. Erika Waak, "*Bowling for Columbine*: Are We a Nation of Gun Nuts or Are We Just Nuts?," review of *Bowling for Columbine*, *Humanist* 63, no. 2 (2003): 41.

3. Patrick Finn, review of *Bowling for Columbine*, *Film & History* 33, no. 1 (2003): 66; Richard Kelly, review of *Bowling for Columbine*, *Sight & Sound* 12, no. 11 (2002): 40; Christopher Sharrett and William Luhr, review of *Bowling for Columbine*, *Cineaste* 28, no. 2 (2003): 37.

4. Wilshire, "Presentation and Representation," 92.

96　　　　*Brian L. Ott and Susan A. Sci*

5. Brian Snee, "Free Guns and Speech Control: The Structural and Thematic Rhetoric of *Bowling for Columbine*," in *Visual Communication: Perception, Rhetoric, and Technology*, ed. Diane S. Hope (Cresskill, NJ: Hampton Press, 2006), 194. For an explanation of expository and participatory styles of documentary, see Bill Nichols, *Introduction to Documentary* (Bloomington: Indiana University Press, 2001), 99–138.

6. Sharrett and Luhr describe Moore's film as "complicated" and "at times, disjointed." Sharrett and Luhr, review of *Bowling for Columbine*, 37. Hoberman calls it "poorly structured, [and] a half-hour too long." J. Hoberman, "They Aim to Please," review of *Bowling for Columbine*, *Village Voice*, October 8, 2002, http://www.villagevoice.com/2002-10-08/film/they-aim-to-please/. Snee says that "the film left many reasonably confused." Snee, "Free Guns and Speech Control," 194.

7. Chris Kaltenbach, "French Hail Their New Hero; Step Aside, Jerry Lewis—Cannes Goes Wild for Michael Moore and His Film, 'Bowling for Columbine,'" review of *Bowling for Columbine*, *Baltimore Sun*, June 2, 2002, http://articles.baltimoresun.com/2002-06-02/entertainment/0206010199_1_michael-moore-cannes-jerry-lewis.

8. Marlowe Fawcett, "Fear and Goading," review of *Bowling for Columbine*, *Times Literary Supplement*, December 13, 2002, http://marlowefawcett.com/wp-content/uploads/2010/06/TLS_bowlingforcolumbine.pdf; Finn, review of *Bowling for Columbine*, 65.

9. The phrase "strangely compelling" is strategically ambiguous. As we argue throughout this chapter, the appeal of *Bowling for Columbine* is largely affective. Because affect is, strictly speaking, asignifying (nonsymbolic), we are suggesting that the film operates primarily on a bodily level or material register. In other words, its "argument" is experienced (felt) as a flow of general atmospheric-like intensities rather than understood (interpreted) as a series of specific step-by-step meanings. To say that the film is "strangely compelling," then, is to suggest that its appeal lies at the very limits of language and symbolicity.

10. Jonathan Curiel, "Moore Captures U.S. Zeitgeist/'Bowling for Columbine' Explains Violence," review of *Bowling for Columbine*, *San Francisco Chronicle*, October 18, 2002, http://www.sfgate.com/entertainment/article/Moore-captures-U-S-zeitgeist-Bowling-for-2761485.php.

11. Snee, "Free Guns and Speech Control," 195.

12. George A. Kennedy, *Aristotle on Rhetoric: A Theory of Civic Discourse*, 2nd ed. (New York: Oxford University Press, 2007), 113–14.

13. Joshua Gunn and Jenny Edbauer Rice, "About Face/Stuttering Discipline." *Communication and Critical/Cultural Studies* 6, no. 2 (2009): 216.

14. There are, of course, exceptions to this general trend. Benson and Anderson's rhetorical analysis of Frederick Wiseman's films, for instance, specifically treats "film as a constructed invitation to a complex experience of thoughts *and* feelings" (emphasis added). Thomas W. Benson and Carolyn Anderson, *Reality Fictions: The Films of Frederick Wiseman*, 2nd ed. (Carbondale: Southern Illinois University Press, 2002), 3.

15. See, for instance, Joshua Gunn, "Maranatha," *Quarterly Journal of Speech* 98, no. 4 (2012): 359–85; Christian Lundberg, "Enjoying God's Death: *The Passion of the Christ* and the Practices of an Evangelical Public," *Quarterly Journal of Speech* 95 (2009): 387–411; Brian L. Ott and Diane Marie Keeling, "Cinema and Choric Connection: *Lost in Translation* as Sensual Experience," *Quarterly Journal of Speech* 97, no. 4 (2011): 363–86; Brian L. Ott and Gordana Lazić, "The Pedagogy and Politics of Art in Postmodernity: Cognitive Mapping and *The Bothersome Man*," *Quarterly Journal of Speech* 99, no. 3 (2013): 259–82.

16. Brian L. Ott, "The Visceral Politics of *V for Vendetta*: On Political Affect in Cinema," *Critical Studies in Media Communication* 21, no. 1 (2010): 41.

17. Jane M. Gaines, "Political Mimesis," in *Collecting Visible Evidence*, ed. Jane M. Gaines and Michael Renov (Minneapolis: University of Minnesota Press, 1999), 92, 90.

18. Renato Barilli, *A Course on Aesthetics*, trans. Karen E. Pinkus (Minneapolis: University of Minnesota Press, 1993), 2.

19. Barbara M. Kennedy, *Deleuze and Cinema: The Aesthetics of Sensation* (Edinburgh, Scotland: Edinburgh University Press, 2000), 114.

20. Charles Altieri, *The Particulars of Rapture: An Aesthetics of the Affects* (Ithaca, NY: Cornell University Press, 2003), 2. As Ahmed explains, "Emotions cannot be separated from bodily sensations." Sara Ahmed, *The Cultural Politics of Emotion* (New York: Routledge, 2004), 12.

21. Ahmed, *Cultural Politics*, 7.

22. Ott, "Visceral Politics of *V for Vendetta*," 50.

23. Kenneth Burke, *A Grammar of Motives* (Berkeley: University of California Press, 1969), 236.

24. Altieri, *Particulars of Rapture*, 2.

25. Raphaël Micheli, "Emotions as Objects of Argumentative Constructions," *Argumentation* 24, no. 1 (2010): 6.

26. Gerald Clore and Stanley Colcombe, "The Parallel Worlds of Affective Concepts and Feelings," in *The Psychology of Evaluation: Affective Processes in Cognition and Emotion*, ed. Jochen Musch and Karl Christoph Klauer (Mahwah: Lawrence Erlbaum Associates, 2003), 346.

27. Sharrett and Luhr, review of *Bowling for Columbine*, 36. Moore, who has been widely criticized for placing "himself at the center of his work" is "dressed in his customary jeans, untucked shirt, and gimme cap." Ibid.; Waak, "*Bowling for Columbine*," 4. See also Hoberman, "They Aim to Please"; Wilshire, "Presentation and Representation," 92.

28. Fawcett, "Fear and Goading"; Sharrett and Luhr, review of *Bowling for Columbine*, 36.

29. Brent J. Steele, "Irony, Emotions and Critical Distance," *Millennium: Journal of International Studies* 39, no. 1 (2010): 96.

30. Berel Lang, "The Limits of Irony," *New Literary History* 27, no. 3 (1996): 579.

31. Ann Marie Seward Barry, *Visual Intelligence: Perception, Image, and Manipulation in Visual Communication* (Albany: State University of New York Press, 1997), 208.

32. Bijana Scott, "Picturing Irony: The Subversive Power of Photography," *Visual Communication* 3, no. 1 (2004): 47.

33. Roland Barthes, *Image–Music–Text*, trans. Stephen Heath (New York: Hill and Wang, 1977), 30–31. For a sustained analysis of our modern obsession with images of atrocities, see Susan Sontag, *Regarding the Pain of Others* (New York: Farrar, Straus and Giroux, 2003).

34. Lisa Nesselson, review of *Bowling for Columbine*, *Variety*, May 16, 2002, https://variety.com/2002/film/reviews/bowling-for-columbine-1200549676/.

35. Edmund Burke, *A Philosophical Enquiry into the Origin of Our Ideas of the Sublime and Beautiful* (New York: Harper & Brothers, 1844), 51.

36. Although the editing of this scene (direct cut) implies that the footage of Heston is from the 1999 NRA rally in Denver, it is actually from a 2000 NRA rally in Charlotte, North Carolina.

37. See Barry, *Visual Intelligence*, 195–212; Susan L. Feagin, "Time and Timing," in *Passionate Views: Film, Cognition, and Emotion*, ed. Carl Plantinga and Greg M. Smith (Baltimore: Johns Hopkins University Press, 1999), 168–79.

38. Snee, "Free Guns and Speech Control," 201.

39. Moore's harrowing use of gun-related fatality statistics is an example of what Woodward calls "statistical panic." Kathleen Woodward, *Statistical Panic: Cultural Politics and Poetics of the Emotions* (Durham: Duke University Press, 2009), 196. A fear-driven form of anxiety based on the probability of mortal risk, statistical panic is an affect that thrives on a feeling of vulnerable. Woodward explains, "Fatally we feel that a certain statistic, which is in fact based on an

aggregate and is only a measure of probability, represents our very future—or the future of someone we love." Ibid., 196. A typical response to statistical panic is the avoidance of risk via preventive measures, since, as the saying goes, you don't want to end up just another statistic.

40. Bill Nichols, *Representing Reality: Issues and Concepts in Documentary* (Bloomington: Indiana University Press, 1991), 44.

41. Nichols, *Representing Reality*, 53.

42. We concur with Snee's assessment that "the film concludes with two memorable sequences that seem misplaced." Snee, "Free Guns and Speech Control," 194–95.

43. Sigmund Freud, "Mourning and Melancholia," in *The Freud Reader*, ed. Peter Gay (New York: W. W. Norton & Company, 1989), 587.

44. See Emily Brady and Arto Haapala, "Melancholy as an Aesthetic Emotion," *Contemporary Aesthetics* 1 (2003), http://hdl.handle.net/2027/spo.7523862.0001.006; Julia Kristeva, "On the Melancholic Imaginary," *New Formations* 3 (1987): 5; David L. Eng, "Melancholia in the Late Twentieth Century," *Signs* 25 (2000): 1276.

45. Eng, "Melancholia," 1276.

46. Christine Ross, *The Aesthetics of Disengagement: Contemporary Art and Depression* (Minneapolis: University of Minnesota Press, 2006), 23.

47. Sharrett and Luhr, review of *Bowling for Columbine*, 36.

48. Glenn W. Muschert, "Frame-Changing in the Media Coverage of a School Shooting: The Rise of Columbine as a National Concern," *Social Science Journal* 46 (2009): 165; Charles R. Acland, *Youth, Murder, Spectacle: The Cultural Politics of "Youth in Crisis"* (Boulder, CO: Westview Press, 1995), 8; Arthur G. Neal, *National Trauma and Collective Memory: Extraordinary Events in the American Experience*, 2nd ed. (New York: M. E. Sharpe, 2005), 165.

49. Jeffrey C. Alexander, "Toward a Theory of Cultural Trauma," in *Cultural Trauma and Collective Identity*, ed. Jeffrey C. Alexander, Ron Eyerman, Bernhard Giesen, Neil J. Smelser, and Piotr Sztompka (Berkeley: University of California Press, 2004), 1; J. William Spencer and Glenn W. Muschert, "The Contested Meaning of the Crosses at Columbine," *American Behavioral Scientist* 52 (June 2009): 1373. One of the most profound "marks" Columbine has had on our collective consciousness is its adoption as "a cultural script," which subsequent school shooters have used to mimic, rationalize, or memorialize with their own violent actions. Ralph Larkin, "The Columbine Legacy: Rampage Shootings as Political Acts," *American Behavioral Scientist* 52, no. 9 (2009): 1312.

50. Although never mentioned in the film, one of the most notorious school shootings in history occurred in Montréal on December 6, 1989. Marc Lépine, an engineering student at the University of Montréal, went to his mechanical engineering class with the intent to kill. Upon entering the class, Lépine told all the men, including his professor, to leave and they complied. Then Lépine murdered six women because they were a "bunch of feminists," after which he entered another classroom and killed eight more women, as well as injuring nine women and four men in the hallway, before killing himself. According to his suicide note, Lépine "blamed feminists for ruining his life" and felt this was a "political act" that had to be done. Sharon Rosenberg, "Neither Forgotten nor Fully Remembered: Tracing an Ambivalent Public Memory on the 10th Anniversary of the Montréal Massacre," *Feminist Theory* 4, no. 1 (2003): 5.

51. E. Ann Kaplan, *Trauma Culture: The Politics of Terror and Loss in Media and Literature* (New Brunswick: Rutgers University Press, 2005), 90.

52. Ibid., 91.

53. Alexander, "Toward a Theory of Cultural Trauma," 10, 24, 27.

54. Judith Butler, *Precarious Life: The Power of Mourning and Violence* (New York: Verso, 2004), 20.

55. Alexander, "Toward a Theory of Cultural Trauma," 14.

56. Butler, *Precarious Life*, 20.

5. The Conversion of Lila Lipscomb in *Fahrenheit 9/11*

Thomas Rosteck and Thomas S. Frentz

O f all the Michael Moore documentaries treated in this volume, none has enjoyed more financial success than *Fahrenheit 9/11*. In the summer of 2004, the film broke box office records for documentaries, grossing over $119 million in the domestic market after winning the Palme d'Or at the 2004 Cannes Film Festival. It remains today the most financially successful documentary film ever produced.[1] This is even more remarkable considering that, released in the midst of a presidential election season, *Fahrenheit 9/11* was taken as an "indictment of the Bush Administration's middle East policies" and as a film "conceived expressly to drive Bush from the White House."[2]

Predictably, given such readings, the reception of *Fahrenheit 9/11* was contentious. Some reviewers celebrated its historic potential as "the first movie to really affect a national election."[3] Others, encouraging Americans to see it, called it "one of the most important films ever made."[4] But clearly the swell of media opinion ran in the opposite direction, and soon even the film itself became an issue in the campaign. Moore was widely accused of playing fast and loose with the facts and producing nothing more than a clever bit of propaganda for strictly partisan political ends.[5] Reports of inaccuracies dominated the coverage, and commentaries reacted as much to Moore's image as political provocateur and celebrity figure as to the material in the film.[6] Thus, ultimately, both filmmaker and film were framed within a discourse of "liberal elitism." *Fahrenheit 9/11* transformed in the public mind from a critique of the Bush administration into a convenient symbol with which to denounce the entire Democratic Party and to flay all versions of "liberal politics."[7]

The response among film scholars has largely followed the same template. For instance, at a meeting of the American Film Historians group, most participants flatly accused Moore of producing a disreputable piece of propaganda.[8] Others cited the film's form and structure as root causes of its "failure."[9] Typical is the comprehensive essay by Shawn Parry-Giles and Trevor Parry-Giles, who claim the film is a "disappointment" because it uses tactics that neither connected with an audience nor encouraged deliberation of major issues. Because the film is both a "deliberative" text and a "campaign" text, they say, and therefore has two "arguments"— namely, the "immorality and illegitimacy of the US wars in Afghanistan and Iraq" and "the illegitimacy of the Bush presidency"—its dual aims and intentions are inconsistent and contradictory.[10]

However, even as commentators were dismissing Moore's documentary because it had no measurable effect on either the 2004 presidential election or the administration's policies in the Middle East, popular critics and reviewers did agree, almost without exception, that the film had one shining moment—namely, the personage of Lila Lipscomb, whose on-screen presence demonstrated movingly intense pathos and profound eloquence. Here is reviewer Denis Hamill's initial reaction: "As an American mother named Lila Lipscomb drowned in anguish over the death of her son in Iraq, the packed Loews Bay Terrace theater in Queens was so silent at the 11 A.M. show of 'Fahrenheit 9/11' on Friday that all you could hear was the rustle of tissues . . . as the movie played, I watched men and women, young and old, wiping their eyes in silhouette."[11]

Carrie Rickey sounds a similar note, recognizing the potential of Lipscomb's example as an element of the film's suasory effects: "Lipscomb is a soft-spoken patriot who loves her country and her children, two of whom enlisted in the armed forces. Her daughter returned safely from Desert Storm in 1991. But the fate of her son, Sgt. Michael Pedersen, stationed near Karbala in Iraq, weighs on her heart like an anvil."[12] Rickey, clearly moved by Lipscomb's on-screen image, contrasts her gentle presence with that of the usually bombastic Moore. "The triumph of *Fahrenheit* . . . is that Moore shuts up and lets Lipscomb eloquently make his point for him. When she reads the final letter her son wrote before he was killed in Iraq, the kicker of which shall not be revealed here, we share her conversion experience from flag-waving, yellow-ribbon-tying soldier's mother into a woman who finds solidarity with protesters in front of the White House. ... I thank Moore for introducing me to Lila Lipscomb. May her son—and all of the fallen in Iraq—rest in peace."

Reviewer A. O. Scott likewise says, "The most moving sections of *Fahrenheit 9/11* concern Lila Lipscomb, a cheerful state employee and former welfare recipient who wears a crucifix pendant and an American flag lapel pin. When we first meet her, she is proud of her family's military service—a daughter served in the Persian Gulf War and a son, Michael Pedersen, was a marine in Iraq—and grateful for the opportunities it has offered. Then Michael is killed in Karbala, and in sharing her grief with Mr. Moore, she also gives his film an eloquence that its most determined critics will find hard to dismiss."[13]

We too think Lila Lipscomb is the key to unraveling some of the less transparent meanings in *Fahrenheit 9/11*, and that her role in the film is part and parcel of its appeal. Moreover, we think that Rickey is on the right track when she says, rather in passing, that Moore shuts up and allows Lipscomb to make his points for him. That he does, indeed. But because the commentators on the film concentrated on its immediate political impact, or lack thereof, the larger significance of Lipscomb's role has yet to be put forth. We want to study Lipscomb's role in the film and see what it might reveal about the larger forms of representation within the political documentary.

In what follows, we closely examine Lila Lipscomb's four scenes in *Fahrenheit 9/11* and argue that Moore does more than just shut up; he allows Lipscomb to personify what it means to be a rhetorical advocate in these polarized political times. More generally, the film draws our attention to the problem of focus and depiction in modern, mediated visual forms. The problem may be briefly described in this way. At the heart of the documentary enterprise is the technological capacity to record a visual and aural record of a particular piece of the world, a recording that comprises the evidentiary quality of the documentary account.[14] From this capacity, critical questions immediately arise—among them, what the relationship is between the record of a "specific reality" and the more general propositions that the specific reality exemplifies. For example, how does the documentary record of one individual worker's situation connect with the more general problem of "unemployment in the Midwest"?

While this tension between particular and general animates most "realist" texts, it is exacerbated in visual forms because of the obvious recognition that what the camera records is radically "particular" and seems initially to foreclose more "general" implications. This bridging of the particular-general gap in documentary film is especially crucial when we consider its role as a political document. As Bill Nichols points out, the problem is that documentary conflates traditional notions of argument and evidence: "documentary has a tension arising from the attempt to make statements about life that are quite general while necessarily using sounds and images that bear the inescapable trace of their historical origins."[15] James A. Wood succinctly describes this inherent tension and argues that while visual forms powerfully present the single example (because of our acceptance of the film image as "tied" to reality), precisely because the film image is so specific, it may prevent generalization, stranding the viewer at the level of the single case.[16] For persuasion to succeed, Wood says, it is essential to invest the specific case with implications beyond the local and singular. Therefore, what gives persuasive potency to the documentary form is an audience's willingness to acknowledge that one "particular" is at the same time "general," "typical," or "representative."[17]

Based on such preliminary considerations, then, these questions frame our investigation. Taking a cue from Wood, we may ask whether Lila Lipscomb transcends the individual story of one person's plight. If she does, how does she come to stand for others who oppose US policy? And further, how does Lipscomb gather the potential to model protest? Beginning with these questions, our reading of *Fahrenheit 9/11* engages two interconnected issues. First, examining the text in terms of its symbolic movement, we discover previously unacknowledged rhetorical action and show how the film strategically solicits our judgment both of the individual tragedy of Lila Lipscomb and, more broadly, of the immorality of the Bush administration's war policies. That is, we note how this documentary constructs specific images of a single case and at the same time builds a more general ideological and oppositional perspective. Second, this angle of approach also obliges us to probe the question of representation and depiction in documentary argument. We contend that *Fahrenheit 9/11* relies on a simultaneous particularizing and universalizing symbolic movement to represent Lila Lipscomb.

Representation itself is a symbolic operation, and the representation of the individual in a form that both magnifies and narrows is the business of synecdoche, the trope of representation. As such, we argue that the symbolic movement called synecdoche prompts our assent to the plight of a single individual while at the same time suggests how that individual can stand for a larger complex of public issues. What we shall see is that such "representativeness" is a textual fabrication—a carefully crafted strategy of this documentary.

Fahrenheit 9/11 bridges the gap between particular and universal by inviting its audience to reconstruct the figure of Lila Lipscomb in three ways: as a historical person (an agent of social activity) within a narrative field, as a character in a conversion story (political advocate), and as a mythic icon or symbol (an idealized and heroic embodiment of shared values and attitudes). That is, the film simultaneously invites its audience to contemplate essentially three Lila Lipscombs: historical person, narrative character, and exemplary persona. Moreover, we suggest that each of these three intertextual dimensions—history, narrative, myth—is necessary for a reading that retains the potential to reconstitute Lipscomb as the locus of audience sympathy with the potential to become a model for political action.[18] And by "passing his mantle" to her, so to speak, Moore simultaneously affects three different kinds of representation for Lipscomb. She becomes a model of a new form of political advocacy, a substitute sign for Moore himself, and a universal critic of the Bush administration's policies.

We do not meet Lila Lipscomb until *Fahrenheit 9/11* is well beyond its midpoint. When we do, she appears in only four scenes, which we might label professional, personal, family, and public. In what follows, we examine each scene in some detail, noting both dialogue and cinematic treatment, all the while paying close attention to the three forms of representation that we feel Lipscomb characterizes.

The Professional Introduction

For the transformation from the real to the ideal to be effective, the text must first encourage us to see the central figure as concrete, specific, and altogether typical. Immediately after a rather muddled discussion of unemployment in Flint, Michigan, we hear a woman's voice-over and then the film quickly cuts to a sturdy, middle-age woman wearing a light blouse and dark sweater.[19] She is framed asymmetrically, suggesting the unbalanced context that surely defines any unemployment office. The intertitle below identifies her as "Lila Lipscomb, Executive Assistant of Career Alliance." She is talking offscreen, presumably to Moore, and she is telling him that the real unemployment rate in Flint is probably closer to 50 percent than the official figure of 17 percent. As she speaks, the camera cuts to the street, where men and women, mostly black, obviously unemployed, and clearly anxious, mill about carrying cardboard boxes of their possessions as they wait to see the Career Alliance people inside. The camera then zooms in on a poster saying, "Attention: Do You Need to File an Unemployment Claim?"

As the camera pulls back, we see some of Lipscomb's coworkers in the background. There is a medium-long shot of Lipscomb laughing and talking on the phone while two coworkers busy themselves behind a counter. The atmosphere seems hectic but well organized and important. Then the camera cuts back to a medium shot where we hear Lipscomb say, "So my family has gone through the welfare system. When it was Jobs Central, in the mid-80s, I came through the job training partnership program here at Jobs Central and went to a secretary school. Years later, I'm the executive assistant to the president of the agency. Interesting."[20]

From the moment of her cinematic introduction, Lipscomb is revealed as a historical person—a woman situated in a community, an institution, embedded in a context. Her specificity is further detailed as she recounts her pragmatic advice to her children. "I started . . . telling my children, 'The military is a good option. I can't afford to have you go to college; I cannot pay your way. Financial aid will not help you.' So, I, as a mother, started teaching my children about the options in that the military could do, that would take them around the world, they would see all the things that I, as a mother, could not let them see. It would pay for their education that I as their mother, and their father, could not pay for." Moore then asks, "The military's a good option for kids in Flint?" to which Lipscomb quickly replies, "Military's an excellent option for the people in the city of Flint" (92).

Lipscomb first appears as a professional and a true patriot. She is openly promilitary, not only for the young people of Flint for whom there is no other job option, but for her own children as well. What seems to be happening here politically, we think, is that Lipscomb is embracing both ends of the political spectrum. Yes, her own professional success grew out of the welfare system, but yes, too, military service is an excellent way to get ahead in periods of economic decline and financial crisis. She represents, in other words, both left and right, red and blue. And because Moore is still offscreen, by speaking *to* him as well as *for* him, she expands and softens his own intractable ultraliberal leanings.

If *Fahrenheit 9/11* really does encourage a reading where Lila Lipscomb is the model for political protest, then it must enrich and magnify the specific and concrete to sustain the potential for greater meaning. This it does through the slippage into the discourses of conversion and myth. But this subsequent transubstantiation into the imagery of narrative and the ideological requires first our assent to the "reality" of the historical. In short, a viewer's willingness to grant a faithfulness or fidelity to the historical could be the crucial element in the potential success of the film's textual argument. The visual substance of the historical person of Lila Lipscomb provides the semiotic substance for her still-to-emerge narrative character and mythic persona.[21]

The Personal Profile

We do not encounter Lila Lipscomb again until several segments later. When we do, she is walking out the front door of her home carrying a rolled-up American flag. As the hand-held camera follows her into the front yard, Moore, still offscreen, asks, "Do you consider yourself a proud American?" Lipscomb replies, "Absolutely. I am an extremely proud American. I think I'm probably more proud than the average Joe. When I put my flag out, I can't allow it to touch the ground, because I know the lives that were lost and the blood that was shed so that I could be here and have a flag." When Moore asks, "Right . . . how often do you put the flag out?" Lipscomb tells him, "Every single day, every single day. I started when my daughter was in Desert Storm. I had the same flag flying on my front porch and the same yellow ribbons, praying and hoping every single day that my child would come home safe and that everybody's child would come home safe" (105–6).

Like all documentary films, this one operates in the crease between life as lived and life as symbolized and represented, and the potential for meaning in *Fahrenheit 9/11* depends on this fragile relationship. From this textual juncture, the film fabricates narrative and character to give meaning to the events of a single life.[22]

They move inside now as the camera frames Lipscomb in her kitchen. She is dressed in a dark shirt with a cross necklace clearly visible. When Moore affirms that hers is a very strong military family, Lipscomb adds, "Very strong. My family was . . . my family is what I consider part of the backbone of America. It's families like mine, and it's not just my family, there's hundreds of families, millions of families out here, that this country was founded on their backs. I have been known to be a conservative Democrat" (107).

Here we see "family values" with real value and, we might add, values very consistent with a conservative political perspective and with the promilitary side of Lipscomb that we previously discovered at her office. We also hear Lipscomb saying that her family is more than a concrete particular; it is representative of "millions of families out here" in America. But then things begin to get politically messy.

For the first time in these scenes, Moore now appears on-screen for a quick shot with Lipscomb out of the frame. Reflecting on Lipscomb's family, he says pensively, "It's a great country. It's a great country," to which Lipscomb replies, almost as a non sequitur, "The cross that I choose to wear, if you notice [here the camera zooms in on the cross, showing that it is decorated with multicolored stones], it's a multicultural, a multicolor cross. That's because I believe that all God's people come in many colors. And my family itself is multicultural" (107). The camera cuts to a still photo of a young woman, Lipscomb's daughter who served in Desert Storm. Then it makes another quick cut to a still shot of a young man in fatigues. As the camera zooms in on him, we learn that he is her son, Michael Pederson, currently serving in Iraq. Moore asks off-camera, "What was your reaction to protesters during, say, the Gulf War or Vietnam, or . . ." Lipscomb interrupts him: "I always hated the protestors. I always hated the protestors [quick cut to a still shot of a protest rally]. It was just a slap in my face. It was just, like, they were dishonoring my son. And I burned in my soul to tell them, 'You don't understand, they're not there because they want to be there.' But then I came to understand that they weren't protesting the men and women that were there, they were protesting the concept of war" (108–9).

Many important things transpire in Lipscomb's kitchen. We discover, as Moore puts it, what a gift her family has given to our country, with two children having served in the military. And we learn that her family, by being multicultural and multiracial, is itself a cross section of America in microcosm. But perhaps most important, *Fahrenheit 9/11* begins to frame its central biographical narrative: the "conversion of Lila Lipscomb." Such biography is "story," however, and by design, biography counters the errant movements of a life with the smooth curve of narrative form. As story, the closure and unity of biographical conversion narrative stand at odds to the open-endedness and incoherence of life as it is lived, and thus every biography is an attempt to imbue reality with meaning and significance.

The story of Lipscomb's conversion within *Fahrenheit 9/11* draws on its viewers' familiarity with the dynamics of narratives found in other "transformation" or "conversion" narratives to layer meaning over the historical life of Lila Lipscomb. In her second appearance in the documentary, she is shown as a person who is about to confront a life-changing experience.

The Family Tragedy

Fahrenheit 9/11 has established Lila Lipscomb as a real-life, specific person and as a figure who has clear political views that run in support of the military and in opposition to protest and antiwar activity. But as we expect in conversion narratives, the convert must undergo a consciousness-raising experience and emerge from that as a different person.[23] As Valeria Fabj notes, "One must dissociate oneself from the past by first deciding not to tolerate the existing order, forgive oneself for having been a part of that order, and promise to adhere to the rules of the new order. Thus, conversion is a process, a transformation that requires at least three distinct steps, rather than an instantaneous change of mind."[24]

Following the trajectory of the conversion narrative, we are now asked to share in Lipscomb's darkest hour. Her son, Sergeant Michael Pedersen, has been killed in a Blackhawk helicopter crash near Karbala in south-central Iraq. The camera frames Lila and her husband, Howard Lipscomb, sitting on their couch in the family living room. As she reminisces about Michael and his feelings about being sent to Iraq, the camera cuts to a long shot of the entire family. We now see what she had described in the previous scene—a truly integrated family of nine spanning three generations. If there was any doubt that this family represented that cross section of America Lipscomb mentioned earlier, this shot dispels that once and for all. As she recounts the phone call from the army telling her that Michael had been killed, the camera moves in closer. She begins to cry. "The grief grabbed me so hard that I literally fell off on the floor and I was alone. I didn't have anybody to pick me up, so I literally crawled over to my desk, and was hanging on, and I remember screaming, 'Why does it have to be Michael? Why did you have to take my son? Why is it my son that you had to take? He didn't do anything! He wasn't a bad guy; he was a good guy, why did you have to take my son?'" she sobs (115).

We now see Lipscomb holding Michael's last letter home. As she begins reading the letter, fighting back tears, the camera cuts to individual shots of the family's grief, first a daughter crying softly while someone out of frame smooths her hair, then the youngest infant, who seems to sense but not quite grasp the gravity of what's going on. "How is everyone?" the letter begins. "I'm doing fine. We're just out here in the sand and windstorms, waiting. What in the world is wrong with George 'trying-to-be-like-his-dad' Bush? He got us out here for nothing whatsoever. I'm so furious right now, Mama. I really hope they do not reelect that fool, honestly" (116).

As she finishes the letter, the camera catches her hand tapping against it with intense frustration. Then the camera tracks right, until it centers in on Howard. To this point, he has done little except to comfort his wife as she relived their son's death. Now he speaks for the first time. "I feel . . . I . . . I . . . I feel sad for my family because we lost our son. But, I really feel sorry for the other families that is [sic] losing their kids as we speak. And for what? I don't . . . That's the, I guess, sickening part. For what?" he asks (117).

It is difficult, perhaps even impossible, not to get caught up in this family's grief, but rhetorically this is more than a family tragedy. It is here, we think, that Lipscomb and her entire family put forth one of the most brutal indictments of the administration's policies in the Middle East. And that indictment, lest we forget, comes not from the living in that living room, but from the words of a dead American son, a marine who, with his own last words home, condemns the war he was asked to fight for no good reason.

The conversion narrative takes the raw materials of history and seeks to reshape these, to give them a familiar structure and hence a potential for expanded meaning. Biography is, as Hayden White explains, the desire to represent the moral under the cover of the aesthetic.[25] And it is by inviting its audience to "read" Lila Lipscomb as a character within a familiar conversion narrative form that *Fahrenheit 9/11* seeks to reconstitute its real central figure both as one "converted" from support to opposition—and as one embodying certain beliefs and values.

But in addition to reframing Lipscomb's individual story, these details encourage a natural pathos for her. It seems reasonable to suggest that viewers might find their emotional reaction intensified as they are invited to perceive Lipscomb caught up in a tragic, even heartbreaking scenario. Such tactics are neither surprising nor novel; even Aristotle's *Poetics* advises that the tragic hero be someone "average." Moreover, Aristotle continues, such tragedy acquires the potential for pathos in that "what we fear for ourselves excites pity when it happens to others."[26]

Public Reconciliation at the White House

But the conversion of Lila Lipscomb is not yet complete. What remains within the conventions of the narrative is to reveal the reborn figure as an icon of change and transformation and, in the process, to depict the mythic and iconic results of the conversion.

Lipscomb's last scene is introduced by Moore's voice-over off-camera: "Lila had called to tell me that she was coming down from Flint to Washington, DC, to attend a jobs conference. On her break, she said she was going to go and pay a visit to the White House" (123). A hand-held camera picks up Lipscomb pausing in front of a makeshift booth in which a young protester is displaying photos of presumed American atrocities. The camera catches Lipscomb and the protester talking past one another, Lipscomb telling about her son being killed in Iraq, the young protester bashing Bush. As the camera records this strange nondialogue, an unidentified woman wearing a fashionable red coat and designer sunglasses comes into the frame to see what might be going on. To the protester's "Bush is a terrorist," she jumps in with, "No he isn't. This is all staged. This is all staged" (124).

Lipscomb turns on the woman, telling her what happened to her son: "He was killed in Karbala. April 2. It's not a stage. My son is dead." To which the woman responds, "Well, a lot of other people, too. Blame al Qaeda!" At this, Lipscomb, now visibly upset, turns away and heads off toward the White House. "What did that woman yell at you?" Moore asks off-camera. Crying now, and having trouble catching her breath, Lipscomb says, "That I'm supposed to blame the al Qaeda. The al Qaeda didn't make a decision to send my son to Iraq. Ignorance . . . that we deal with . . . with everyday people. 'Cause they don't know. People think they know, but you don't know. I thought I knew, but I didn't know" (125).

As Lipscomb makes her way toward the White House, the camera backs off, leaving us with a chilling shot from behind Lipscomb as she sobs in front of the fence before the White House. In the background, we see the Washington Monument looming up on the left, a billowing Old Glory on the right, and if we look closely, two armed personnel, either military or White House security, walking across the roof.

As we watch, Lipscomb bends over, apparently overcome with grief. Then she rights herself and says, with her back still to the camera, "I need my son. God, it's tougher than I thought it was gonna be to be here, but it's freeing also, because I finally have a place to put all my pain and all my anger and to release it" (125). Once ignorant, now wise, once blind, now enlightened, Lila Lipscomb emerges as a model for protest and political action. Insofar as she has demonstrated the conversion from "conservative," "supporter of the war," to doubter, questioner, opponent of "George," she stands as the representative of the political conversion of an entire public. In this final scene, all three forms of representation seem to come together. As a model for political action, not just thought and reflection, Lipscomb brings her anger, pain, and frustration to the very doors of the White House. As a sign for Michael Moore, she continues to stand in for the filmmaker in ways that his own tarnished and rigidified image will no longer allow. And in confronting the banal ignorance of the "woman intruder," she models what being a spokesperson for those few "in the know" might look like.

Private Tragedy as Representative of Public Policy

Beyond this specific yet evocative story of a particular woman, we have argued that *Fahrenheit 9/11* invites us to see, in the private and individual tragedy of Lila Lipscomb, the realm of the universal and to give a grander ideological significance to her story. Lipscomb's private tragedy becomes representative of our public policies, and this universality makes her plight that much more evocative. It is interesting that we find this same notion of representation defined in the rhetorical figure of synecdoche that launched our analysis.[27]

In describing what he calls an "evanescent moment," Kenneth Burke addresses the classical tropes of metaphor, metonymy, synecdoche, and irony, considering them not in their figurative use, but for "their role in the discovery and description of the truth."[28] As for synecdoche, while the tradition defines it as one of the figures of substitution, "genus for species or species for genus for the sake of vividness of effect," or as "given persons or people, given places or times, [standing as] tabernacles for greater wholes,"[29] Burke is far more expansive. For him, synecdoche is "representation," and by this he means the representing of "part for the whole, the whole for the part . . . cause for effect, effect for cause, etc." Every synecdoche,

Burke concludes, implies a "convertibility between the two terms . . . an individual is treated as a replica of the universal, and vice versa."[30]

How then does *Fahrenheit 9/11* invite us to see beyond the individual case of Lila Lipscomb? In this "small story," the case of one particular woman is given larger ideological meanings, while at the same time the ideological is enacted in the particular—given names, places, actions, attributes—naturalized within commonsense wisdom. We may describe these operations as synecdoche in the following ways.

First, the appeal of the *Fahrenheit 9/11* rests on the synecdochic amplification from particular to general. By now it should be clear that for Moore, the "representativeness" of the "case" of Lila Lipscomb is a careful and necessary fabrication. As we have seen, the film seeks to fix the Lipscomb story by attending to details and to the specifics of her case. As a firm believer in "my country right or wrong," Lipscomb first appears as an enthusiastic supporter of war in Iraq.

Second, the appeal of the film reverses this generalizing valence of the synecdoche and depends on the systematic reduction from general to particular. Using the story of Lipscomb as the index of a complex oppositional political ideology, *Fahrenheit 9/11* articulates more universal ideological themes in terms of a specific and intelligible representation. Moreover, we suggest, it is via this less acknowledged synecdochic movement that Moore may potentially accomplish his ideological work.

In sum, we are invited to read *Fahrenheit 9/11* in terms of its archetypal frames, so the documentary layers a signification drawn from conventions of the conversion "story" or "myth" over the nonfiction archival evidence of Lipscomb's life. The film imposes an order on the real that is a function of an alternation between conventions of the nonfiction "reality" and a symbolic reading that promises a resolution paralleling that of other conversion stories.

This text represents, then, an intersection of two sorts of signifying codes: the one based on our assent to the indexical relation of image and world, an acknowledgment of the ontological potency of the nonfiction document, and the other based on the mythic and narrative, drawn from a cultural stock of characters and soliciting us to read the conversion biography as myth, as the acting out of an allegory or parable.

But in saying this, we are not saying that this documentary is read like a "fictional" conversion discourse. On the contrary, the viewer is constantly pulled back by the "stickiness of the indexical image" to the notion that this is a real person, in a real situation, experiencing genuine emotions. It is this difference between the imaginary and the indexical that separates the nonfiction discourse from the mythical or fictional. As Nichols has said, the ground of documentary resides in the relation between character and social agent; a person acts as an agent in history, not a narrative, no matter how much we give meaning to the former by way of the latter.[31] Yet it is also this confluence of symbolic forms that suggests the potential of *Fahrenheit 9/11* to elicit audience reaction.

The Trope of Synecdoche and the Rhetoric of Documentary

In this chapter, we have fastened on the single feature of *Fahrenheit 9/11* that critics and reviewers alike applaud: the performance of the "every person," Lila Lipscomb. We have argued that if we attend to her screen appearances carefully, she participates in three types of representation. She is a "historical person" embedded in time, from which she emerges as a new form of political advocate embracing both sides of the political spectrum. But she is also a "character" in a conversion narrative, where she is transformed from ignorance to activism. And finally, she is an "icon," modeling the results of transformation and opposition to the Iraq War. In this guise, she becomes a more moderate and complex stand-in for Moore's inflammatory extremism, all the while affirming his own devastating critique of President Bush, the Iraq War, and the administration's policies in the Middle East.

In taking up this tentative reading, we have also identified one potential explanation. Employing the trope of synecdoche, Moore is able to endow the historical person, Lila Lipscomb, with layers of potential meaning by allowing viewers to read her story through the more familiar narrative conventions of the conversion narrative and the rebirth myth. The work of this text thus depends on its ability constantly to prompt its audience to reconstruct this synecdochic equivalence, this perfect symmetry between the individual person and the wider problem of opposition to a war in Iraq. Synecdoche enables an understanding of how *Fahrenheit 9/11* prompts our assent to the plight of an individual while at the same time suggesting how that individual can stand as a "small picture" of a larger complex of historical and situational problems. As an individual, Lila Lipscomb stands for the universal, and as representative of the universal, her individual plight invites a more generalized pathos.

As *Fahrenheit 9/11* demonstrates, Burke's conception of synecdoche has the potential to enrich our understanding of documentaries. It also suggests implications for the more general problem of representation and depiction in documentary argument, and it offers up a lasting lesson and legacy for this political documentary that goes far beyond its insertion into arguments over the 2004 presidential campaign. The documentary lodges between the blunt "evidentiary" film and the imaginative constructions of creative invention, and its potential for public effect seems dependent on this genial relationship. On the one hand, such documentary argument is based on the ontology of the photograph itself, "the indexical relationship with the pro-filmic event."[32] But to engage the public mind, documentary must enrich and magnify this specific historical moment. As Nichols has put this point, "The subject of the documentary must be presented as an agent or event in history by way of a filmic representation that introduces ideology and myth without overturning indexical reference."[33] And as *Fahrenheit 9/11* makes clear, this transubstantiation into the imagery of the ideological or mythic requires our assent to the "reality" of the historical.

The shuttling back and forth between the indexical or historical and the symbolic, ideological, or mythic that defines such documentary action seems to have its equivalent in the two-way movement between the specific and the universal. This approach gives us leverage to disable one crucial problem of the rhetoric of documentary: How does documentary argument escape the tyranny of the specific case?

When seen this way, the trope of synecdoche is perfectly suited to describe the persuasive dimensions and rhetorical action of many documentaries. For it seems that it is via the cognitive operations described by synecdoche that the documentary magnifies the specific case while enacting the universal within the concrete through the layering of the conventions of narrative over it. In this regard, Michael Osborn once predicted, "As knowledge becomes more complicated and remote, and as more people become responsible for informed judgments and decisions, synecdoche, which makes the world accessible through concrete representation, seems likely to become increasingly vital."[34]

As the pundits would have it, *Fahrenheit 9/11* was a total failure as a political film. It did not, as some had hoped, alter the results of the 2004 presidential election, stop the war in the Middle East, or seriously affect the administration's policies there. And except for perhaps a brief moment after its initial release, it did not even stimulate political dialogue in the country. But sometimes, as we have tried to show here, the rhetorical significance of a text resides in something other than its immediate impact on various audiences, and that significance does not always emerge clearly until long after the text first appeared in public.

Notes

1. Box Office Mojo, "Documentary: 1982–Present," Internet Movie Database, last modified June 12, 2014, http://www.boxofficemojo.com/genres/chart/?id=documentary.htm.

2. Mary Corliss, "A First Look at *Fahrenheit 9/11*," review of *Fahrenheit 9/11*, *Time*, May 17, 2004, http://www.time.com/time/arts/article/0,8599,638819,00.html#ixzz0y775XCdW; Carrie Rickey, "Fire Starter: Filmmaker Michael Moore Lobs Grenades at President Bush with 'Fahrenheit 911,' Accusing Him of Putting War Contractors before U.S. Soldiers," review of *Fahrenheit 9/11*, *Philadelphia Inquirer*, June 20, 2004.

3. David Elliott, "Burning Point," review of *Fahrenheit 9/11*, *San Diego Union-Tribune*, June 24, 2004.

4. Joe Williams, "'Fahrenheit 9/11' Goes to War against Bush," review of *Fahrenheit 9/11*, *St. Louis Post-Dispatch*, June 25, 2004.

5. Jon Scott Oberacker, "The People and Me: Michael Moore and the Politics of Political Documentary" (PhD diss., University of Massachusetts, 2009), 490–92, http://scholarworks.umass.edu/cgi/viewcontent.cgi?article=1061&context=open_access_dissertations.

6. David Denby, "George and Me," review of *Fahrenheit 9/11*, *New Yorker*, June 28, 2004, http://www.newyorker.com/archive/2004/06/28/.040628crci_cinema?currentPage=2#ixzz0y72CEIor; David Sterritt, "George W. and Me," review of *Fahrenheit 9/11*, *Christian Science Monitor*, June 25, 2004, 14; Michael Isikoff and Mark Hosenball, "Terror Watch: More Distortions from Michael Moore," review of *Fahrenheit 9/11*, *Newsweek*, June 29, 2004, http://www.newsweek.com/2004/06/29/terror-watch-more-distortions-from-michael-moore.html.

7. E.g., Bill O'Reilly, "Rank Propaganda," review of *Fahrenheit 9/11*, *Chicago Sun-Times*, June 29, 2004; Williams, "'Fahrenheit 9/11' Goes to War."

8. Maarten Pereboom and John E. O'Connor, "Michael Moore: Cinematic Historian or Propagandist?" *Film and History 35*, no. 2 (2005): 7–16.

9. Lynn A. Higgins, "Documentary in an Age of Terror," *South Central Review* 22, no. 2 (2005): 20–38.

10. Shawn J. Parry-Giles and Trevor Parry-Giles, "Virtual Realism and the Limits of Commodified Dissent in *Fahrenheit 9/11*," in *The Rhetoric of the New Political Documentary*, ed. Thomas W. Benson and Brian J. Snee (Carbondale: Southern Illinois University Press, 2008), 26.

11. Denis Hamill, "Moore's Message Delivered," review of *Fahrenheit 9/11*, *New York Daily News*, June 29, 2004.

12. Rickey, "Fire Starter."

13. A. O. Scott, "Unruly Scorn Leaves Room for Restraint, but Not a Lot," review of *Fahrenheit 9/11*, *New York Times*, June 23, 2004.

14. John Corner, ed., preface to *Documentary and the Mass Media* (Baltimore: Edward Arnold, 1986), xiv.

15. Bill Nichols, "The Voice of Documentary," in *Movies and Methods*, vol. 2, ed. Bill Nichols (Berkeley: University of California Press, 1985), 262.

16. James A. Wood, "An Application of Rhetorical Theory to Filmic Persuasion" (PhD diss., Cornell University, 1967), ProQuest (AAT 6800681); see also Lawrence Behrens, "The Argument in Film: Applying Rhetorical Theory to Film Criticism," *Journal of University Film and Video Association* 31 (1979): 3–11; John Harrington, *The Rhetoric of Film* (New York: Holt, Rinehart and Winston, 1973); Roger Silverstone, *The Message of Television: Myth and Narrative in Contemporary Culture* (London: Heinemann, 1981).

17. Wood, "Application of Rhetorical Theory"; Corner, preface to *Documentary and the Mass Media*, vii–xiv.

18. See Bill Nichols, "History, Myth, and Narrative in Documentary," *Film Quarterly* 41 (Fall 1987): 9–20; see also Thomas Rosteck, "The Intertextuality of the Man from Hope: Bill Clinton as Person? Bill Clinton as Persona? Bill Clinton as Star?," in *On Stump, State and Stage: Bill Clinton and Political Communication*, ed. Stephen A. Smith (Fayetteville: University of Arkansas Press, 1995), 231–37.

19. Sarah Kozloff, *Invisible Storytellers: Voice-over Narration in American Fiction Film* (Berkeley: University of California Press, 1988).

20. Michael Moore, *The Official "Fahrenheit 9/11" Reader* (New York: Simon & Schuster, 2004). All subsequent quotes from the film are from this source, with text references to page numbers given in parentheses.

21. Bill Nichols, *Representing Reality: Issues and Concepts in Documentary* (Bloomington: Indiana University Press, 1991), 251.

22. Bill Nichols, "Questions of Magnitude," in *Documentary and the Mass Media*, ed. John Corner (Baltimore: Edward Arnold, 1986), 114.

23. Charles J. G. Griffin, "The Rhetoric of Form in Conversion Narratives," *Quarterly Journal of Speech* 76 (1990): 152–63; James L. Golden, Goodwin F. Berquist, and William Coleman, "Secular and Religious Conversion," in *The Rhetoric of Western Thought*, 4th ed., ed. James L. Golden, Goodwin F. Berquist, and William Coleman (Dubuque, IA: Kendall-Hunt, 1989), 565–86.

24. Valeria Fabj, "Intolerance, Forgiveness, and Promise in the Rhetoric of Conversion: Italian Women Defy the Mafia," *Quarterly Journal of Speech* 84 (1998): 191.

25. Hayden White, "The Value of Narrativity in the Representation of Reality," in *On Narrative*, ed. W. J. T. Mitchell (Chicago: University of Chicago Press, 1981), 14.

26. Aristotle, *Poetics*, trans. Ingram Bywater (New York: Random House, 1954), 242, 38–9, 100.

27. See also Thomas Rosteck, "Synecdoche and Audience in *See It Now*'s 'The Case of Milo Radulovich,'" *Southern Communication Journal* 57 (1992): 229–40; Thomas Rosteck, *"See It Now" Confronts McCarthyism: Television Documentary and the Politics of Representation* (Tuscaloosa: University of Alabama Press, 1994), 77–82.

28. Kenneth Burke, "Four Master Tropes," in *A Grammar of Motives* (Berkeley: University of California Press, 1969), 503.

29. Richard A. Lanham, *A Handlist of Rhetorical Terms: A Guide for Students of English Literature* (Berkeley: University of California Press, 1968), 97; Arthur Quinn, *Figures of Speech: 60 Ways to Turn a Phrase* (Salt Lake City: G. M. Smith, 1982), 58.

30. Burke, "Four Master Tropes," 503–17.

31. Nichols, "Questions of Magnitude," 121.

32. Andre Bazin, "Ontology of the Photographic Image," in *What Is Cinema?*, ed. Hugh Gray (Berkeley, CA: University of California Press, 1967), 13.

33. Nichols, "Questions of Magnitude," 122.

34. Michael Osborn, "Rhetorical Depiction," in *Form, Genre, and the Study of Political Discourse*, ed. Herbert W. Simons and Aram A. Aghazarian (Columbia: University of South Carolina Press, 1986), 99.

6. The Phenomenal Text of Michael Moore's *Sicko*

Edward Schiappa, Daniel Ladislau Horvath,
and Peter B. Gregg

How does one write about the meaning and significance of a film such as Michael Moore's 2007 film *Sicko*? As the first chapter co-author has noted previously, "We do not have access to the Pure Text, or to its single correct interpretation, all we have is the *phenomenal* text—the text as its various readers perceive and experience it. Each textual encounter is *partial* in the sense that it represents one of many possible ways to encounter any given text, and in the sense that our individual histories, abilities, values, and interests influence the 'meaning' that we glean from a text."[1]

All accounts of textual encounters necessarily involve selective perception and description. Since it is theoretically possible to talk about a given experience ad infinitum, we have to decide *which* aspects of an experience to talk about and *how* to talk about them. What we find salient about a text is guided by what Hans-Georg Gadamer unapologetically calls our "prejudice"—the combination of personal and professional experiences and commitments that come into play every time we make meaning.[2] For that reason, we suggest that the experienced reception of *Sicko* is every bit as interesting and important as the film itself.

This chapter offers multiple accounts of the experience of *Sicko*. We begin with a reception of the very idea of *Sicko* that occurred before the film was even released. Second, we provide a brief synopsis of the film that highlights which aspects of the film were most salient for the goal of "denotative conformity."[3] Third, we describe the critical reception of the film by paid and unpaid critics. Fourth, we provide our own account of what we find rhetorically and culturally significant about *Sicko*. Last, we explore the empirical question prompted by the receptions we describe throughout the chapter: Does *Sicko* change minds? What does it accomplish with viewers?

Before *Sicko*: A Presumption of Persuasiveness

Years before the film was released, *Sicko* was understood as potentially persuasive by the health insurance industry that is *Sicko*'s putative subject. Wendell Potter, former vice president of Cigna turned whistleblower, details the intricacies of the public relations machine of the health-care industry, including an exposé of the campaign against *Sicko*.[4]

Potter reveals that as early as 2004, before a single scene of *Sicko* was shot, the health-care industry began a concerted effort to prepare for its filming and release. In anticipation of Moore's ambush-style interviews, the companies scheduled meetings with corporate security to develop plans in case Moore "showed up at their doorsteps." At the same time, top executives attended media training sessions designed to equip them with pithy things to say and give them pointers on "how not to look like a deer caught in the headlights if they got ambushed." Furthermore, given the way memos often ended up on Moore's website, the companies made an effort to cleanse all internal memos of any reference to the filmmaker, henceforth known only as "Hollywood."

Potter notes that the health-care industry's research pointed to a decline "and alarming erosion" in America's opposition to government-run health-care systems. Thus the timing of *Sicko*, slated for release the year before a presidential election, and the success and perceived persuasiveness of Moore's previous movies led to a PR campaign involving "hundreds of thousands of dollars" designed to discredit the idea of universal health care. Health insurers were to promote themselves as part of the solution rather than part of the problem, with statements about their support for efforts to reform the US health-care system. At the same time, using "third party allies," their goal was to reactivate the public's fear of "government takeover," "which tested extremely well over the years," a new fear trope designed to replace the effective yet tired warning about "socialized medicine." The backup plan for the "worst case scenario" was, to use Potter's words, "to push Moore off the cliff" in an all-out effort to depict Michael Moore as a person bent on "destroying free-market health care and with it, the American way of life."

Synopsis of the Film

Michael Moore's *Sicko* was released on June 22, 2007.[5] Made for a budget of about $9 million, the film reportedly had grossed over $36 million as of August 2011.[6] The movie begins with a scene about Adam sewing up his own wound, because he is uninsured and cannot afford to go to an emergency room, and Rick, who lost two fingers in an accident but had to choose to reattach only one because of the prohibitive expense of reattaching both. Moore makes it clear that his focus is not so much about the fifty million Americans without health insurance, of whom an estimated eighteen thousand die annually because of the lack of insurance, as it is about the health insurance industry's poor treatment of those who *do* have insurance. In the early planning stages of the film, Moore had issued a call for personal stories of problems with health insurance coverage, and he reports in *Sicko* that he and his staff received more than twenty-five thousand such stories. The movie argues through a series of examples that the drive for profit motivates the health insurance industry to deny coverage systematically. Admissions by former industry officials that company policy was to avoid paying when possible makes these personal anecdotes, some of which are heartbreaking, credible as evidence of general trends. Financial ruin, suffering, and deaths result from such practices.

Moore traces the current health-care crisis to the Health Maintenance Organization Act of 1973, which fostered the creation of managed care networks and gave HMOs the authority to deny payment for care recommended by licensed doctors. An audio clip involving Richard Nixon and John Ehrlichman from 1971 is featured, with Nixon pleased with Ehrlichman's description that HMOs make more money the *less* care they provide to patients.

Sicko describes how the health insurance industry spent $100 million to defeat proposed health care reform in 1993. Moore notes that Hillary Clinton, who as First Lady was the point person on health-care reform at the time, went on to become one of the top recipients of campaign contributions from the health-care industry. He continues by documenting the influence of lobbying, punctuated by examples of former congressional aides who were later hired by the insurance industry.

Following an implicit problem-solution approach, Moore then travels to Canada, Great Britain, France, and Cuba to contrast the failings of US health care with the humaneness and availability of single-payer systems in those countries. US health statistics are provided to underscore how poor our average health care and life expectancy are compared with those in the rest of the industrialized world. Moore uses these trips as a form of counterargument to debunk the myths propagated by the insurance industry about the dangers of "socialized medicine." French protests are featured to illustrate the relative complacency of US citizens when it comes to national policies. A group of Americans who became ill from volunteering at 9/11 Ground Zero, but were refused health coverage for their illnesses, are ferried by Moore to Cuba. They appear to attempt (unsuccessfully) to receive care at the US Guantanamo Bay detainment facility that is comparable to the free care the "evildoers" receive. Instead, the group goes to Havana, where they receive free medical attention and the 9/11 rescue workers are honored by a local fire station.

Moore ends the film by addressing the audience, saying that people ought to take care of each other. To practice what he preaches, Moore makes a $12,000 contribution to Jim Kenefick, conservative webmaster of MooreWatch.com, to cover medical costs that were threatening to shut down Kenefick's website. The film ends with Moore walking toward the US Capitol with his laundry, claiming he will get the government to clean his laundry until better health care is made available to all Americans.

The Critical Response to *Sicko*

With a Rotten Tomatoes score of 93 percent, 88 percent from "top critics," *Sicko* received a glowingly positive nod from professional viewers.[7] Several themes emerge from a thorough reading of the professional reviews of *Sicko*. Moore's argument is perceived as persuasive. Bob Mondello writes that Moore's "usual humor and force," deployed through tactics "as provocative as always" and peppered with instances of grandstanding, "most of it very funny," marks a persuasive union between the filmmaker's particularly successful and controversial style of filmmaking and a subject of concern for us all.[8] In Amy Biancolli's view, *Sicko* is a "damning, touching, darkly comical exposé" on the United States health-care system, "a deeply impassioned appeal for change."[9] Joe Morgenstern claims that Michael Moore's "argumentative blogumentary" is "shockingly funny—and sometimes genuinely shocking." For him, the movie's appeal "lies at the intersection of its timing and style." In the end, he says, *Sicko* "may help stimulate the debate."[10] For James Berardinelli, although the points made by the film "aren't revolutionary," they are presented "in a compelling manner." With "a good mix of humor and pathos," *Sicko* "is flawed but effective."[11]

More than being persuasive, *Sicko* is also perceived as distinct from all of Moore's previous movies. Ty Burr maintains that *Sicko* is "Moore's best, most focused movie to date."[12] Part of the reason for its distinctiveness and its appeal is a perceived change in style. On the principle that less is more, the reviewers celebrate in *Sicko* a less conspicuous Moore. Lisa Schwarzbaum notes that Moore approaches the topic of health care "with considerably less personal bombast than he laid on in *Fahrenheit 9/11*."[13] Similarly, David Ansen contends that "this time around, Moore spares us the spectacle of himself storming the offices of his villains, his camera ever ready to capture their clench-jawed embarrassment."[14] Biancolli calls this visible absence from the screen "a shrewd move for a filmmaker who understands his role as cultural irritant."[15]

In the critical reports, the argument of the movie seems split. The professional critics celebrate the first part, where the litany of harrowing personal stories is difficult to refute, while expressing reservations about the second part, almost exclusively dedicated to Moore's "comparison and contrast" travels through Canada, France, Cuba, and so on. Mick LaSalle contends that Moore makes two arguments—health care in America is in a state of escalating crisis, and we need a single-payer system—"one that's entirely persuasive and another that's at least intriguing."[16] For Peter Howell, Moore's international travels make *Sicko* "completely lacking in journalistic rigor."[17] Andrew Sarris argues that the second part of the movie leaves Moore "open to the assaults of the naysayers."[18] Asking himself if *Sicko* is one-sided, Ansen answers with a prompt "You bet." He concludes that Moore's "broad, simple strokes" are bound to raise skeptical eyebrows.[19] More often than not, it is the Cuban excursion that irks the reviewers. Tom Charity asserts that the boatlift to Cuba is "Stunt Man Mike at his crudest, and not as effective as he intended."[20] For Stephanie Zacharek, though *Sicko* is "the most persuasive and least aggravating of all of Moore's movies," the deliberately simplistic desire to render everything in black and white hinders the argument by betraying a distrust in his audience's ability to follow him into the complex gray areas.[21]

The success of *Sicko*, as partially indicated by the overwhelmingly positive reviews, was precisely what the health insurance industry feared. Wendell Potter recounts that a staff member was sent for a scouting report of the film's reception at its premiere at the Cannes Film Festival. When the film's ending was greeted by a fifteen-minute standing ovation, the industry's fears were confirmed: "It was very, very well received. We were very scared."[22] According to Potter, "from that moment on, [the industry] developed a very, very sophisticated communications campaign" to discredit the film and its message. "We felt that this movie would be—have such an impact that it would really pave the way for legislation to be passed that could be very detrimental to the insurance industry. So it was very important for the insurers to attack this movie as fiercely as possible."

Specifically, Potter describes the creation of Health Care America, a front group funded by health-care industry dollars—from insurance premiums—with the sole purpose of attacking Moore. Potter notes that the industry had succeeded in "getting their talking points into most of the stories that appeared about the movie," including those by such news organizations as the *New York Times* and CNN, without a single reporter doing enough investigative work to expose Health Care America as a front for the health insurance industry.

Probably the most well-known incident of a major media outlet acting as an unwitting mouthpiece for this campaign was the Moore-Gupta exchange. On July 9, 2007, CNN anchor Wolf Blitzer aired a segment on *The Situation Room* titled "Reality Check," filed by the network's chief medical correspondent, Dr. Sanjay Gupta. The report ran as a preview for the scheduled interview with Moore about *Sicko.* The Gupta report challenged Moore's factual evidence, chiefly the figures pertaining to medical spending per capita in the United States and Cuba.[23] Gupta concluded his report with this controversial remark: "But no matter how much Moore fudged the facts—*and he did fudge some facts*—there's one everyone agrees on. The system here should be far better." During the interview, Moore unleashed a harshly critical tirade denying all allegations of factual inaccuracies posited by Gupta's report. Moore ended up demanding apologies from CNN, for himself as well as for the American people, "for not telling the truth."[24]

The controversy found a new venue, *Larry King Live,* the following day as a direct debate between Moore and Gupta. The show began with the airing of a slightly modified version of the Gupta report. As a result, King opened up the discussion by allowing Gupta to explain the revisions. "Yes, we made a mistake, Larry," admitted Gupta, "with regards to the per capita spending for Cubans. Michael correctly—he said $251 in the movie."[25] Despite this admission, Gupta maintained his criticism regarding Moore's use of factual evidence. The tone of the discussion alternated between being appreciative of Moore's bringing the issues of health care to the forefront and critical of Moore's "cherry-picking" the evidence.

On July 15, CNN published an eleven-point rebuttal of the two fact-check reports published on Moore's website in response to the two televised debates. CNN corrected and apologized for two errors but defended the core of Gupta's argument yet again. A triumphal document titled "CNN Throws in Towel, Admits to Two Errors, and States That All 'Sicko' Facts Are True to Their Source (or Something like That) . . . ," published on Moore's website, underlined CNN's admission of error affirming that, while it is still possible to question the research method used, all of Moore's statistics were the correct numbers from the sources cited.[26] CNN's position transformed from a vigorous challenge of the hard factual evidence to a quibble on sources as well as on Moore's alleged misuse of the term "free healthcare." In light of the overwhelming pro-Moore comments found on CNN's website discussing the exchange, the Gupta report and the subsequent highly visible scandal may have legitimized Moore as a public spokesperson on health care rather than undercut his authority.

Clearly, *Sicko* is a provocative text. The simple idea of a movie about health care already casts a shadow over the entire industry, prompting PR campaigns and corporate training sessions. *Sicko*'s place as the second highest-grossing political documentary,[27] its positive critical reception, and the intense controversies surrounding its factual evidence complement the persuasive potential of *Sicko* as a discrete text. In the next section, we provide our own rhetorical reading of the movie with a focus on how it persuades, noting, however, that the same elements that account for its punch may reduce its efficacy as a political instrument.

The Rhetorical Grammar of Moore's Style: Blue-Collar Irony and Affective Politics

By *grammar of style*, we mean an identifiable cluster of recurring rhetorical elements and a discernible pattern of relationships among them. Along these lines, we propose *the story, the socialist comparison*, and *the impossible conversation* as staple stylistic elements constituting the morphology of this grammar. We also contend that *blue-collar irony* can be thought of as *the* syntactic relationship defining much of Moore's style. Irony, with its strident juxtapositions and stark contrasts, making it evident and broadly appealing, is a trope that works through discordant interplays;

the incongruities on-screen are designed to reveal, accentuate, or engender cognitive dissonance. The intended audience of the movie, those secure in the knowledge of having health insurance, is confronted with abundant evidence of a predatory health-care system inimical to all. In this respect, irony is deeply unsettling and, as such, intimately linked to *affect*. Indeed, affect forms the very texture of each of these morphological elements and emerges as the effect of their ironic interplay. Working in conjunction, irony and affect are the building blocks of Moore's radical rhetoric. While we maintain our focus on one particular "utterance," namely *Sicko,* we are tempted to go beyond it and propose this grammar as a useful lens, complementing the other theoretical approaches presented in this book, for understanding Moore's decades-long efforts to directly intervene in the most visible and contentious political debates of the day.

From *Roger and Me* to *Sicko* and *Capitalism*, through harrowing stories of suffering "neighbors," through unflattering comparisons with "socialist paradises," and through the spectacular dramatization of the impossibility of a real dialogue between the downtrodden and powerful elites, Moore paints a bleak image of contemporary life. Through spectacle and ironic contrast, these morphological elements are juxtaposed and made to expose the absurdities of a society ruled by, with, and for the powerful. Saddened by people dying for corporate profit, perplexed by the cluelessness and carelessness of the elites, distraught by the ominous feeling that the stories unfolding on-screen could be our stories, or even angered by his "fudging the facts," by his cherry-picking the evidence, or by his shameless emotional manipulations, *affect* constitutes the texture and the effect of Moore's rhetoric.

However, his is not a hopelessly depressing chronicle of the status quo. The *socialist comparison* provides a positive alternative to this bleak image; the success stories of other countries doubles as an account of the possible. At the same time, Moore's efforts toward individualizing blame, toward identifying "the enemy" and thus providing an outlet for our rage, serve the same purpose of forestalling the closure of affect into its negative iterations (fear, powerlessness, anger). The contrast between the official ideology peddled as the American Dream and the disheartening reality of its nightmarish manifestation is meant to enrage and, through affective mobilization, engender *action*. Moore does not bracket his rage and sadness so that quiet reason might prevail; his rhetoric injects the blood of affect into the politics of the day, laying the emotional ground for a revolution. We argue for the relevance and ubiquity of the three morphological elements—the *story*, the *socialist comparison*, and the *impossible conversation*—concluding with discussions of irony and affect as defining features of Moore's rhetorical politics.

The Story: Our Suffering Neighbor

George W. Bush, opening the movie with his (in)famous diagnosis of the health-care system—"Too many good docs are getting out of the business. Too many OB-GYNs aren't able to practice their love with women all across this country"—stands here less as Moore's usual "wanted poster" for political and corporate culpability and more as a nostalgic moment for the era of great nemeses, a humorous nod to the cluelessness of the "decider." The laughter (or anger) cascading in the wake of Bush's one-liners is instantly suffocated. *Sicko* begins in the raw. The spectators' first gaze lingers on an open wound. The man, without health insurance, is forced to stitch his own bleeding cut. We see Adam repurposing his living room into an operating room. This is in fact our first "morphological" unit: the story. These are first and foremost stories of suffering, of exploitation, of silencing and marginalization. Rick, as a "hopeless romantic," "chooses" to have the top of his ring finger reattached for $12,000 and give up on the middle finger, valued at $60,000. "It's an awful feeling" chimes Rick's wife, visibly distraught, "to just try to put a value on your body."[28] But this is exactly what Moore reveals to be happening. Dollar amounts and the customary noise of a cash register accompany the drawings of reattached limbs; behind the closed doors of insurance companies, our bodies are carved up and price tagged.

"The story" functions rhetorically to personalize suffering. A third of the movie is devoted to parents, grandparents, children, wives, and husbands thrown in the midst of insurance tragedy. Kenneth Burke has said, "You persuade a man only insofar as you can talk his language by speech, gesture, tonality, order, image, attitude, idea, identifying your way with his."[29] These are heartbreaking and personal stories. We do not witness anonymous torment; these are not strangers. These are the stories of our suffering neighbors. Identifying with the victims on-screen is not difficult. Critic Dana Stevens notes, "We don't need Michael Moore to tell us this. . . . We get the clue from the ruinous medical bills that arrive in our mailboxes, from our friends' gruesome stories of conditions untreated and claims denied, and even from the mouths of our own doctors."[30]

From the first scenes, we are confronted by the "sick" reality of the US health-care system. "However," interjects Moore, "this movie is not about Adam," nor is it about Rick, for that matter. While the appalling account of fifty million uninsured people has its place in an argument against the current health-care system, Moore intends to confront us with a different one: the underside of the American Dream. This is "a wise choice from a rhetorical point of view," Stevens says, for by exploring the drama engulfing the insured, Moore can show that "our status quo doesn't just have a few soft spots—it's rotten to the core."[31] What this movie is about, Moore informs us, is the lucky, the insured, those of us living the dream. For the first half hour, we are bombarded with story after story of anguish, of denied medical treatments, and of tragedies where profit-driven health insurance companies act as mercantile "grim reapers." These stories are not brushed over. This is a slow and highly detailed emotional journey through suffering and sufferance.

We follow Larry and Donna Smith, who, despite having health insurance, lost their house to medical bills and were forced to move into their daughter's "storage room." Parents and children, perplexed and almost defeated, stage the all-too-common drama of medical bankruptcy. Even when their grandchildren wholeheartedly cry for a seemingly unrelated reason—the father is forced by the economic situation to look for work in Iraq—the camera lingers unashamedly. Moore refuses to separate the intertwining tragedies of an economic downturn and a predatory health-care system. These stories build on each other to paint a dismal picture of a health insurance system where math supersedes basic human rights. Laura Burnham, while being unconscious from a head-on collision, should have "preapproved" the ambulance ride to the hospital. This can happen only in a system where the bottom line overrules common sense.

From these distressing stories, we slowly descend into tragedy. Maria, Diane, Laurel, and Caroline are happily insured as long as none of them needs actual medical care. As soon as they are diagnosed with different forms of cancer, the insurance companies fight tooth and nail *not* to save their lives. Tragically, as we find out, in some of these cases, the insurance companies succeed. From Adam, "the first story ever told," we arrive at wounds that can no longer be sewed up in one's living room. Moore places these accounts in succession, without interruption, rhetorically building toward an affective and sensorial overload. Evidently, the emotional aftermath of this tragic inventory of suffering runs the risk of coagulating into despair. With pity, fear, and anger characterizing much of the first half of the movie, Moore turns to other countries in an attempt to show a possible way out.

The Intense Shade of Green of the Socialist Grass

The second prominent morphological feature of Moore's stylistic grammar, complementing the personal story of suffering, is the parallel account of countries where social policies, utterly demonized in US public discourse, are shown *not* to inevitably lead to a 1950s communist nightmare. The United States is juxtaposed with these working "socialist" systems in order to expose the falsity undergirding the conservative ideological assault on any policy proposal based on solidarity. Most of the time, it is precisely here where Moore gets accused, at worst, of "fudging the facts" and, at best, of being "purposely naïve" in painting an idyllic picture of foreign health-care systems where nothing seems to go wrong. Most of the reviewers, regardless of their overall appreciation of the movie, point to these comparisons as problematic. Andrew Sarris contends that while medical care is "free" in all of these countries, Moore does not "adequately address" the quality of care.[32] For Lisa Kennedy, although the journeys are interesting, even moving, "they feel too often like comparing apples and oranges."[33] The individual testimonies are dismissed under the guise of mathematical precision. As the Gupta-Moore exchange demonstrates, what matters is the arithmetic. While these comparisons might fail the ethics of a proper demonstration, we contend that Moore's is not an objective argument based on facts, even though statistics are provided, but an emotional journey. More than simply confronting the conservative equation of solidarity = evil, these comparisons present the success stories of health care.

For the rest of the movie, the citizens content with their health insurance turn out to be living in Canada, Great Britain, France, or Cuba. American citizens pretending to be Canadians to get medical treatment, Canadians frightened of coming into the United States without supplemental health insurance, French citizens getting services bordering on the unthinkable by US standards, such as government-employed housekeepers doing laundry—these represent the "other" story, the account of the possible. In a roundtable with US citizens living in France, Moore shrinks in disbelief, covering his ears, while being bombarded with the long list of "free" benefits—education, vacations, and health care—enjoyed by these people. "And they'll come to your house and do your laundry," says Moore with a laugh, trying to push this account to the absurd. To his and our dismay, the answer is evidently yes. In the very next scene, Moore stands, humbled, side by side with a government employee washing clothes for a new mother.

The difference between them and us is fear, suggests Moore. While in France the government is afraid of the people, in the United States the people are afraid of the government, contends one of the participants in the roundtable. A series of images of French protest for housing, salaries, and vacations follows. These are peaceful marches of citizens entitled to basic human rights. An upbeat French song accompanies these images. The mood is positive. Protest is healthy, Moore suggests. This is the resolution to the anguish experienced during the first part of *Sicko*. The French riots of 2005, where North African Arabs of Algerian, Tunisian, and Moroccan heritage burned the outskirts of Paris, are conveniently left out. If revolt is what Moore is after, as these images indicate, then this revolt is a velvet one. This is a carefully orchestrated emotional journey through individual contentment. If the first morphological unit, *the story*, is designed to elicit pity, stimulate fear, and ultimately provoke anger toward a predatory health-care system, the second one—*the socialist comparison*—is designed to engender hope. Moore does not analyze in detail the minutiae of what makes these other health-care systems work. What he wants to do is to paint in broad affective strokes the picture of the possible. Finding a way out of the current health-care system is complicated by abundant evidence of the barriers preventing a real dialogue between people and corporate-political elites.

The Impossible Conversation

One of Moore's most recognizable rhetorical techniques is the guerrilla-style ambush interview. As we have seen in Potter's account, the training of executives of health insurance companies and security personnel was designed to defend against this spectacular and controversial method of staging culpability. In *Roger & Me*, Moore's stated goal is not to mediate the grievances of the autoworkers to GM's CEO, but to bring Roger Smith to the town of Flint. Moore's interest in bringing to the same table bosses and workers seems contrived from the start. He has no interest in forming a meaningful dialogue with the agents of corporate power. Rather, his goal is to perform for his audience the inherent impossibility of that very fantasy.

This stylistic feature makes its debut in his first documentary. What Moore dramatizes is the political problem of *access*. His goal as a documentary filmmaker is never to secure conversations with the representatives of corporate power, but to perform the impossibility of such conversations and thus dramatize social inequalities. His attempts to "just talk" with Roger Smith in *Roger & Me* are stopped at the door, literally as well as metaphorically. In *Bowling for Columbine*, a duped Charlton Heston wanders off camera—in his own home!—as Moore raises awkward questions about the prevalence of youth violence in the United States.

Reviewers, however, seem to agree that in *Sicko*, Moore is tamed, that his staple interview technique is missing. Moore "may be an imp, a manipulator and a provocateur, but he keeps his vaudevillian antics to a minimum,"[34] sparing us this time of "the spectacle of himself storming the offices of his villains"[35] making *Sicko* a movie where there is less "cheap-shotting of such eye-level piñatas as Charlton Heston in *Columbine*."[36] Judged by this standard, *Sicko* appears to be less confrontational. However, the theme of the impossible conversation permeates this documentary as well. Right from the beginning, the mere mention of Moore making a movie about health care is used to force a health insurance company to reverse a previous denial. Doug, after receiving the news that Cigna would not cover two implants to stop his nine-month-old daughter from going deaf, writes a letter stating, "Noted filmmaker Michael Moore is in the process of gathering information for his next film. I've sent information concerning Cigna's lack of caring for its policy holders. Has your CEO ever been in a film before?" Though Moore is careful to point out that this is happening without his permission, in the following scene we hear the recorded message where Cigna reverses the previous denial of treatment. The scene is at once self-serving, showcasing Moore's cultural leverage, as well as revelatory of the lack of dialogue between people and corporations: a positive resolution to our health insurance problems can occur only through the threat of a third party. This is not dialogue but blackmail. To drive the point home, if Cigna thought that its reversal of denial would buy some goodwill and have this case stricken from the *Sicko* record, in actuality it finds the entire incident laid down on celluloid for all to see—an ambush if ever there was one.

The barriers between corporations and people are everywhere in *Sicko*. Becky Malke, an insurance company employee "in charge of keeping sick people away," testifies about the dubious practices of the insurance industry, and to the invisible walls erected to protect profit. A long list of conditions moves up the screen with dizzying speed; countless diseases, with names few could pronounce, move faster and faster until our ability to read them all but disappears. Moore's message seems clear: it is not about the items on the list, but the existence of the list itself, that makes any dialogue with the insurance companies a futile endeavor. If there was ever any doubt that the conversation is indeed impossible, Moore shows us that corporations and people speak different languages.

Lee, the industry's "hit man," sent to retrieve corporate money after the insurance company paid for an operation by looking into preexisting conditions as a way of denying coverage, details the legality of what is known in some states as "a prudent person preexisting condition." His attempts to translate this term do not make it any more intelligible. "If," he says, "prior to your insurance kicking in, you had any symptom which would incline a normally prudent person to have sought medical care, then the condition of which that symptom was a symptom is excluded." The perplexed silence of the interviewer is followed by the character's admission: "It's labyrinthine, isn't it? But that's how it works—you're not slipping through the cracks. Somebody made that crack and swept you towards it." The power imbalance and the unintelligible language reinforce the drama of a deeply divided society segregated by power and money.

Communication is not what brings the masses and the powerful together, but what tears them apart; language, words, definitions become tools of mystification and oppression. We can only witness, thanks to the wonders of magnetic tape, Moore informs us, the origins of this health-care disaster. Nixon stills accompany his gleeful remarks—"fine" and "not bad"—to John Ehrlichman's report about "Edgar Kaiser running this Permanente thing for profit . . . all the incentives are toward less medical care, because the less care they give them, the more money they make." The next scene depicts Nixon giving a speech on the formation of HMOs with this seemingly sincere and patriotic message: "I want America to have the best health care in the world."

This is the hypocrisy that Moore forces us to metabolize. These are conversations that decide the fate of millions, that lie at the root of bankruptcy, of destroyed lives, of tragedies; these dialogues behind closed doors literally kill, and the only way we can "participate" is by silently witnessing them, all too late, on the screen. Moore wants to make his audience feel the sting of the "impossible conversations" not so much to demoralize it, although this might very well be the unintended consequence, but to show that when it comes to "regular channels," to a proper deliberative participation, the game is rigged in favor of the powerful. Moore performs the impossible conversation through the interwoven modes of irony. His journeys to the closed doors of corporate and political apathy enhance the inconsistencies, contradictions, and incongruities between what we know and what really happens. The ironic "edge" becomes necessary for convening Moore's message in the context where "speaking truth to power" does not make it so much as flinch.

Blue-Collar Irony

One of Moore's most prominent rhetorical strategies is the use of irony's incongruity. Irony, in its most basic definition, is "the expression of one's meaning by using language that normally signifies the opposite, usually for humorous or emphatic effect,"[37] a "contradiction or incongruity between appearance or expectation and reality,"[38] a trope acting through dissonance between the manifest content and the latent one. Throughout Moore's documentaries, the optimistic worldview of social elites is juxtaposed with the bleak realities of the downtrodden. In *Sicko*, what we thought we are entitled to by having health insurance is constantly contrasted through disturbing stories with the consequences of actually testing the extent of one's health coverage at the hospital's gate.

However, irony is not simply a matter of strident juxtapositions. Beneath the use of irony lies a strong political will. Linda Hutcheon defines irony as having an edge, involving "the attribution of an evaluative, even judgmental attitude." Certainly, "the emotions provoked by irony as it is both used and attributed, as it is felt as well as deployed are probably not to be ignored."[39] Irony cannot be divorced from attitudes and emotion; the very deployment of irony, in any context, engages attitudes and stirs emotion. Affect, whether uneasy laughter or unrelenting anger, becomes a way of paying attention, a way of being concerned and involved; the emotional aftermath of irony is what actualizes its political valence.

Moore introduces us to the American Dream via clips of homemade movies. The juxtaposition of celebratory music and images of a 1960s middle-class paradise, a Reaganite rendition of the shining city on a hill, is, in Moore's world, ominous. The images of middle-class abundance, from the young capitalist delivering the morning paper to the family converging around their own living room cornucopia to the suburbs gleaming in all their Saturday morning glory and barbecue smoke, are exposed for what they are: an ideological construction. These glorious images are juxtaposed with story after story of families forced to sell their house to pay medical bills, of seventy-nine-year-olds forced to work in order to maintain their insurance, and of unconscious victims of car accidents who should have "preapproved" the ambulance ride to the hospital. *Sicko* is deliberately designed to overwhelm the viewer with evidence of the discrepancy between our expectations, as one of the 250 million insured, as one of those people living the 1960s black-and-white homemade middle-class dream, and the disheartening reality. The tragedy of *Sicko* lies not just in the stories of corporate neglect we witness on-screen, but also in the realization that these characters, experiencing the absurdities of health insurance, could very well be us.

While Moore shies away from the camera for the first part of the documentary, neither his goal nor his tools have significantly altered. In Moore's case, the use of irony, by turns humorous and tragic, has a clear political edge. Commercials of health insurance companies with humane tag lines such as "Every American deserves affordable health care" are followed by dreadful stories. "Let's meet some of these happy insured customers," gleefully interjects Moore. Maria, Diane, Laurel, and Amy have health insurance from Blue Shield, BCS, and MEGA Life as well as tumors and cancer. Medical need is met by rubber-stamped vocabulary such as "denied treatment," "not medically necessary" or "not life-threatening brain tumors." While trying to cope with the absurdity of the insurance vocabulary of denial mapped onto these real conditions, Moore informs us that Diane died from her non-life-threatening tumor, Laurel's cancer has spread throughout her entire body, and Amy's cancer found a way to her brain and killed her. The strident juxtaposition of joyful music and women being denied treatment is not meant to conceal but to expose, to accentuate. The punch line of the joke of being insured is death. If there is a rude awakening to be had in this case, it unfortunately can now only belong to the viewer. This is yet another example of a scene, of a movie, that, through disquieting discrepancies, is meant to revolt as in "cause to feel disgust" as well as in cause to "rise in rebellion."[40]

Such discordant juxtapositions help expose the haunting vocabulary of the political right. Moore meets head-on the well-known conservative refrain, "socialized medicine." What we find out is that Reagan lives on embedded in our political vocabulary. Moore tells us that a record "made by a well-known actor" was distributed in order to warn the population of the evils of socialized medicine. Reagan's voice warmly cautions us of the subtle ways in which the United States can transform into a socialist country. The first step toward such a nightmare is, evidently, *health care for all*. The black-and-white images portray people being evicted, bureaucratic dystopias, unreasonable working quotas, and young children exercising in unison as signifiers of the communist misery soon to follow the cardinal sin of solidarity. Moore's ludic engagement with the socialist nightmare continues with a musical number portraying Russian peasants singing optimistically about their work. The subtitles speak of wheat quotas and proletarian enthusiasm. But, Moore's voice interjects, "then it occurred to me that back home in America, we've socialized a lot of things." The complex ironic juxtaposition of sound, images, and text is deployed to reveal our hypocrisy. While the Russian song continues, the images change. Instead of Russian peasants gathering wheat, we see American firefighters marching, teachers in classrooms, mail being delivered, and libraries being used. The subtitles, mockingly "translating" the Russian lyrics, point to "your firemen" saving lives and rescuing cats from trees, your teachers providing free education, and so on. At the end of the song, underneath a statue of Karl Marx, Moore wonders out loud, "Why don't we have more of these free, socialized things. Like health care?" This is the (political) cognitive dissonance that Moore forces us to grapple with.

Moore's most famous "stunt" in *Sicko*, his attempt to enter the Guantanamo Bay military base, is designed to expose the hypocrisy behind the 9/11 hero veneration. He associates key words used by the Bush administration to designate the enemy in the War on Iraq narrative—such as al Qaeda and "evildoers"—with free medical assistance, while the 9/11 rescue workers literally and metaphorically are left floating outside the base, outside our government's concern. Pointing out that suspected terrorists benefit from free medical assistance while the 9/11 rescue workers do not, Moore uses irony's sharp edge to expose the contrast between official sentiments of appreciation toward 9/11 heroes and the institutional realities of health-care injustice. If, contends Moore, you cannot judge the US society by how it treats its worst—the uninsured, in this case—this play of indifference staged outside the government's base show us that you cannot judge US society by how it treats its best, either. Images of large rallies celebrating the 9/11 heroes are juxtaposed with present-day raffle fund-raisers held in desolate bars. The once celebrated 9/11 volunteers are barflies dragging behind their oxygen masks. "Which way to Guantanamo Bay?" asks Moore in their name from a boat full of destitute Americans. This is not the subtle irony of great literary works, where contextual knowledge is essential for its decoding; this is *blue-collar irony*, not dumbed down but direct and broadly appealing, based on strident juxtapositions jumping out from the screen. Moore uses it not to make us laugh but to make us cringe, not to mystify but to reveal.

Kenneth Burke notes that the "methodology of pun," or metaphorically applying words that belong to one category to a different one, offers a revised perspective, a "comic synthesis" that transcends the individual elements. He argues that perspective by incongruity is not "demoralizing" but is "remoralizing" a situation "already demoralized by inaccuracy."[41] Moore's work represents the working-class version of perspective by incongruity. He constantly places next to each other, in stark contrast, things that do not belong. This constant effort to mix and match categories, this strident juxtaposition, is not subtle but a direct and affective blow to our worldview. These impossible juxtapositions are designed to show the ridiculousness of the social world, the chasm separating us from those having the power to decide our fate. The discrepancy between what is said and what is meant, between what is said and what is shown, and between what is shown and what is heard is at times amusing, at times sad, but always directly and simply revelatory. Irony is not simply a way of organizing an argument; for Moore, it is a way of affectively mobilizing the masses. While our discussion necessarily treats them separately, in practice irony and affect are inseparable.

The Affective Politics of Sicko

Joshua Gunn and Jenny Edbauer Rice, in a "brief provocation," chart the history of rhetorical studies with an eye on its efforts to cleanse itself of affect. While early communication scholars shared the assumption that "speech is a meeting place of the human body and language, of both affect and the word, of both feeling and meaning," Gunn and Rice posit that "uncomfortable with the instability of its object and desirous of institutional approbation, the stuttering discipline gradually muffled the voice of feeling, renaming itself 'Communication Studies' and turning its back on the understanding of affect betokened by the object of speech." Consequently, they contend, the "affective turn" in communication studies can be better described as an "about face." Apart from the difficulties of representing and quantifying affect, the authors point to the efforts of a discipline to define itself against the elocutionist movement, with the elocutionist regarded as "histrionic," "effeminate aesthetes," as well as defining itself, with the rise of wartime propaganda and the rise of demagogues, as a discipline concerned with "combating negative emotions and controlling unruly affect."[42] Affect can be conceptualized as "emotions or, more specifically, short-lived states and feelings such as anger, disgust, pride, and fear."[43] Specifically in relation to cinematic experience, Brian Ott's understanding of affect in his analysis of *V for Vendetta* as "direct sensory experiences (of color, light, sound, movement, rhythm, and texture), along with the feelings, moods, emotions, and/or passions they elicit" is particularly useful.[44]

Moore's documentaries are not just about conveying information; the attitudes embedded in irony's edge make them about affect and provocation as well. Facts do not speak for themselves. In Moore's case, they scream. His aim is not simply to provide evidence for the magnitude of the problem and let the viewer decide. Moore wants to dramatically expose the inner workings of a corrupt state and corporate apparatus. His use of irony is most suited to expose the inconsistencies and the contradictions of a public sphere opened to all in theory yet closed to marginalized voices in practice. Irony is not affectively indifferent. Humor, pity, anxiety, and anger are the intertwining effects of Moore's deliberately discordant juxtapositions. One cannot maintain neutrality, Moore implies, when watching these images. In *Sicko*, the close-up of Adam's wound in the very first scene sends a powerful message: this will not be an easy film to watch. As if Moore wants to be sure of our "revolt," the camera descends at the level of skin. The wound covers our field of view; the screen is split by human suffering. The horror of this overproximity of anguish does not wane. Story after story builds on the initial shock, adding pity, the perplexity of those secure in the knowledge of being insured all the while being denied treatment, the horror of finding out that some of the people testifying to their ordeal are already dead, the intense fear when realizing the similarities between their stories and ours, and ultimately anger. We find out that we are fortune's toy, that we are trapped in the deliberately capricious and arbitrary health-care insurance system without any recourse.

As reviewer Claudia Puig notes, *Sicko* is a film that will arouse "surprise, outrage, sadness and heated discussion."[45] Moore has struck a "socio-psychic nerve in the body politic," says Sarris, "generating a feeling of outrage that seems to be reverberating in every theater in which the movie is being shown."[46] Jonathan F. Richards describes Moore as barreling into theaters like a "ringmaster of the Circus of Broken Dreams," using "humor, sarcasm, pathos, outrage, and a barrage of case histories and facts to make his case that America's health care system is sick."[47] Even Moore's critics are unable to dismiss the affective nature of these stories. Stephen Hunter agrees that although the American health-care system is busted, Michael Moore is not the guy to fix it, but the anecdotes "are the best parts of the film; Moore has an empathetic gift, and he's able to draw eloquent tales of anguish and a sense of abandonment among blue-collar folks who aren't used to complaining out loud about the tough breaks they've caught."[48] David Denby makes an analogous point by stating that while Moore "scrapes bottom in his new documentary," *Sicko* "starts out strongly, with Moore interviewing families who have been betrayed or neglected by HMOs and insurance companies."[49] The series of stories is a blatant manipulation of our emotions, but Moore's work arguably transcends the ethics of filmmaking. He is not making a documentary; he is desperately trying to revolt in order to make us revolt. Moore does not want simply to make us cringe but to repurpose this horrified recoil, to refashion it into a political tool.

Experiencing compassion, fear, and anger in a society characterized by the impossibility of a real dialogue can lead to despair and feelings of powerlessness. Nonetheless, Moore provides an outlet for our anger. He seldom indicts without putting a face on the enemy. In "Maria Watanabe vs. Blue Shield," for example, we see Glen Hollinger, MD, the medical director for the Good Samaritan Medical Practice Association (GSMPA), a contracted group for Blue Shield California, admitting under oath that he does not see or read any of the denial letters sent bearing his signature. Furthermore, in *Sicko*, more than in any of his other movies, some of the culprits confess. Becky Malke, in charge of rejecting applications, breaks down and cries while telling the story of a couple rejoicing in the prospect of having health insurance; all the while, Malke was wholly aware they would be rejected. Similarly, Linda Peeno's congressional testimony unfolds in front of our eyes. "I am here today to make a public confession," she states. "In the spring of 1987, I denied a man a necessary operation that would have saved his life, and thus caused his death." This particular act, adds Peeno, "secured my reputation as a good medical director. . . . I went from making a few hundred dollars a week as a medical reviewer to an escalating six-figure income as a physician executive." These rare examples provide a positive spin to this otherwise frightening diagnosis.

In Moore's stunt trip to Cuba, the camera lingers on the Cuban firefighters standing at attention and giving a respectful salute to the 9/11 volunteers. "It is a great honor to have you visit our station," begins the chief Cuban firefighter, adding, "We all learned about this terrible moment on September 11. And it gave us a great sadness. And from the human point of view, *we would've liked to have helped with the rescue operations* that were under way at that moment. Firefighters around the world are family" (emphasis added). Moore chimes in, "If this is what can happen between supposed enemies, if one enemy can hold out his hand and offer to heal, then what else is possible?" Inspired by the Cuban firefighters, Moore writes an "anonymous" check for the person running the biggest anti-Moore website and whose poor financial situation owing to his wife's illness is prompting him to shut down the website. The widely publicized "anonymous" check is both a gracious gesture and a stunt some considered in bad taste. Behind these artificial stunts, behind the political theater staged for our benefit, behind these most hated and criticized scenes, however, the affective message lingers: even enemies can reach out.

Moore is explicit in using our emotions to prompt a call for radical change. At the end of *Capitalism: A Love Story*, Moore states, "You know, I can't really do this anymore unless those of you who are watching this in the theater want to join me. I hope you will, and please speed it up." "I am tired of feeling like I'm doing this alone," says Moore in an interview, adding, "It doesn't work with Michael Moore and Sean Penn and Ted Kennedy and a few others. The people have got to get involved in their democracy."[50] What we see here is Moore spelling out the message of his movies: these are not the efforts of someone trying to transform us into informed citizens, but of someone who is trying to start a social revolution; this is Moore's affective politics. Moore's rhetoric is one designed primarily to mobilize affective energies and engender social action. Whether he succeeds is a matter of debate. In the next section, we explore such empirical questions (whether and how does *Sicko* persuade?), usually left unanswered by a rhetorical reading.

Does *Sicko* Change Minds?

Sicko is intended to be a persuasive message. To explore whether *Sicko* actually changes minds, we conducted a modest research project in the fall semester of 2010. Eighty-one undergraduate students with an average age of 20.6 years, sixty females, twenty males, and one subject of unreported gender, completed a pretest labeled "Health Insurance Attitude Survey," with seven statements that participants were asked to answer, using a seven-point scale that ranged from "strongly agree" to "strongly disagree":

1. I consider myself politically conservative.
2. I consider myself very healthy.
3. Before passage of the ACA (Affordable Care Act), health insurance in the US was in need of serious reform.
4. Before the passage of the ACA, too many Americans were denied health insurance coverage unfairly.
5. Before the passage of the Affordable Care Act, too many Americans lacked access to adequate health care.
6. I am glad the Affordable Care Act was passed into law.
7. I consider myself well informed about the Affordable Care Act.

Items 3 through 6 were at the heart of our study, as they tapped into core attitudes about the status of health insurance and whether the Affordable Care Act, the comprehensive health insurance reform bill now often referred to as "ObamaCare," was a policy option that viewers would favor more or less after seeing *Sicko*. Thus the empirical question is whether watching *Sicko* would change answers to those four items; we hypothesized that it would.

The eighty-one students who completed the pretest were shown *Sicko* between ten and fourteen days after completing the pretest to minimize the chances that they would recall their exact answers to the pretest items. A few days after viewing *Sicko*, students completed a posttest that included the four core pretest questions along with other questions about health care and insurance and a series of open-ended items: Did your attitudes about Michael Moore as a filmmaker change as a result of seeing *Sicko*? Why or why not? What did you find as the *most* persuasive part of *Sicko*? What did you find as the *least* persuasive part of *Sicko*? What could Michael Moore have done differently to make *Sicko* more persuasive to the general public?

Focusing first on the core items and using paired t-test analysis, we found that viewing *Sicko* did in fact lead to a statistically significant attitude change on all four items. Those viewing the film on average moved from "slightly agree" ($M = 3.04$, $SD = 1.31$) to "agree" ($M = 1.94$, $SD = .86$) on whether health insurance in the United States was in need of serious reform, $t(80) = 9.9$, $p < .001$. Given the examples in the film, it is not surprising that students similarly moved from an average "slightly agree" (*M* = 3.06, *SD* = 1.27) to "agree" (*M* = 2.09, *SD* = .98) on the statement that too many Americans were denied health insurance coverage unfairly, $t(80) = 8.8, p < .001$. The next item pertained to health care rather than health insurance, per se, but a similar shift from an average response of "slightly agree" (*M* = 2.91, *SD* = 1.24) to "agree" (*M* = 2.19, *SD* = 1.01) occurred with respect to the statement that too many Americans lacked access to adequate health care, $t(80) = 6.05, p < .001$. Our last item asked participants if they were glad that the Affordable Care Act, which was the focus of enormous national attention in the early months of 2010, had passed. Despite the contentiousness of the debate a few months earlier, we found that attitudes still shifted after viewing *Sicko*, from an average response between "slightly agree" and "uncertain" (*M* = 3.41, *SD* = 1.4) to "slightly agree" (*M* = 2.83, *SD* = 1.48), $t(80) = 5.85, p < .001$.

Participants tended to *disagree* with the statement "I consider myself well informed about the Affordable Care Act" both on the pretest (*M* = 4.59, *SD* = 1.5) and the posttest (*M* = 4.16, *SD* = 1.54), though, interestingly, there was a small shift closer to "slightly disagree" that was weaker than the other changes but still statistically significant, $t(80) = 2.27, p < .01$.

Many film critics assume that Moore is preaching to the choir in his films and that only similar-minded liberals would view them and agree with their messages. To explore that claim, we repeated the paired t-test analysis just described but limited the data to that drawn from the thirty-three participants who agreed (from "slightly" to "strongly") with the statement "I consider myself politically conservative." Not surprisingly, self-identified conservatives generally drifted toward "uncertain" or "slightly agree" to the four items on the pretest. Nonetheless, not only did we find statistically significant changes on all four items again, but also they often were *larger* shifts of opinion than found among those who did not self-identify as conservative. The single largest change was on the statement that health insurance in the United States was in need of serious reform, where the average response by conservatives moved from an average of 3.73 (*SD* = 1.2) to 2.33 (*SD* = .82), a shift of 20 percent on a seven-point scale, $t(32) = 8.29, p < .001$. Equally noteworthy was the shift on the statement that they were glad the ACA had passed. In the pretest, the average answer was on the "slightly disagree" side (*M* = 4.36, *SD* = 1.34), but in the posttest, the average answer had moved to the "slightly agree" side (*M* = 3.79, *SD* = 1.45), and this shift also was statistically significant, $t(32) = 3.17, p < .005$.

In fact, if one considers *Sicko* purely as an instrument of persuasion and attitude change, it was arguably most effective with those who identified as conservative. We found a positive correlation between how strongly viewers rated themselves as conservative and their agreement with the claim that health insurance in the United States was in need of serious reform—Moore's basic thesis ($r = .30$, $p < .001$). A correlation of .30 compares very favorably with the effects found with most mass media attitude change research. A comprehensive meta-analysis of ninety-seven studies of the "cultivation" effect of heavy viewing of television, for example, found an average correlation between viewing and content-related attitudes of .10. Experimental studies have found higher correlations between viewing hours of television programs featuring gay men and attitude changes about homosexuality, for example, that are in the .30 range.[51] That we found a .30 correlation with attitude change among self-identified conservatives based on one viewing of a movie is, in fact, remarkable.

To be sure, getting self-identified conservatives to pay money to see a Michael Moore film is not necessarily easy. Natalie Jomini Stroud found, for example, that those with "unfavorable impressions of [George] Bush were more than six times more likely" to see *Fahrenheit 9/11* than those with favorable attitudes toward him.[52] And not every person who watches *Sicko* will experience a change in attitude. In participant comments, some conservative students described the film as "propaganda," "manipulative," "biased and one-sided," and even "anti-American." But most self-identified conservative participants were more likely to praise Moore, calling him "a great film-maker" who did a "great job" and "got enough evidence to support his claim." In response to the question "Did your attitudes about Michael Moore as a film-maker change as a result of seeing *Sicko*?," one student wrote, "Before watching this I thought he was a pushy, loudmouth, sticking his nose where it does not belong guy. I was wrong. He was genuine in the issue and in the cases he dealt with. Also, I don't think he was pushy." Another participant wrote, "I thought he was some crazy left wing democrat who wanted communism, but really he is just exposing truths."

In short, there is no question that *Sicko* is an effective persuasive message. At the same time, this brief detour into quantitative analysis can serve as a useful reminder that when we talk about media persuasion, we are not talking about radical change in consumers' attitudes. Persuasion research in general, and mass media effects research in particular, virtually never find sudden and dramatic reversals of beliefs and attitudes.

The most one can hope for is that an individual message "nudges" those who hear it in a particular direction. The available evidence suggests that *Sicko* provides a nontrivial nudge.

Although Moore has expressed a certain amount of angst that his films are not accomplishing more, he may simply be overestimating the power of individual mass-mediated messages. Our modest quantitative analysis suggests that *Sicko* accomplishes with viewers all that can be expected—a nontrivial shift of opinion that is particularly pronounced with those who were *not* already true believers. To expect that a film could have a more profound effect, such as helping affect the outcome of a presidential election, is simply unrealistic. Moreover, it is entirely possible that the very tools of Moore's success with audiences also function to undercut the political efficacy of the film. Our analysis of Moore's affective grammar suggests that his films evoke a strong emotional response, but by relying on irony and a dramatization of the impossible conversation, they do not provide a template for practical action; the form belies the content. We are provoked to outrage, but the film demonstrates the futility of expecting change. *Sicko* can be read as calling for the revolution, but it ends with the symbolic, harmless gesture of carrying a load of laundry toward the US Capitol.

Moore's films are persuasive entertainment. They reinforce beliefs among fellow liberals, they are significant artistic achievements, and when conservatives have the occasion to experience them, many are moved. That is not a bad day's work.

Notes

1. Edward Schiappa, *Beyond Representational Correctness: Rethinking Criticism of Popular Media* (Albany: State University of New York Press, 2008), 61.

2. Hans-Georg Gadamer, *Truth and Method*, trans. Garrett Barden and John Cumming (New York: Continuum, 1975), 235–53.

3. Edward Schiappa, *Defining Reality: Definitions and the Politics of Meaning* (Carbondale: Southern Illinois University Press, 2003), 29.

4. Wendell Potter, *Deadly Spin: An Insurance Company Insider Speaks Out on How Corporate PR Is Killing Health Care and Deceiving Americans* (New York: Bloomsbury Press, 2010). All quotations from Potter can be found in chapter 2, "The Campaign against *Sicko*," 29–44. Cigna was created when the Insurance Company of North America and the Connecticut General Insurance Corporation combined in the early 1980s. A publicly traded corporation, it claims total assets around $100 billion.

5. We encourage anyone who has not seen this film to do so, as it is available at low cost in DVD format or free on the Internet, including in thirteen segments on YouTube.com. A complete transcript of the film's dialogue is available at http://www.script-o-rama.com/movie_scripts/a1/sicko-script-transcript-michael-moore.html.

6. Box Office Mojo, "Sicko," Internet Movie Database, accessed August 16, 2011, http://boxofficemojo.com/movies/?id=sicko.htm.

7. Rotten Tomatoes is a website that collects movie reviews and provides aggregate scores from all reviews, their top expert reviewers, and audience responses. See Rotten Tomatoes, reviews of *Sicko*, accessed August 16, 2011, http://www.rottentomatoes.com/m/sicko/.

8. Bob Mondello, review of *Sicko*, NPR, June 22, 2007, http://www.npr.org/templates/story/story.php?storyId=11285928.

9. Amy Biancolli, "A Fiercely Effective Call to Arms," review of *Sicko*, *Houston Chronicle*, June 29, 2007, http://www.chron.com/entertainment/movies/article/Sicko-re-release-1555210.php.

10. Joe Morgenstern, "Pixar Cooks with Joy, Inventiveness in 'Ratatouille,' a Comic Tour de Force; 'Sicko' Is Political Theater with Some Blind Spots," review of *Sicko*, *Wall Street Journal*, June 29, 2007, http://online.wsj.com/news/articles/SB118307125242752135.

11. James Berardinelli, review of *Sicko*, *ReelViews*, June 22, 2007, http://www.reelviews.net/php_review_template.php?identifier=480.

12. Ty Burr, "Moore at his Feverish Best in Hilarious, Sobering 'Sicko,'" review of *Sicko*, *Boston Globe*, June 29, 2007, http://www.boston.com/ae/movies/articles/2007/06/29/moore_at_his_feverish_best_in_hilarious_sobering_sicko/.

13. Lisa Schwarzbaum, review of *Sicko*, *Entertainment Weekly*, June 29, 2007, http://www.ew.com/ew/article/0,,20044198,00.html.

14. David Ansen, "Michael Moore's Cure for What Ails Us," review of *Sicko*, *Newsweek*, June 22, 2007, http://www.newsweek.com/david-ansen-reviews-sicko-102123.

15. Biancolli, "Fiercely Effective Call to Arms."

16. Mick LaSalle, "Need a Doctor? That's Too Bad," review of *Sicko*, *San Francisco Chronicle*, June 29, 2007, http://www.sfgate.com/movies/article/Need-a-doctor-That-s-too-bad-2554436.php.

17. Peter Howell, "Prescription for Trouble," review of *Sicko*, *Toronto Star*, June 29, 2007, http://www.thestar.com/news/2007/06/29/prescription_for_trouble.html.

18. Andrew Sarris, "License to Ill," review of *Sicko*, *New York Observer*, July 17, 2007, http://observer.com/2007/07/license-to-ill/.

19. Ansen, "Michael Moore's Cure."

20. Tom Charity, "'Sicko' a Tonic, Even with Flaws," review of *Sicko*, CNN, June 29, 2007, http://edition.cnn.com/2007/SHOWBIZ/Movies/06/28/review.sicko/index.html?iref=newssearch.

21. Stephanie Zacharek, review of *Sicko*, *Salon*, June 22, 2007, http://www.salon.com/2007/06/22/sicko/.

22. Quotations in this section are from a transcript of Wendell Potter's appearance on the radio show *Democracy Now*, hosted by Amy Goodman, November 11, 2010, http://www.democracynow.org/2010/11/17/push_michael_moore_off_a_cliff.

23. Gupta claimed that Moore had said medical spending per capita was $7,000 per year for the United States and $25 for Cuba, but that the real figures were $6,096 a year for the United States and $229 for Cuba.

24. Wolf Blitzer, *The Situation Room*, CNN, July 9, 2007, http://transcripts.cnn.com/TRANSCRIPTS/0707/09/sitroom.03.html.

25. Larry King, *Larry King Live*" CNN, July 10, 2007, http://transcripts.cnn.com/TRANSCRIPTS/0707/10/lkl.01.html.

26. Michael Moore, "CNN Throws in Towel, Admits to Two Errors, and States That All 'Sicko' Facts Are True to Their Source (or Something like That) . . . ," July 17, 2007, http://www.michaelmoore.com/words/mikes-letter/cnn-throws-in-towel-admits-to-two-errors-and-states-that-all-sicko-facts-are-true-to-their-source-or-something-like-that.

27. Box Office Mojo, "Documentary–Political: 1982–Present," Internet Movie Database, accessed August 16, 2011, http://boxofficemojo.com/genres/chart/?id=politicaldoc.htm.

28. All subsequent quotes from the film are taken from Michael Moore, *Sicko* (New York: Weinstein Company, 2007), DVD.

29. Kenneth Burke, *The Rhetoric of Motives* (Berkeley: University of California Press, 1969), 55.

30. Dana Stevens, "Sick Joke: Michael Moore Gathers Our Rage at America's Health-Care System," review of *Sicko*, *Slate*, June 29, 2007, http://www.unz.org/Pub/Slate-2007jun-00312.

31. Ibid.

32. Sarris, "License to Ill."

33. Lisa Kennedy, "'Sicko' Isn't Strong Enough for Health Care Ailment," review of *Sicko*, *Denver Post*, June 28 2007, http://www.denverpost.com/movies/ci_6245558.

34. LaSalle, "Need a Doctor?"

35. Ansen, "Michael Moore's Cure."

36. Bruce Newman, review of *Sicko*, *San Jose Mercury News*, June 28, 2007, http://www.mercurynews.com/movies/ci_6252211.

37. *New Oxford American Dictionary*, 3rd ed., s.v. "irony."

38. *The Bedford Glossary of Critical and Literary Terms*, 1st ed., s.v. irony.

39. Linda Hutcheon, *Irony's Edge* (New York: Routledge, 1995), 41.

40. *New Oxford American Dictionary*, 3rd ed., s.v. "revolt."

41. Kenneth Burke, *Attitudes toward History*, 3rd ed. (Berkeley: University of California Press, 1984), 309.

42. Joshua Gunn and Jenny Edbauer Rice, "About Face/Stuttering Discipline," *Communication and Critical/Cultural Studies* 6, no. 2 (2009): 215–17, doi:10.1080/14791420902868029.

43. Shelley Wigley and Michael Pfau, "Arguing with Emotion: A Closer Look at Affect and the Inoculation Process," *Communication Research Reports* 27, no. 3 (2010): 218, doi:10.1080/08824091003737901.

44. Brian L. Ott, "The Visceral Politics of *V for Vendetta*: On Political Affect in Cinema," *Critical Studies in Media Communication* 27, no. 1 (2010): 42, doi:10.1080/15295030903554359.

45. Claudia Puig, "Moore Wields a Sharp Scalpel in Ambitious 'Sicko,'" review of *Sicko*, *USA Today*, June 22, 2007, http://usatoday30.usatoday.com /life/movies/reviews/2007-06-21-sicko_N.htm.

46. Sarris, "License to Ill."

47. Jonathan F. Richards, "Sicko: Documentary," review of *Sicko*, *Film-Freak.be*, July 15, 2007, http://www.filmfreak.be/index.php?module=filmfreak &func=viewpub&tid=9&pid=424&title=Sicko.

48. Stephen Hunter, "'Sicko': Michael Moore's Anemic Checkup," review of *Sicko*, *Washington Post*, last modified June 29, 2007, http://www.washingtonpost .com/wp-dyn/content/article/2007/06/28/AR2007062802280.html.

49. David Denby, "Do No Harm: 'Sicko' and 'Evening,'" review of *Sicko*, *New Yorker*, July 2, 2007, http://www.newyorker.com/magazine/2007/07 /02/do-no-harm.

50. David Germain, "Michael Moore: I May Quit Documentaries," *Huffington Post*, September 15, 2009, http://www.huffingtonpost.com/2009/09/15 /michael-moore-i-may-quit-_n_286854.html.

51. See Schiappa, *Beyond Representational Correctness*, 11–12, 102–10.

52. Natalie Jomini Stroud, *Niche News: The Politics of News Choice* (Oxford, UK: Oxford University Press, 2011), 45.

7. The Ghosts of Michael Moore's Future Past; or, The Many Failures of *Slacker Uprising*

Davis W. Houck and Joseph Delbert Davenport

By the fall 2004 general election season, documentary filmmaker Michael Moore was at the top of his game. His 2002 documentary, *Bowling for Columbine,* had garnered glittering critical acclaim, including the Academy Award for Best Documentary Film. Two years hence, his next project, *Fahrenheit 9/11,* catalyzed antiwar sentiment in the United States and across the world; in so doing, the Palme d'Or–winning film grossed over $100 million, making it the highest-earning documentary film on record. Moore's critical and commercial successes could not have surprised many; by the turn of the millennium, he was already America's foremost political documentarian—an iconic presence with an iconic style.

Whether his decision to go on the road during the fall 2004 presidential campaign was driven by political hubris, the need to gather material for his next film, a genuine sense of electoral urgency, megalomania, or some combination of the four, to the road Moore and his production team went. In a five-week, twenty-state, sixty-two-city bender, Moore's Slacker Uprising Tour had a simple aim: persuade the nation's college students, a demographic vastly underrepresented at the polls, to get out and vote— for the Democratic nominee, John Kerry, so that he could become the country's next president.

An audacious undertaking, Moore's sprint around the country urging slackers to the polls, averaging nearly two cities a day, generated in the press and among partisans a predictable blend of applause, disdain, and controversy. Moore rather kairotically concluded the tour in our adopted hometown of Tallahassee, Florida, on November 2, 2004, the so-called "scene of the crime" of the infamously disputed 2000 presidential election. But despite Moore's cross-country rhetorical efforts, Kerry lost badly to George W. Bush, including the state of Florida. Although Moore might have motivated some of his targeted collegiate slackers to vote, his larger purposes clearly were frustrated. End of story—or so Michael Moore watchers might have thought.

Four years later, as the 2008 campaign season heated up to a fever pitch, Moore did an unexpected thing: on September 23, he released a film documenting his 2004 Slacker Uprising Tour, making it available for free download on his website. That film, titled *Slacker Uprising*, was offered as a free gift to his fans, said Moore, who had supported him throughout his career as a filmmaker. Whether or not the freebie functioned as a marker of filmic recompense—after all, it was available to those who loathed him, too—the project met with unequivocally bad reviews. From the left and the right, from the margins to the mainstream, critics denounced the film as an extended and distended admixture of political speech and celebrity music videos; it was simultaneously bloated *and* lacking in content. "*Slacker Uprising*," Ben Walters notes, "offers neither analysis . . . nor lessons from Kerry's defeat. In fact, it offers no argument whatsoever, just a lot of shots of Moore's name on digital marquees and his face preaching to the choir."[1] Joe Leyden of *Variety* opines, "This repetitive and self-indulgent hodgepodge comes across as a nostalgia-drenched vanity project, with far too much footage of various celebs at assorted gatherings introing Moore as the greatest thing since sliced bread."[2] Similarly, Josh Tyler holds little back, claiming that *Slacker Uprising* "just has nothing going on. It's hard to get mad at Moore, when we know he's capable of so much more. I doubt he really put any effort into making this one. He doesn't even bother with much of a voice over. Right now, with the American economy crumbling around us and the country seemingly on the ropes, I can't imagine a more depressing, wasteful way to spend an afternoon than by watching the most half-assed documentary of the year, *Slacker Uprising*."[3]

In our estimation, with or without a price tag, *Slacker Uprising* is by far the worst film in Moore's oeuvre. But that judgment should not foreclose critical comment; in fact, the unequivocal failure of the film makes it a prime candidate for critical investigation.[4] In this essay, we argue that *Slacker Uprising* failed for several reasons—none of which had anything to do with John Kerry's electoral loss. We offer four interrelated arguments. First, even as the text positions political speech as a vital good in democratic deliberation, engaged and deliberative speech is foreclosed throughout the documentary. The opposition is allowed to speak only in a caricatured manner, a trademark of Moore's films, and one that seemingly preempts any need for further debate. Perhaps more important, Moore's speechmaking is punctuated less by an invitation to deliberate and more by the verities and altar calls of the true believer. That Moore is often framed visually as the singular avatar of a mass audience (fig. 1) mitigates and even dismisses formally the possibility of dissent.

Second, Moore's instrumentalist aims—getting so-called "slackers" to the polls to vote for John Kerry—are called into question by the subject position imposed on said slackers; that is, Moore's college interlocutors are allowed no room to explore the modern political process, nor are they

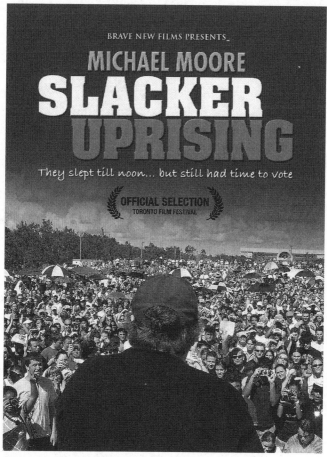

Figure 1. *Slacker Uprising* DVD cover

given any policy positions to adjudicate. All that matters to their reasoned political judgment, we are to assume, is Michael Moore's presence and the performances of his celebrity friends. While calling on young slackers to buck the trend of voter apathy, he manages to re-create the same stale campaign of personality over policy; in other words, in a film about politics, unexamined ethos dominates. Third, the narrative thread of voting for John Kerry is badly fractured by Moore's repeated attempts to suture America's iconic protest movements involving civil rights, women's rights, and the antiwar movement to the 2004 presidential election; in other words, voting for Kerry-Edwards is never explicitly linked to these consequential events.

Fourth, viewers are presented with wildly fluctuating production qualities, suggesting that Moore and his production company were gambling on an electoral outcome that failed to materialize. Without a crucial Kerry triumph, the story falls apart, and certain audiovisual inconsistencies that could be forgiven or overlooked in service of a stronger narrative are only highlighted by the ramshackle structure of the film. The only consistent production decision seems to have been to keep the camera or cameras on Moore at all times. From beginning to end, our attention during this ambitious coast-to-coast voter turnout campaign is focused directly on the omnipresent everyman from Flint, Michigan: Michael Moore. Which prompts the question: Who is running for president?

Before engaging each of these claims in detail, we begin our analysis by offering an overview of *Slacker Uprising*, which begins at journey's end. The film opens with television footage of President Bush and Senator Kerry on the campaign trail while text dramatically announces, "It was the presidential election of 2004 . . . The fate of the world was in America's hands."[5] "When Johnny Comes Marching Home" hums and swells beneath a recap of the campaign to date: Kerry had the early lead, but then came the Swift Boat Veterans for Truth, and George W. Bush made a resurgence. Things were looking grim for Senator Kerry, but the fight was not over yet, for at that very moment, "a cadre of rock musicians, hip-hop artists, and citizen groups went out on the road with their own 'shadow campaigns' to save John Kerry and the Democrats from themselves." This, we are told, is "one filmmaker's failed attempt to turn things around."

As the sound of screaming slackers begins to rise beneath the martial score, the cameras come up on the Leon County Civic Center in Tallahassee, Florida, on election night. Someone is yelling Moore's name, and as the camera follows him onstage, we get our first glimpse of the "slacker in chief." (We will be seeing a lot of him over the next ninety-seven minutes.) Wearing his trademark baseball cap, he exhorts the cheering crowd to skip work and take all their friends to go vote the next day in the general election. Amid chants of "One more day, one more day," the screen fades to black, and we are whisked back in time, five weeks earlier, to the beginning of the Slacker Uprising tour in Elk Rapids, Michigan.

The Slacker Uprising has begun, blazing a trail across the country with the stated aim of urging "slackers all across America to get up off the sofa and give voting a try, just this once, because we want George W. Bush out of the White House!" And Moore even sweetens the deal: civic participation not being a worthwhile reward in itself, if you register to vote, Moore will personally provide you with a change of underwear or a package of freeze-dried ramen noodles, or both. Over the heavenly strains of Handel's Hallelujah Chorus, Father Moore bellows forth an altar call to the nation's prodigal sons and daughters: "Who amongst you will pledge to vote this year? Will you vote? Will you vote? Let's hear it for the nonvoters who are going to vote . . . and let's get their noodles!" Can I get a hallelujah? Can I get an *R*?

And so it goes for the next hour and a half as we join Captain Mike—the film was originally released as *Captain Mike across America*—on his quest through America's twenty swing states to save John Kerry (who is conspicuously absent) from himself. Cameras follow Moore as he heads west to Arizona, then to Ames, Iowa; Los Angeles; Portland and Eugene, Oregon; and Seattle. Then it's on to Nashville, Tennessee; Philadelphia and Wilkes-Barre, Pennsylvania; Athens, Ohio; and Bethlehem, Pennsylvania. The tour pauses in Utah; moves on to Reno, Nevada; returns to southern California, Ohio, and Pennsylvania; and then makes the final big push in Florida. By the film's close in Tallahassee, viewers are exhausted and vertiginous from the sixty-plus venues that Moore has visited.

The visual plot lines from each venue are nearly identical: a long and enthusiastic queue of college students forms outside of a large stadium, Moore appears at a lectern amid a massive throng of cheering spectators, a small portion of a speech excoriating George W. Bush and the Iraq War is featured to loud applause, often a singer performs an entire song, Moore is reintroduced to loud applause, and quick video segments from local television news stations, CNN, and FOX are employed to move the dramatic narrative of the road film forward. Viewers know where they are in the film only by dint of frequent superimposed titles that highlight locales and venues; nothing in the physical landscape orients viewers to a particular place.

The camera infrequently leaves Moore, as he is typically framed as a singular and heroic figure within a mass of loudly adoring students. By the film's close, it seems unclear whether viewers are being asked to vote for John Kerry or Michael Moore. There is remarkably little pro-Kerry discourse in the film. As Scott Tobias points out, "Based simply on what he has to say in support of John Kerry—nothing—some young voters must have been surprised to learn that Moore's name wasn't on the ballot."[6] The idea is not too far-fetched: aside from the constant visual grammar of a triumphant Moore basking before cheering crowds, those crowds often feature adoring fans wearing "Michael Moore 4 Prez" T-shirts (fig. 2) or waving signs that declare "The Facts Don't Lie: Moore '04" (fig. 3).

Indeed, as Richard Corliss summarizes it, *Slacker Uprising* functions as the "hagiographic record" of Moore's five-week tour.[7] The film's narrative, in sum, is cobbled together with new venues, a loose chronology, large crowds, an acerbic and stage-hogging Moore, celebrity musicians—and a protracted silence on just what voters might be voting for.

The many failures of *Slacker Uprising* transcend its reception by the general public and the film's popular reviewers. We argue that the film's failure is far more consequential, especially in its implicit commentary on American politics in the early twenty-first century. As an instance of

Figure 2. Fans at a rally in Tallahassee

Figure 3. The sign reads "The Facts Don't Lie: Moore '04"

unapologetically partisan politics, *Slacker Uprising* fails its audience in the most fundamental of ways, and that failure is not without hazards to American political discourse. In making this claim, we are aware that a visual medium is not often the best way to advance complex claims with careful grounds leading to logical conclusions. That Moore flouts any semblance of reasoned and reasonable discourse, though, makes *Slacker Uprising* a troubling text that does not augur well for a polity desperately in need of careful argument and meaningful engagement.

We were repeatedly struck by the overwhelming lack of speech by college students—the slackers in question. Yes, we see them by the thousands in long lines and jam-packed venues clamoring to see and hear Michael Moore, but never do we hear the question haunting the entire documentary: Why should we vote for John Kerry and John Edwards? Like a zoo worker at feeding time, Moore is seen throwing to nameless and often faceless male audience members bags of underwear and packages of ramen noodles (fig. 4). The quid pro quo? Voting for Kerry-Edwards. As for his female audience, Moore is implored by one particularly voluptuous Arizona co-ed to "sign my boobies" (fig. 5). The politics of celebrity and the promise of free underwear and food "motivate" the collegiate slackers in question. At this point so early in the film, we are indeed a very, very long way from the Habermasian public sphere. The implications are that collegiate men and women are not much for hygiene, are easily bribed, and are more likely to seek celebrity autographs than "I Voted" stickers.

Figure 4. Feeding the slackers

Figure 5. Keeping their eyes on the prize

But if Moore and his gifts are not enough to motivate his audience to the polls, there is always the prospect that popular musicians can get them there. In a ninety-seven-minute film, we see and hear performances from Pearl Jam's Eddie Vedder, Robert Ellis, Steve Earle, Rage against the Machine's Tom Morello, and Joan Baez. The film features not twenty- to forty-second highlights, but typically an entire song as each gives an extended performance that comments negatively on the Bush administration and its policies. Twenty-five minutes of screen time are thus dedicated to celebrity performances and speeches, nearly one-third of the film. Rhetorically, the performances function both as critique and as celebrity-driven endorsement of Kerry-Edwards; the musical celebrities also explicitly endorse Michael Moore and his political objectives, and their prominence in the film assumes that celebrity status ranks higher than expert credentials in the minds of his slacker patrons. In her appearance at UCLA, for example, Baez compares Moore to Bob Dylan, while in Seattle, Vedder lauds Moore for his thick CIA file.

But perhaps the oddest celebrity appearance occurs midway through the film at a stop in Cincinnati, where we are introduced to Michael Stipe and his R.E.M. bandmates. In one of the few outdoor venues, Stipe speaks eloquently of growing up in the military and having a veteran father. Later, he introduces Michael Moore and the two are shown exchanging a protracted hug. Just when we expect to listen to Moore speak (again) or to hear R.E.M. blast out a raucous "It's the End of the World as We Know It (And I Feel Fine)" to the assembled University of Cincinnati students, the film cuts to an entirely new venue. Unlike the other celebrity appearances, the members of R.E.M. do not even contribute a musical performance (ostensibly their area of expertise); rather, their celebrity status is used as an unspoken guarantee of their expertise about the veteran experience. But would any of the veterans present at these rallies not have a far more credible voice than these rockers from Athens, Georgia? Moore does give veterans a chance to speak, but R.E.M. gets the last word, however secondary their own expertise on the subject may be.

Throughout the film, celebrity status provides an unquestioned, supreme ethos. Later, still more celebrities join the tour. In Columbus, Ohio, Viggo Mortensen gives an impassioned speech after being introduced by Moore for his "great" *Lord of the Rings* films. Still later, north and west of Columbus, in Toledo, we are given five seconds of a Gloria Steinem address. Each of these A- and B-listers is emphatic that George W. Bush does not deserve another term. Reasons for voting for John Kerry and John Edwards remain in the rhetorical void—a void made even more problematic by Moore's explicit denunciation of Kerry for voting to authorize the war, even with poor national and international intelligence. So despite the near-constant denunciations heaped on George W. Bush and his administration for the war in Iraq, viewers are never informed how a vote for Kerry might change the nation's conduct of the war. The cult of celebrity thus telescopes a complex policy argument down to a frightening lowest common denominator: vote as we say because we are celebrities and we know best. Ethos trumps argument at every phase of the Slacker Uprising tour. And in the rare instances where ethos does not win the day, assertion does. "My movies are the antipropaganda," intones Moore before a small contingent of media assembled in Seattle. Even that bald assertion is premised on ethos: Michael Moore would never lie.

Slacker Uprising begins and ends with the assumption that the nation's college students are overwhelmingly on Moore's side—and not simply because they are seeking free underwear and a few packets of ramen noodles. Packaged safely in between is the idea that dissent can be segregated from the rest of the film. Moore offers a ten-minute section of the film in which ideological disagreement is broached—and swiftly dispensed with, but not with argument. Moore's rejoinder is not to speak and rebut, but simply to allow those on the right to speak on camera; refutation is beside the point. In *Slacker Uprising*, dissent is not something that is organic to electoral politics, but something that can be isolated, exposed, and in this case lampooned.

That the right fares badly in a Michael Moore film certainly will not surprise. But the manner in which that dissent is represented would be risible were it not so potentially consequential. Midway through the film at the University of Florida in Gainesville, for example, a vocal opposition heckles Moore during his speech; it is the first such heckling we have witnessed in the film. "Four more years" is chanted loudly, to which Moore responds, "Four more wars." His audience laughs and the hecklers are reduced to a surly silence. Thus have we entered political debate in *Slacker Uprising*.

Immediately after the heckling scene, and in one of the very few scenes in which we hear more than a few words from a college student, a young woman states, "George Bush is a Christian and he prays, uhm, every night for the wisdom of what to do, and being a Christian as well I feel that, you know, God would be the right person to follow in this election, and he follows God and basically I'm going to be following him" (fig. 6). Armed with her syllogism from hell, this young woman functions synecdochically to represent the collective intelligence of Moore's dissenters. But Moore is just getting his camera warmed up. Another young woman is shown wearing a homemade "Jesus and GW [George W. Bush] Freedom Fighters" T-shirt (fig. 7). She remains silent as the camera lingers sarcastically over her visage; the tortured syllogism is still fresh in our minds.

Figure 6. A caricature of dissent

Figure 7. God and country

Other Republicans—identified by their Bush-Cheney placards—are made to look foolish: one young man is syntactically obtuse, while another mutters with great exasperation that Moore's hidden agenda "is just wrong." Yet another encourages us to be educated on the candidates by following the lead of "talk radio and Fox News." A snarling young woman yells at Moore, "You hate the American flag; you hate what America represents." We are next introduced to an older man sporting a black-and-yellow National Rifle Association (NRA) ball cap (fig. 8). "I think the man is a communist, just plain and simple," he says of Moore. The hoary Cold War allusion fits with the on-screen demographic. Later, just to make sure that his audience did not miss the point, Moore's camera zooms in on the hat's NRA logo. And again we hear, "I think he's a communist." While the comparison is not explicit, those who have viewed Moore's *Bowling for Columbine* cannot help but see and hear the NRA ghost of Charlton Heston.

Moore closes the dissent section of the film with two additional caricatures. In the first, a college-age woman states without even a trace of irony or self-awareness, "I actually hate that man cuz anybody who's against our commander in chief should honestly be like sent out of the country and like put in Iraq and Afghanistan and like blown up." And to close this section by returning to how it began, Moore takes us to an event in Fairmount, West Virginia, where several students stand and interrupt him in midspeech by reciting the Lord's Prayer and part of the Holy Rosary. Echoing his earlier visual commentary on the link between the right and Christianity, Moore yells to the hand-holding and chanting students, "What would Jesus bomb?" WWJB as a retort represents the refutative quality of the film: a sound bite functions to silence the opposition and win the argument, while the underlying critique is left, as usual, to implication.

The hyperbolic excesses and rhetorical deficiencies of these dissenting men and women, carefully packaged and sequestered within the text of the film, function rhetorically as the right's collective reaction to Michael

Figure 8. Rifle owners hate communists and vice versa

Moore. They are frothing and grammatically challenged buffoons, rational illiterates, the real "slackers" for their inability to think and speak; too, they are cast as Christian know-nothings blindly following their evangelical leaders. And yet they are positioned as the principal dissent to Moore's views offered in the film. What is even more remarkable about this filmic interlude—and that is how it functions within the larger narrative unfolding—is that a refutation is absent. The opposition has so thoroughly and completely condemned itself at the level of utterance and appearance that to engage in an argument with them would be to miss Moore's overweening point: arguments are not really needed here.

One might plausibly interject, though, that at least the opposition gets a voice and a face, however caricatured and contorted, while Michael Moore's ostensible supporters infrequently get much of a chance to speak. They are, from beginning to end, a largely faceless, cheering, or quiescent, adoring mass. Writing the day before Election Day 2008, Richard Corliss notes that *Slacker Uprising* bears the visual vestiges of Leni Riefenstahl's *Triumph of the Will*, the aesthetic icon of the Third Reich.[8] Moore frequently cuts to a crowd shot during his many stadium appearances. There are 414 separate crowd shots, many of which are slow pans that signify the sheer size of Moore's audiences (figs. 9–11).

The bulk of the film comprises these crowd shots, a visual signature that even is reproduced on the DVD's cover. Often Moore is framed from behind, his ample figure superimposed on the audience. As with

Figure 9. Captain Mike at the podium

Figure 10. The crowd goes wild

Figure 11. The "slacker in chief"

Riefenstahl's visual troping of Hitler's adoration, the same filmic aesthetic holds true in *Slacker Uprising*: time and time and time again, Moore and his speechmaking constitute both the cause and the effect of his mass audience. If ever a contemporary film conspicuously overdetermined the visual politics of assent, this is it; form and content merge in a haze of cheering "massness." That massness overwhelms dissent is keenly evidenced when Moore confronts his tiny, not very audible, and insignificant hecklers (fig. 12).

Figure 12. Marginalizing dissent

In noting a visual parallel between *Triumph of the Will* and *Slacker Uprising*, we are not trying to argue for Moore's latent fascism nor yet his furtive führerism. Featuring Moore amid adoring fans, given the size of his speaking venues and the frequency with which he spoke during the tour, seems altogether fitting at one remove. But 414 separate iterations? Whether this is megalomania, lack of content, or uninspired editing on a time quotient, we do not know. The film itself suggests megalomania as a frame in one of the few scenes shot on a much smaller scale. During Moore's visit to California State University, San Marcos, an event that got moved to a much larger venue at the last hour, we observe Moore outside of the stadium after the event. As he kibitzes across a barrier with a small group of admirers, a young man thrusts a small box toward Moore's entourage. The microphones and camera lean in, and we hear that the box contains his uncle's World War II Bronze Star. He wants Moore to take it, which Moore does with some initial reluctance. It is a moving gesture made more so by the private, impromptu, and vernacular ceremony. But by featuring it in the film, Moore has transformed this private and highly personal moment of memory and death into a public spectacle that functions rhetorically to validate his own bravery (fig. 13).

This is precisely where intention becomes an important cleavage point for parsing a filmmaker's argument. Was this scene included as homage to the man who donated his uncle's medal? As testimony to the patriotic nature of service? Or as aggrandizement of Moore's

Figure 13. Symbol of someone else's bravery

heroic politics? The hodgepodge nature of the film's set pieces provides little context or directorial voice outside of the tour narrative. On the meaning of the particular scene, we can assertively state at best that it happened.

A final, formal repetition that also comments on Moore's audience deserves mention. Moore's entrances are conspicuous; he is met repeatedly, we witness, by loud and sustained applause, and typically we follow Moore very closely into these venues (fig. 14).

Figure 14. Following Mike onstage

These are the filmic equivalents to the DVD's cover shot. Literally are we following Michael Moore. Literally our collective subject position is to follow Michael Moore. Thus do form and content again merge in a manner that comments devastatingly on slacker nation. There is an uprising, but it is limited to getting out of one's seat to cheer and follow a man largely barren of any well-argued policies. Again, the cult of personality is ascendant in *Slacker Uprising*.

While the film unequivocally fails its viewers by how and what it argues, it also fails to present anything resembling a coherent narrative. That failure is curious, given that the film begins with such a clear and urgent message. The message, though, quickly becomes enmeshed in the vicissitudes of the second Iraq War. Following the dissent interlude, the narrative turns to several different attempts to block Moore from speaking. A Fox News segment reports that George Mason University has "dis-invited" Moore from speaking on campus. At Utah Valley University in Orem, student leaders reject a $25,000 gift to prevent Moore from speaking. Similar well-moneyed efforts to keep Moore from speaking are rebuffed in Reno and San Diego. The narrative has turned from getting out the student vote to Michael Moore's First Amendment rights. Instead of linking his right to speak to the issues of the 2004 election, Moore keeps a tight focus on facing down these threats.

But perhaps the most consequential narrative fracture occurs at Kent State University in northeast Ohio. Intermixing black-and-white stills of the tragic events of May 4, 1970, in which Ohio National Guard troops killed four people and wounded nine others, the camera follows Moore and his entourage as they take a guided tour of the campus tragedy. Moore wanders silently and pensively through the landmarks in the chilly, dark, and damp Ohio night—but we can hardly see him and the campus. Only the still photographs allow us to imaginatively bridge 1970 and 2004. Speaking that same night on campus, Moore solemnly encourages his listeners not to forget the tragic events. And then we are on to Columbus and the next crowd of slackers.

But what does the Kent State tragedy have to do with the larger narrative of college students exercising their right to vote in 2004? Explicitly, and according to the film, nothing. But perhaps a clue lies in what visually precedes Moore's visit to Kent State, which took place on October 23. Nearly two weeks earlier, on October 11, Moore was joined onstage by Joan Baez at UCLA. Viewers of the film are not privy to this chronology, since the editors cut from Southern California to Ohio without the hint of a twelve-day time lag. In an interview with Baez, she waxes nostalgic for the days when songwriters like Bob Dylan fueled the student antiwar movement. Today, she argues, "it's Michael Moore" who's mobilizing students. After hearing her sing Finland's national anthem and a brief comment by Moore, we are quickly in the dark and damp of Ohio. Diegetically speaking, Joan Baez, with her iconic status as a leader of sixties-era student protest movements, provides the tenuous narrative link for *Slacker Uprising*'s viewers. Enthymematically, perhaps the students will lead us again—as they did in the halcyon days of campus protest. And yet that very enthymeme is largely undercut by the entirety of *Slacker Uprising*: only by following the sheer force of Moore's personality might students rally to a cause; built on the flimsy cornerstones of free underwear and ramen noodles, along with promised appearances by Michael Moore's celebrity sidekicks, this nascent movement hardly stands a chance.

How many cameras are focused on Michael Moore at any given time? *Slacker Uprising* is ostensibly a road movie, crisscrossing America's vast geographic and cultural landscapes, but instead of overt references to them, we get three cameras trained on our tour guide. Slackers and diplomats alike are relegated to two-second sound bites while we cut across three different angles of celebrities introducing and reintroducing Captain Mike to an adoring audience. As we have demonstrated, there are plenty of sweeping shots of screaming fans to highlight Moore's points but few one-on-one interviews of any depth. For a real-time record of a grassroots uprising, it takes a remarkably incurious director to devote most of his resources to recording his own speeches. Was there nothing else to record? It casts the whole "uprising" as something of a Potemkin revolt. And the event footage is not the only thing to become repetitive.

During a press conference in Seattle, a reporter asks, "Are your movies propaganda? Or do you really feel that they are truthful?" Moore answers, "The propaganda that exists appears every night on the nightly news . . . my movies are the antipropaganda." And yet, in that very scene, footage of that reporter reacting to Moore is repeated twice within ten seconds. On the surface, an editing decision like this seems harmless, but here the reporter in question is smiling in reaction to his answer (fig. 15).

By repeating that smiling footage, is the implication that she has been won over by his response? This opens the door to ask where else he has lifted reactions out of sequence—a slacker laughing, an elderly couple

Figure 15. Does she agree?

nodding along in agreement. These shots tell us something by implication, either that a good point has been made or that people trust the man
speaking, so what does it mean to place those reactions out of order with
the sentiments being expressed? What does it mean to do so under the
heading of "antipropaganda"?

Here we see the often subtle cleavage point between documentary
and propaganda, helpfully highlighted in a scene purporting to make that
distinction for us. Films like Riefenstahl's notorious *Triumph of the Will*
represent one extreme on this spectrum, using carefully staged public
events to give the impression of a mighty and unquestionably superior
Third Reich ascendant. On the other end of that spectrum, we find films
such as Frederick Wiseman's *Titicut Follies*, a painstaking examination of a
modern mental institution shot in the fly-on-the-wall, observational *cinéma
vérité* tradition. Both extremes have been regarded as documentary, and
both claim to present reality, but at what point does a filmmaker's agenda
eclipse his or her claim to reality? The medium of film requires cuts, and
it is important to note that even the most transparently produced documentary must leave some scraps of reality on the editing-room floor. But
are today's documentary audiences literate enough in the technical aspects
of filmmaking to catch a disingenuous edit? Or does the documentary
label quiet any suspicion of manipulative intentions? The question is not
whether Moore is a Nazi. The question is whether propaganda can be used
to refute propaganda, and whether Moore's so-called "antipropaganda,"

in reacting to the perceived whitewashing of mainstream news reporting, utilizes the same ethically compromised techniques to make a point. Oversimplification, disingenuous editing, careful omission of key counterarguments—these are the tools of the propagandist. Considering the weight of his claim as the antipropagandist, Moore ought to be mindful of his frequent use of those same tools.

Yet the most fruitful discussion of this film's production values lives in the big picture. The technical quality of the movie—in terms of audio and video quality, numbers of cameras, or types of shots—varies wildly from beginning to end. (By "beginning" here, we mean the chronology of the tour, not the movie, as the movie begins with footage obtained at the end of the tour.) Footage from the first stop on the tour appears to come from a single camera, perhaps two, and the video is shaky and low-resolution. The final stop on the tour, at the Leon County Civic Center in Tallahassee, features four or five high-definition cameras and moving crane shots, quite a disparity in production values. It is entirely possible that this occurred organically, as an election night concert in Tallahassee featuring an obstreperous Roseanne Barr is perhaps more exciting and photogenic than a small gathering of folks in Elk Rapids, Michigan, a town with a population of 1,721, according to Moore. And by the time Pearl Jam's Eddie Vedder shows up to serenade Seattle, the production has upgraded to better-quality cameras and our first crane shot. Yet even between Seattle and Nashville, the audiovisual seems to take a step back, getting shakier and lower-resolution.

The on-again, off-again production values suggest an ambivalence about what Moore's team is doing with *Slacker Uprising*. Did they know they were making a feature-length movie when they started the tour? Surely, they would have packed a decent camera or two when they took to the road, but the early footage suggests otherwise. Was it a priority to have high-end camera work only for performances from big names like Vedder or Rage against the Machine's Tom Morello? The video quality stabilizes after Nashville, so perhaps that was the point where they decided to fully commit. Questions like these become chickens and eggs: Which came first, the movie or the tour? It can be tricky trying to deduce a filmmaker's intentions by parsing decisions or by imposing our own narrative on available evidence. In the end, dumb circumstance frequently trumps grand theories on why a director did this or that. Viewers may make the justifiable decision simply to stop watching an uncompelling film, but such lukewarm output from an acclaimed director raises numerous questions. And since Moore offers so little by way of analysis or narrative, we must ask what happened.

Perhaps these technical fluctuations are what you get, as a filmmaker documenting current events, when you make a bet and lose. These bits and pieces are stitched together by something that failed to materialize: a Kerry victory. At about twenty-five minutes into the film, Kerry makes his last substantial appearance, in some humorous campaign ads, until the last twenty minutes, when he shows up to lose. The footage that makes up the main narrative of *Slacker Uprising* was originally meant to serve a different master, a tale wherein Michael Moore clears the path for John Kerry to take the White House. The film is haunted by this ghost of future past, by what could have been: "a cadre of rock musicians, hip-hop artists and citizen groups [going] on the road with their own 'shadow campaigns' to save John Kerry and the Democrats from themselves." It would have started in a community center in tiny Elk Rapids, recorded on someone's camcorder. It would have built up steam, gathering momentum and celebrities and HD cameras, riding roughshod over the opposition, until that culminating moment when Kerry assumed the throne—except it never happened. The rhythm of that underdog narrative is irresistible to the American psyche, and Moore did his best to place his chips where he thought they would best serve him after the election. It would have made for a great story if the bet had paid off. But it did not. And the raw materials of *Slacker Uprising*, scattered across the table like poker chips after a bad hand, had to be gathered and reassigned to a new tale.

After one and a half hours of *Slacker Uprising*, we are left with a vexing contradiction: for a movie so bloated and aspirational, it departs with little in the way of lessons learned or wisdom gained. We knew before we began that Moore's quest would fail, yet he does little delving into that sad fact other than to blame it on the slackers' parents and the loss of a single state's electoral votes. The timing of the film's release suggests that it was meant to rally the troops—again—for the 2008 general election, but that call to action hardly surfaces before the end credits begin to roll; like most of the movie's assertions, it is made more by inference than by argument.

And that is the ultimate problem with a film so light on critical content: while we have drawn attention to the number of crowd shots and their relationship to propagandistic intention, the very shallowness of the film suggests that any deeper analysis gives it more credit than it is due. The preemptive discourse, the disingenuous editing, the oversimplification of a complex national election—each of these is cause for concern. A documentary, by aspiring to the rigors of nonfiction, must educate and illuminate, must present its case through credible witnesses and verifiable evidence, and must do so transparently lest it cast a shadow over its own endeavor. Moore's road film substitutes celebrities for statesmen, caricatures for counterarguments, and tries to stitch it together in a cloak of America's sacred cultural movements. In a heftier film, we may draw more urgent conclusions about its intentions and its effect on the discourse of an increasingly divided nation, but this is not propaganda. It does not try hard enough. For twenty weeks in 2004, the slackers rose up, and then, with a sigh, they sat back down. Nobody really knows why or what happened; perhaps someday, someone will make a documentary about it.

Notes

1. Ben Walters, review of *Slacker Uprising*, *Guardian*, September 23, 2008, http://www.guardian.co.uk/film/2008/sep/23/review.slackeruprising.

2. Joe Leydon, review of *Captain Mike across America* (reedited and re-released as *Slacker Uprising*), *Variety*, September 8, 2007, http://www.variety.com/review/VE1117934650.html?categoryid=31&cs=1&p=0.

3. Josh Tyler, review of *Slacker Uprising*, *Cinema Blend*, accessed June 15, 2010, http://www.cinemablend.com/dvds/Slacker-Uprising-3375.html.

4. In researching Moore's documentaries more generally, we were struck by the fact that so few rhetoricians have engaged Moore's influential and widely distributed work. We are aware of only one journal article—published out of the discipline proper—that engages his work only tangentially: see G. Thomas Goodnight, "*The Passion of the Christ* Meets *Fahrenheit 9/11*: A Study in Celebrity Advocacy," *American Behavioral Scientist* 49 (2005): 410–35. Three important book chapters on Moore include Shawn J. Parry-Giles and Trevor Parry-Giles, "Virtual Realism and the Limits of Commodified Dissent in *Fahrenheit 9/11*," in *The Rhetoric of the New Political Documentary*, ed. Thomas W. Benson and Brian J. Snee (Carbondale: Southern Illinois University Press, 2008), 24–53; Jennifer L. Borda, "Documentary Dialectics or Dogmatism? *Fahrenhype 9/11*, *Celsius 41.11*, and the New Politics of Documentary Film," in Benson and Snee, *Rhetoric of the New Political Documentary*, 54–77; and Brian J. Snee, "Free Guns and Speech Control: The Structural and Thematic Rhetoric of *Bowling for Columbine*," in *Visual Communication: Perception, Rhetoric, and Technology*, ed. Diane S. Hope (Cresskill, NJ: Hampton Press, 2006), 193–209.

5. All quoted discourse and video stills from the film are from Michael Moore, *Slacker Uprising* (Culver City, CA: Brave New Films, 2008), DVD.

6. Scott Tobias, review of *Slacker Uprising*, *A.V. Club*, accessed June 15, 2010, http://www.avclub.com/articles/slacker-uprising,2763/.

7. Richard Corliss, "What's Michael Moore Doing This Election?," Michael Moore website, accessed June 15, 2010, http://www.michaelmoore.com/words/mike-in-the-news/whats-michael-moore-doing-this-election.

8. Ibid.

8. "I'm Sorry to See It Go": Nostalgic Rhetoric in Michael Moore's *Capitalism: A Love Story*

Kendall R. Phillips

ichael Moore's *Capitalism: A Love Story* represents the apex of his particular form of documentary polemic and his most ambitious critique of the American political and cultural system. Released at the height of the financial collapse of 2009, the film is a full-scale indictment of Reagan-era "trickle down" economics and the kinds of economic policies championed by the Republican Party and other fiscal conservatives. In her review of the film for *USA Today*, Claudia Puig writes, "This is quintessential Moore, with a clear-cut agenda: Capitalism has superseded democracy, encouraged corruption and greed, and failed our nation. Political bigwigs and wealthy executives may love it, but it's not working for the majority of Americans."[1] *Capitalism*, as Puig notes, is an ideal example of Moore's rhetoric, a rhetoric that gains force from his polemical stances and ability to combine grave political points with humor. Film critic Amy Biancolli contends, "What Moore does—feature-length partisan invectives, dressed up with comically apt archival footage—he does better than anyone. Call them documentaries, but consider them essays: one-sided, hyperbolic, heatedly persuasive works that broadcast a single viewpoint for a single cause."[2]

Scholars have long recognized that documentaries are not transparent representations of truth, but by their very nature are distinctly interested and biased. The cloak of "nonfiction" wrapped around the documentary film has at times merely obscured the fact that, as Bill Nichols points out, "it may entertain or please, but it does so in relation to a rhetorical or persuasive effort aimed at the existing social world."[3] At other times, and certainly the case for the films of Michael Moore, documentary films have more explicitly stated their political purposes. As Thomas Benson and Brian Snee explain in the introductory chapter to *The Rhetoric of the New Political Documentary*, by the early 1990s, "filmmakers and politicians began to explore the persuasive possibility of film in both fiction and documentary."[4] While the history of film is replete with social issue films and overt propaganda, the new era of the political documentary, as Benson and Snee observe, was ushered in by the films of Moore, especially *Bowling for Columbine* (2002) and *Fahrenheit 9/11* (2004).

Although it was less successful at the box office and with critics than these earlier films, *Capitalism* still resonates with a strong rhetorical force that invites us to share in moments of indignation at the state of the American political and economic structure.[5] In this essay, I argue that one of the rhetorics drawing audiences through *Capitalism* is the rhetoric of nostalgia. Images of the past ground the broader moral critique being offered by Moore, and while the critique is both familiar and fragmented, the rhetorical force of nostalgia provides an underlying, though complicated, coherence to the film. A close reading of *Capitalism* suggests that longing for the past asserts itself at key and crucial moments within the film's scattered narratives, and these are the moments to which I attend in this essay.

The rhetoric of nostalgia serves as a principal motif in *Capitalism* and arguably can be seen as one of Moore's overarching tendencies. Even a cursory glance at the other films discussed in this volume suggests Moore's almost obsessive interest in his own childhood and the ways in which his childhood home and way of life represent a kind of moral touchstone against which the ills of the present era are highlighted. *Roger & Me* is perhaps the clearest example, as Moore seeks to understand the dramatic changes in his hometown and uses these changes as an indictment of broader American economic trends. Across his oeuvre, Moore demonstrates a tendency to return to Flint, Michigan, and to reference the idyllic nature of his own childhood era as a counterpoint to the social ills he is investigating. In *Bowling for Columbine*, for instance, Moore confronts Charlton Heston about a National Rifle Association (NRA) rally in Flint, and in *Fahrenheit 9/11*, he follows two marine recruiters as they seek to persuade impoverished youth from Flint to enlist. In these and other examples, Moore demonstrates a recurrent longing for a return to the home of his childhood.

Nostalgia, originally conceived as a physical ailment consisting of a pain (*algos*) related to separation from home (*nostos*), is a deeply ambivalent concept. For some critics, nostalgia is a feeling embedded within the isolation and speed of modern life; for others, it is a reactionary impulse that thwarts progress toward new life. In *The Future of Nostalgia*, Svetlana Boym teases out the ambiguity and ambivalence of nostalgia into two broad themes: restorative and reflective nostalgia. Restorative nostalgia, which can be thought of as the more conservative and reactionary strand, "does not think of itself as nostalgia," she says, "but rather as truth and tradition." If restorative nostalgia can be thought of as more focused on the stability of a perceived home of tradition and truth, reflective nostalgia is conceived by Boym as dwelling "on the ambivalence of human longings and belonging" and thus can be thought of as a more progressive and creative form of the sentiment.[6] The two senses of nostalgia can be productively contrasted: whereas reflective nostalgia opens a space for thinking about where we are and how we got here, restorative nostalgia can be thought of as foreclosing that space with a reliance on received tradition. While it would be easy to think of nostalgia in only one of these senses in examining Michael Moore's *Capitalism*, I suggest that both strands can be seen, and that in analyzing both strands of nostalgia and the tension created between them, we can gain insights into Moore's rhetorical work as well as the broader dimensions of nostalgic rhetoric and its place in critical rhetorical practices.

Nostalgia: Reactionary and Radical Rhetorics

Although nostalgia is a seventeenth-century term, it is generally conceived as deeply embedded in the twentieth century and the cultural dynamics of modernity. As Alastair Bonnett notes, "The modern era is characterized by change and a far more intense and urgent relationship with loss," and as such, nostalgia became a deeply ingrained dimension of modern sentiment.[7] The complexity and rootlessness of modern life established the conditions for a widespread emergence of sentimental nostalgia. David Lowenthal writes that "a perpetual staple of nostalgic yearning is the search for a simple and stable past as a refuge from the turbulent and chaotic present."[8] The expansion of capitalism further fostered a reactionary focus on the past. Capitalism's inevitable push toward new products, experience, and consumptions has surrounded us, Bonnett contends, with "messages that extol the future and warn of the dangers of stasis, the failure to change."[9]

Hence, nostalgia's emergence as a general cultural trend can be mapped alongside the rise of modern bureaucratic, urbanized, and mobile life and the expansion of capitalist impulses toward future desires and consumption.

Nostalgia, in this way, can be seen as a reaction against the sense that the present is accelerating and leading toward greater fragmentation. Thus, in contemporary nostalgia, we often long not so much for a lost home as for the simpler time we imagine that home represents. As Aaron Santesso explains, nostalgia "is more often imagined in temporal terms (one longs for the past) than in the spatial or geographical terms at the heart of Hofer's original definition."[10] In most cases, we long not for a specific site or even an earlier time period, "but rather a state of mind," Malcolm Chase and Christopher Shaw observe. Chase and Shaw contend that the emergence of this longing for a past "state of mind" is contingent on three broad cultural conditions: First, we must view time in a linear fashion, since a belief in cyclical time makes nostalgia less about longing and more about waiting. Second, we must have "some sense that the present is deficient," and out of this dissatisfaction, we are drawn to yearn for a time when these deficiencies were not present. Finally, there must also be objects that connect us to some sense of this past. These objects "become talismans that link us concretely with the past," and with them we craft an ever-changing narrative of that earlier time and its cultural state of mind against which we compare the failures of the present.[11]

Flint and Moore's childhood during the city's boom times, to which he continually returns, can thus be thought of as talismans not so much of a physical home as a state of mind. As is typical of nostalgia, Moore's childhood home stands in for a time of stability, prosperity, safety, and justice, and broadly speaking, his nostalgia is not so much for Flint as for the Flint of his childhood memories. As Santesso points out, "It is atypical . . . to encounter a depiction of nostalgia for middle age; childhood is the usual object of nostalgia."[12] The individual interest in childhood as an idyllic time of joy and wonder is paralleled in collective nostalgia through a longing for a simpler time for the country, and in this way, the collective experience of nostalgia is often associated with nationalism. In these yearnings, both individual and collective, lies a desire to return to an innocent and idealized way of life, suggesting a strong connection between nostalgia and utopia.[13]

This sense that the ideal era lies in the past hints at the overarching structure of nostalgic narratives, which generally are arranged around an idealized past state of affairs. Nostalgic narratives typically suggest a particular cultural failure—or lapse—that bifurcates time so that there we are separated from the earlier, idealized "prelapsarian" era and instead exist within the desolate "postlapsarian" state of the present.[14] The idealized prelapsarian past is often portrayed as utopian in the sense that it is, as Susan Stewart argues, "a utopia where authenticity suffuses both word and world." The narratives of nostalgic utopia, for Stewart, bear the distinct danger of becoming totalizing and therefore erasing their own status as narrative. She notes that "nostalgia, like any form of narrative, is always ideological: the past it seeks has never existed except as narrative, and hence, always absent, that past continually threatens to reproduce itself as a felt lack."[15]

For many cultural critics, nostalgia's at times dogmatic insistence on a utopian past gives license to reactionary and overtly conservative political impulses. Karl Marx famously wrote, "The social revolution of the nineteenth century can only create its poetry from the future not from the past. It cannot begin its own work until it has sloughed off all its superstitious regard for the past."[16] Contemporary commentators have generally followed Marx's lead. Frederic Jameson, for instance, objects to the "costume-party self-deception," whereby we are "wearing the costumes of the great moments of the past," and Richard Sennett warns that "regret is a dangerous sentiment. Whilst it produces empathy for the past, and so a certain insight, regret induces resignation about the present, and so a certain acceptance of its evils."[17] Among progressive theorists and critics, Sean Scanlan observes, nostalgia is viewed as "a sort of political crime causing well-intended leftists to flee even the appearance of any connection."[18] The fear of nostalgia, especially among progressives, seems driven by two interlocking concerns: reactionary politics and a warped view of the past. Christopher Lasch, for example, worries that the individual caught up in nostalgia is "worse than a reactionary; he is an incurable sentimentalist. Afraid of the future, he is also afraid to face the truth about the past."[19] Timothy Barney summarizes these concerns: "Nostalgia, for theorists in this vein, is an obstacle to knowledge, clouding 'real' history with inauthentic emotion."[20]

For Barney and a growing number of scholars, however, the simple dismissal of nostalgia as an inherently dangerous and conservative sentiment is unsatisfactory. In his reading of the film *Good Bye Lenin!*, Barney wonders, "Can not nostalgia be employed as a basis for social change, rather than simply trying to live within a rose-hued era?"[21] He contends that nostalgia should not be judged by notions of authenticity or consensus, but rather recognized as having the capacity to spur genuine reflection and the potential for progressive action. Alastair Bonnett argues along similar lines, contending that nostalgia's yearnings for the past "are not a cancerous or alien intrusion but integral to the radical imagination." Bonnett notes that leftist politics typically strive "to overcome alienation and return humanity to authenticity," and that these are also the trappings of nostalgic yearnings.[22]

The debate over nostalgia's political valence, however, might lead us toward oversimplifying the sentiment. Nostalgia—whether reflective or restorative, radical or reactionary—is embodied in rhetorical appeals, and while it might be tempting to spend time classifying nostalgic appeals as either reflective or restorative, this would miss the complexity provoked by any appeal to utopian images of the past.[23] The past, as numerous scholars have observed, is neither simple nor fixed, but rather, always a subject for contention and revision.[24] As Bonnett writes, "Any attempt to fashion nostalgia to our political needs is also complicated by the way memory and affiliation are culturally cross-cutting."[25] The rhetoric of nostalgia entails these complications as cultural meanings, forms of social identity and affiliation, and broader ideological structures become intertwined with the appeal. Thus an attempt to simply classify one appeal as reflective and another as restorative may miss the complexities by which our yearning for the past is implicated in other cultural dimensions. A more appropriate critical approach is to consider the ambivalence and ambiguity that may inhere in a given rhetorical appeal to nostalgia. This is the approach recommended by Marouf Hasian, who suggests "critical memory studies" as a means of employing "a self-reflexive method that balances the need for inquiry with tolerance for alternative perspectives."[26]

In what follows, I seek to take this critical approach to the nostalgic rhetoric in Michael Moore's *Capitalism: A Love Story*, with particular attention to the points in the film that seem to most explicitly gesture toward nostalgia. In order to capture the ambivalent relationship between reflective and restorative nostalgia, I read these scenes first in light of their progressive/radical potential, and then provide a subsequent reading focused on elements of restorative/reactionary nostalgia. Following these parallel readings, I provide some thoughts about the dynamic interplay between these divergent rhetorical orientations contained within the film and the implications of these readings for future studies of nostalgic rhetoric.

Moore's Nostalgic Rhetoric

The overall narrative structure of Moore's *Capitalism* is a jumble of divergent incidents and storylines all orbiting around a general condemnation of contemporary multinational corporations and their collusion with the government to foster policies that exploit the working and middle classes. While nostalgia suffuses all of the film, here I want to focus on three moments in the film in which nostalgic appeals are both most evident and most crucial to the overall argument of the film. The first establishes the idyllic world of 1950s middle-class America; the second focuses on the ruin and devastation wrought by contemporary capitalist policies; and the third involves a prophetic call to return to earlier policies. The first two moments are driven largely by Moore's own childhood memories and his relationship to his father, who appears briefly in the second segment. The third nostalgic moment substitutes symbolic fathers in the form of Franklin Delano Roosevelt and other heroic historic figures for Moore's real father, and they provide concrete examples of the way America could have been, the road not taken. In addition to serving as transition points in the overall film structure, it is also clear that these moments parallel the general structure of nostalgic narratives: the idyllic prelapsarian childhood, the economic corruption of the lapse, and the postlapsarian world of the contemporary American political economy. These three filmic moments also contain elements of both reflective and restorative nostalgia, thus crafting a complicated, ambivalent, and conflicted rhetorical orientation.

Reflective Nostalgia in Moore's Radical Rhetoric

The opening moments of Moore's film announce its nostalgic tone. After a credit sequence featuring footage of various bank robberies, the film cuts between scenes from an educational film about the fall of ancient Rome and scenes from contemporary America. The voice-over from the original educational film carries on throughout this sequence, so that descriptions of spectacles and gladiators are intercut with images from the television show *American Idol* and bouts of mixed martial arts, the description of the tyrannical dictator is connected to former vice president Dick Cheney, and the abuse of rights and torture of prisoners reveals images of detainees in Guantanamo Bay. Suggesting an analogy between the fall of Rome and contemporary America is nothing new, but the analogy is usually employed in critiques of American liberalism and moral decadence. Moore's film reconstructs this narrative and, while still borrowing imagery from the past, constitutes a radical nostalgia. In this way, Moore is crafting what Jennifer Ladino has called "counter nostalgic narratives," which serve "to revisit a dynamic past and to invert or exploit official narratives in ways that challenge dominant histories."[27] The fall of Rome, and by analogy America, came not from moral failings but from governmental corruption and an economy of greed.

Moore's use of home movies in this first phase of the film offers clear visual evidence of the idyllic prelapsarian era—the young Moore on vacation in New York, visiting a fake movie studio, gleefully donning a new baseball mitt—and his youthful exuberance in these moments underscores the film's voice-over narrative. "We lived a good life. If this was capitalism, I loved it. And so did everyone else," the adult Moore intones over the rapid flow of clips from his own childhood. Edited into these images of Moore are other familiar popular cultural images from the 1950s, clichés reminiscent of television shows like *Father Knows Best* and *Leave It to Beaver*. Representations of the 1950s typically focus on domestic tranquility, family values, and American ascendancy and are most often used, as Christine Spengler notes, "to bolster support for socially conservative legislation."[28] This is especially true of depictions of the American family from the 1950s. Daniel Marcus observes that "the nuclear family as presented in the family sitcoms of the 1950s took on documentary value to illustrate the stable realities of American life before the disruptions of Sixties social movements."[29] Moore is here seeking to reformulate this clichéd vision of American innocence in a counternostalgia founded on a different economic vision. In his voice-over, Moore emphasizes what he presents as the real basis of this idyllic era. During this period, Moore informs us, the wealthy "had to pay a tax rate of ninety percent," providing a basis for the nation's infrastructure. For families like Moore's, things were even more positive: "Middle class families only needed one income to survive. Our union family had free health care and free dental. The kids could go to college without getting a loan from a bank. Dad had four weeks paid vacation every summer. Most people had a savings account and little debt." In this way, Moore provides a different vision of America's golden age, one founded on high taxes, strong unions, and a growing American middle class.

In his portrayal of the idyllic childhood of American innocence, Moore establishes a focal point for nostalgic yearning. The combination of clichéd images with radical economic revisioning of the era lays the groundwork for the film's next major section—a focus on the "lapse," or America's fall from grace. The film introduces American decline through a very brief snippet of a speech by President Jimmy Carter haranguing America for its focus on consumerism and material goods; the voice-over refers to the former president as "Debbie Downer." Immediately following this brief segment, the narrative turns to the rise of Ronald Reagan, the "most famous corporate spokesman of 1950s," who is positioned into the presidency by a vast conspiracy of wealthy Americans. Following the nostalgic logic of the preceding section, Moore inverts the received wisdom about President Reagan—returning America to strength and prosperity—through a series of interposed graphs and statistics revealing rising debt, flat wages, increased bankruptcies, and a growing prison population. Moore indicts the Reagan administration with the "wholesale dismantling of our industrial infrastructure."

In these initial nostalgic gestures, Moore is providing the kind of nostalgia that, as Bonnett argues, provides the imagination with a yearning for radical traditions and the kinds of associations and communal commitments evident in the progressive movement's past.[30] In this way, Moore presents the labor unions of the 1950s as not merely a political instrument but a unique way of life. Moore seeks to recover this idyllic way of life from both our overly conservative popular memory and from the politically conservative policies ushered in by the Reagan administration. In so doing, Moore decenters the conservative nostalgic narrative by offering a different sense of the prelapsarian world and a different sense of the lapse that brought us to our present state.

Reagan's arrival in the film's narrative announces the moment of the lapse—the crime that ends the idyllic era and produces the corrupt world in which we now experience nostalgic yearning. This second segment, occurring approximately twenty-two minutes into the film, begins with a self-reflective moment of nostalgia: a recollection of Moore's own work as a filmmaker. Moore here casts himself as the prophetic voice as he employs clips from his first film, *Roger & Me*, to demonstrate his prescience about the coming disasters. There is even a nostalgic moment as he once again seeks entrance into the GM headquarters to see the company's CEO, an effort that once again fails. The most poignant moment of this section is the appearance of Moore's own father as the father-and-son duo tour the rubble of the old factory where the elder Moore used to work. As the two men survey the devastation of twisted metal and crushed concrete, Moore recalls with his father the happier times when Moore's mother would wait with her children outside the factory for their father to appear after work. Underscoring the nostalgic yearning for the earlier, idyllic time is the camera's focus on the debris left in the wake of the plant's destruction—an almost fetishistic interest in the ruins of the postlapsarian world. This is a clear trope of reflective nostalgia. As Boym notes, "Reflective nostalgia lingers on ruins, the patina of time and history, in the dreams of another place and another time."[31] The remnants of the former ACDelco spark plug factory here provide material evidence of the absence of the lost community and way of life that Moore painted in the film's earlier sections.

The lapse is followed in Moore's film by a focus on the postlapsarian world of the present, a place in which children are imprisoned for profit, airline pilots are underpaid and overworked, companies seek to profit from the death of their employees, and multinational corporations predict the end of democracy in favor of a new system of "plutonomy," rule by the wealthy. For the next hour, Moore's film careens through a variety of examples punctuated with moments of levity (an animated backdrop showing the country literally falling apart behind President George W. Bush as he speaks) and sadness (the painful scenes of families devastated to learn that their loved one's death added to a corporation's profit line). The contrast between the earlier world of the American 1950s and the harsh economic climate of the present is cast in stark terms, and Moore even employs a series of religious leaders who conclude that capitalism is a sin.

An explicit appeal to nostalgia returns during the film's third act. Here Moore employs historic examples to contrast our current corrupt state with prelapsarian examples of moral purity and authority. Dr. Jonas Salk, inventor of the polio vaccine, chose to give his vaccine away rather than profit from it, making clear the moral superiority of the past. Contrasted with the short-term profit expectations of corporate traders, Salk's noble lifesaving gesture stands as a paragon of virtue and a condemnation of contemporary capitalism. The moral authority of the past is also employed in the film's final moments, its call-to-action phase. The election of Barack Obama is used by Moore as a signal of the potential for times to change. (There is perhaps some irony, however, in the fact that Obama was a prominent supporter of the corporate bailout of Wall Street that is criticized in the film.) Scenes of Obama's election are immediately followed by a series of more optimistic examples—people resisting evictions and strikers overcoming corporations—and these scenes in turn are followed by another movement to the past. Moore's uncle, we are told, was one of the union members who staged a massive sit-down strike against General Motors at its factory in Flint, Michigan, in 1936–37. As corporate thugs and police sought to break the strike, says Moore, the governor, with the support of Franklin Delano Roosevelt, sent in the National Guard to protect the workers' right to strike, and this, in Moore's moral universe, constitutes a clear example of democracy trumping capitalism. The movement of scenes suggests an analogous relationship between Obama, who is shown supporting a sit-in strike in a Chicago factory, and Roosevelt, and in this way Moore's nostalgic past provides a moral roadmap for the future.

Moore's use of the GM strike demonstrates what might be thought of as the overarching theme of the film: the potential of politics to disrupt the encroachment of capitalism. Bonnett observes that radical nostalgia may be employed as a disruption of modernity, and Moore's film embraces just such a political logic. The sympathetic portrayal of the strikers and the heroic efforts of Roosevelt to support workers against a large corporation open a space for thinking differently about the relationship between democracy and capitalism. Bonnett notes, "If modernity is a time of alienation then all attempts to speak of human sympathy and solidarity are likely to offer a politics of transgression in the form of a sense of loss."[32] In Moore's film, this politics of sympathy and solidarity is reinforced by triumphal examples like the successful contemporary workers' action against the owners of a window manufacturing company and the bread company owned by its employees.

The epitome of the democratic spirit Moore wants to see revived comes in the film's final and most compelling nostalgic moment. In recently uncovered newsreel footage, we see President Roosevelt declaring the need for a "second Bill of Rights," one focused on economic rights like medical care, housing, minimum wages, and freedom from unfair corporate monopolies. While Obama's election signals the possibility of a populist uprising, the figure of Roosevelt provides the underlying moral authority for this movement. The roots of American democracy, Moore argues, are not bound to a free-market economy—a point he makes when scouring an original copy of the Constitution for the word "capitalism." In these earlier champions of democracy—the founders and Roosevelt—Moore seeks to recapture a political spirit capable of combating the growth of multinational capitalism, and in so doing, he seeks a nostalgic rhetoric capable of disrupting the habits of contemporary thinking and opening a space for creativity. It is telling that in the film's final defiant moments, after reviewing the devastation of Hurricane Katrina and the crimes of corporate greed, Moore declares, "I refuse to live in a country like this, and I'm not leaving." The film ends with Moore pronouncing Wall Street a crime scene and urging us to replace the evils of capitalism with "something that is good for all people. And that something is called democracy."

As the screen goes black, Moore urges the audience to participate—"Y'know, I can't really do this anymore, unless those of you who are watching this in the theater want to join me. I hope you will and, please, speed it up"—though he leaves uncertain and open the way this participation might take place. Critics of the film condemned Moore for raising so many questions without providing many answers, but if Moore's nostalgic rhetoric is understood as reflective nostalgia, then it can be read not as a call to action so much as an effort to create what Bonnett describes as "a moment of displacement and, hence, creativity."[33]

Restorative Elements in Moore's Nostalgic Rhetoric

The rhetoric of Moore's *Capitalism* is strongly tied to the kind of nostalgic appeal that Boym calls "reflective" and Bonnett would call "radical." Moore uses the past to disrupt habitual attitudes toward contemporary economic justice by painting an idyllic portrait of an innocent, prosperous, and more equitable past. Moore explicitly invokes the moral authority of the architects of that golden age to motivate and justify dismantling the systems of the present. In many ways, it would be simpler and easier to declare Moore's film an example of reflective, radical nostalgia and leave it at that. Making such a categorization, however, would oversimplify the complexities of nostalgia as an orientation toward the past and fail to recognize the ways in which more conservative, restorative nostalgic elements appear in Moore's film.

Restorative nostalgia, I argue, not only is present in Moore's film but also serves as a powerful animating force within his overall appeal. To be clear, I pursue this reading not so much to undermine Moore's nostalgic rhetoric—or my reading of it—but as a means of exploring the complex relationship between reflective and restorative nostalgia and the ways this complexity animates the rhetoric of *Capitalism* and is implicated in our general political responses to our past.

In her discussion of the rhetorics of nostalgia, Boym notes, "Restorative nostalgia knows two main narrative plots—the restoration of origins and the conspiracy theory."[34] Even a cursory viewing of Moore's *Capitalism* reveals these elements. The conspiracy theory Moore constructs is vast and disturbing. In Moore's account of the lapse, the election of Ronald Reagan is the result of a conspiracy of the wealthy engineered by Don Regan. In one disturbing snippet, Regan is seen instructing the president to hurry up during an address to Wall Street. This example of impropriety is used by Moore as evidence of powers behind the Reagan presidency pulling the strings and crafting policies benefiting wealthy Americans.

There is a long rhetorical tradition of incorporating conspiracy theories into appeals for changes. Charles Griffin, for example, observes the power of conspiracy theories to provide the moral grounds for cultural condemnations.[35] Thomas Goodnight and John Poulakos argue that conspiracies constitute fantasies designed to disrupt the normal, pragmatic views of the world by projecting expansive counterrationalities that render social reality in dramatically contrary ways. They observe, "History, contemporary social institutions, and the future begin to be seen as determined by secret and powerful groups."[36] Moore's depiction of the Reagan presidency clearly follows this form of conspiracy, as the filmmaker constructs a fantasy in which not only Reagan's election was engineered by powerful secret forces, but so too were the subsequent economic changes imposed on the country.

Moore's filmic narrative erases the economic turmoil of the 1970s with its combination of economic stagnation and inflation—or "stagflation"—as well as the energy crisis, which brought a great deal of economic hardship to Americans. The brief appearance by President Jimmy Carter is dismissed by Moore as a message from "Debbie Downer," and Carter's message about the need for economic self-restraint is used merely as a setup for the appearance of Reagan as the "nation's corporate spokesman." In this way, Moore's nostalgic conspiracy completely erases the economic and political history of the late 1960s and 1970s in favor of painting a picture in which the utopian boom economy of the 1950s was intentionally dismantled by the ascendancy of Ronald Reagan in 1980.

The dismissal of the economic hardships of the 1970s is not the only time Moore demonstrates selective recollection of American history. He handles the unpalatable historical realities of his childhood by saying, "Yes, of course not everything was perfect. We didn't mind having to put up with a little bit of this and a little bit of that." Visually, "this" is fire hoses being turned on civil rights protesters in the South, and "that" is the war in Vietnam. As Boym writes regarding restorative narratives, "The stronger the rhetoric of continuity with the historical past and emphasis on traditional values, the more selectively the past is presented."[37] In Moore's efforts to reconstruct the idyllic past of his childhood, the complications of racial and gender politics or of war are only distractions. The class structure of the 1950s, at least the class structure of the middle-class working white family, serves as Moore's rhetorical point of origin. In his efforts to reconstruct that utopian, prelapsarian state, the interference of economic and cultural history must be bracketed.

In Moore's efforts to construct a radical nostalgia, he resorts to various techniques of the more reactionary restorative narrative—an emphasis on the purity of origins, a dismissal of contrary evidence or complicating issues, and a reliance on conspiracy fantasies to craft blame for the current state of affairs. It would be hard to imagine a powerful or persuasive narrative along the lines Moore lays out without the use of these restorative techniques. A more nuanced view of historic, economic, and cultural relations would render his polemic toothless and his efforts to force open a transgressive and reflective space less effective. Moore's reliance on origins, selective history, and conspiracy theories may be more about the limits of his rhetorical style than an indictment of his politics.

His politics, however, do come into some question after a closer viewing of the origins of his nostalgic utopia. Moore's reconstruction of his past is powerfully connected to images of fathers. Fathers or father figures loom large in Moore's nostalgic rhetoric, and it is notable how often Moore refers to his father as the foundation of his idyllic childhood home throughout his films. The father stands as the primary moral figure in Moore's films, and quite explicitly in *Capitalism* we see the distinction between good fathers and bad fathers as Moore seeks to reground the nation's morality in the prelapsarian utopia of his childhood imaginings. A careful reading of Moore's father obsession in *Capitalism* reveals a close parallel with Jacques Lacan's notions of the different forms of the father. For Lacan, the real father, the actual physical father, is recast in two other, more powerful forms: the imaginary and the symbolic fathers. The imaginary father is a fantasy created around the dead father and can take the form of either the "good father," who embodies virtue and protection, or the "bad father," who is the source of privation and terror. An even more abstracted notion of father occurs in Lacan's conception of the symbolic father, who exists as a fundamental component of the structural order of society and, as Joshua Gunn puts it, "as a legislative function articulates the 'rule of law.'"[38] Moore's nostalgic construction of the father uses all three forms in a carefully constructed appeal for the return to the idealized childhood home of the imaginary father and the equating of this imaginary father with a return of the moral order of the symbolic father.

In the first of Moore's nostalgic moments, the imaginary father provides the foundation for not only the home but also the nation as a whole. "Dad had a secure job and mom could work if she wanted but didn't have to." In this first phase of the film, Moore utilizes the imaginary father as a generic and open rhetorical figure whose presence brings security, prosperity, and strength to the family and, in that way, to the country as a whole. Visually, this is underscored by the numerous generic images of the 1950s father rapidly edited into the narrative sequence. These images are not so much of Moore's father as of the generic, symbolic father figure complete with sweater, bowling ball, and pipe.

In the film's second nostalgic movement, we view the world through the eyes of Moore's real father, and yet, even in this appearance of Moore's father, he remains more imaginary than real. While Moore's father offers a few recollections of his days in the now dismantled plant and some regret, lamenting, "I'm sorry to see it go," it is Moore who offers the more nostalgic recollections. "I remember Mom bringing us kids here to pick you up . . . we'd see you come down the ramp and we got real excited each time we saw you." The real father is here mainly as a rhetorical prop to provide credence to the imaginary father figure Moore continues to see as the moral center of his childhood universe, and in some ways the aged and wizened figure of Moore's father suggests a parallel to the destroyed ruins of the factory in which he worked and, by the film's account, which gave him his identity and importance. In *Capitalism*, Moore seeks to recover the moral authority of the father by reconstructing the time in which the father was vital and potent. The fall of the real father from this position of authority and potency underscores the film's narrative of the "lapse," and the lament of Moore and his father at the site of the former ACDelco plant underscores the degree to which the father has fallen. Thus, one might argue, the appearance of Moore's real father actually serves to reinforce a sense that the imaginary father has replaced the "dead" real father, and it is the imaginary father who provides hope of a return to the prelapsarian idealized world.

The remainder of the film entails a search for the imaginary father in American history. Dr. Jonas Salk, for instance, is portrayed as a moral authority in large part because he eschewed the potential gains of capitalism and instead insisted on giving away the polio vaccine for free. One of the shots of Salk shows him with his large family, and Moore says, "This man could have been rich many times over had he sold his vaccine to a pharmaceutical company. But he thought his talents should be used for the greater good and the decent salary he made as a doctor and a research professor was enough for him to live a comfortable life." Salk and the other imaginary fathers from history rise as essential figures in our hopes for salvation from the postlapsarian world, their importance echoing Lacan's declaration that "this imaginary father, it is he, and not the real father, who is the foundation of the providential image of God."[39] Moore's uncle also serves as an imaginary father in the battle between the unions and General Motors, which signals the film's most optimistic note.

Perhaps the most potent rhetorical imaginary father emerges at the film's conclusion. Roosevelt arrives in filmic form at the conclusion of *Capitalism* to provide the moral authority necessary to open a space in which capitalism can be openly challenged politically. The rhetorical effort to pit democracy against capitalism is tied in large part to the moral authority invoked by the words of Roosevelt, and in this way, the former president becomes the embodiment of the Progressive movement. The "second Bill of Rights" presented by Roosevelt suggests a powerful directive from a fallen father, but in the nostalgic narrative of Moore's film, it is this alternative moral logic that suggests a route back to the prelapsarian world of prosperity, solidarity, and clarity. It is also most clearly in the figure of Roosevelt that we see the conflation of the imaginary, idealized father figure with the legislative, ordering power of the symbolic father who appears to grant right and protections for the nation.

Moore's reliance on father figures as the primary—indeed, in some ways, sole—arbiters of political morality is troubling. The figure of the father stands not only as the foundation of Moore's nostalgic utopia but also as the only figure with the authority to open a space for reflection on the current "lapsed" state of the world. This yearning for a father figure to return and lead us back to our home has the potential to foreclose the possibility of a creative space of reflection, since we are waiting for our leader rather than seeking a new path ourselves. As Gunn observes, "An ideology of paternal sovereignty is problematic because it promotes the concentration of political power into a single figure or leader."[40] The collapse of imaginary father into the symbolic father whose authority undergirds our social order also suggests a kind of infantilizing nostalgia, one in which our hope lies not in a populist eruption of democratic creativity, but in the potential for a new father figure to arise—perhaps Obama, whose election is used to signal the film's final optimistic turn.[41]

Implications

In her genealogy of the rhetoric of nostalgia, Kimberly Smith observes the ways in which nostalgia arose as a site of resistance to industrialization but has since developed a complex relationship to notions of modernity and progress. Nostalgia, Smith notes, possesses both conservative and progressive potentials, and in this way, the analysis of what she calls "nostalgic tropes" may "give us better insight into the political role of memory—not simply as an escape from reality or a source of social cohesion, but as an enduring wellspring of transformational politics."[42]

My reading of Michael Moore's *Capitalism: A Love Story* suggests the importance of embracing these complexities. While it would be easy to demonstrate that Moore's film is either radical and reflective or reactionary and restorative, what is more important is that the film's rhetoric demonstrates both dimensions of nostalgia; indeed, these different dimensions can often be read in the same filmic element. The ambivalence of Moore's nostalgic rhetoric—being both radical and reactionary—is not so much a failure as a reminder that our invocations of the past are rarely simple or unidirectional. The film's nostalgic rhetoric provides the viewer with a vision of a return to an idyllic past while simultaneously deferring this return until the emergence of a new father figure to lead us.

I suspect that these nostalgic threads are evident in most, perhaps all, of Moore's earlier works. Certainly, nostalgia is evident in Moore's *Roger & Me*—a film nostalgically referenced in *Capitalism*—but Moore's reliance on the 1950s as a source of both nostalgia and moral authority seems evident in most of his other films as well. It might also be useful to consider how other documentary filmmakers engage the politics of nostalgia. It seems likely that a close reading of the films of, for example, Errol Morris would render a different, though perhaps no less nostalgic, rhetorical stance. The tendency of many documentary films to engage the past, whether the historical epics of Ken Burns or the more localized records of resistance of Barbara Kopple, seems to call for more careful rhetorical attention. There may also be interesting rhetorical constructions of public memory within the recent spate of mockumentaries. Alexandra Juhasz and Jesse Lerner argue, "Documentary lends itself to a nostalgia of authenticity, while fake documentary acts to inoculate against such easy revival and reclamation of what are, always, only images."[43] It seems that the rhetorical construction of public memory within documentaries, and specifically the use of nostalgia within these constructions, may be a fruitful area for future investigation.

Thought of in terms of the broader study of public memory, this analysis of Michael Moore's *Capitalism* urges care in our engagement with nostalgia. Scholars of public memory have long insisted that our memories of the past are always framed in relation to the needs of the present, and nostalgia is one way of framing our relation to the past, an affective orientation that situates the past in ideal terms and our present as one of yearning and loss. From a rhetorical perspective, then, nostalgia is a way of inviting audiences to share this framework, of collectively orienting themselves to the past. This reading of Moore's rhetorical presentation suggests that the invocation of nostalgia is rarely simple, our feelings of loss in relation to the past are rarely uncomplicated, and our view of an idyllic past rarely urges us in one direction.

Notes

1. Claudia Puig, "'Capitalism' Markets in Impassioned Outrage," review of *Capitalism: A Love Story*, *USA Today*, September 24, 2009.

2. Amy Biancolli, "Moore's Stirring 'Story,'" review of *Capitalism: A Love Story*, *San Francisco Chronicle*, October 2, 2009, F1.

3. Bill Nichols, *Introduction to Documentary* (Bloomington: Indiana University, 2001), 69.

4. Thomas W. Benson and Brian J. Snee, "New Political Documentary: Rhetoric, Propaganda, and Civic Prospect," in *The Rhetoric of the New Political Documentary*, eds. Thomas W. Benson and Brian J. Snee (Carbondale: Southern Illinois University Press, 2008), 3.

5. See, for example, Manohla Dargis, "Greed Is Good? He Begs to Differ," *New York Times*, September 23, 2009, C1; Ann Hornaday, "Moore's Passion Yields Dividends in 'Capitalism,'" *Washington Post*, October 2, 2009, C4.

6. Svetlana Boym, *The Future of Nostalgia* (New York: Basic Books, 2001), xviii.

7. Alastair Bonnett, *Left in the Past: Radicalism and the Politics of Nostalgia* (New York: Continuum, 2010), 20.

8. David Lowenthal, "Nostalgia Tells It like It Wasn't," in *The Imagined Past*, eds. Christopher Shaw and Malcolm Chase (Manchester, UK: Manchester University Press, 1989), 21.

9. Bonnett, *Left in the Past*, 3.

10. Aaron Santesso, *A Careful Longing: The Poetics and Problems of Nostalgia* (Newark: University of Delaware Press, 2006), 15.

11. Malcolm Chase and Christopher Shaw, "The Dimensions of Nostalgia," in Shaw and Chase, *Imagined Past*, 1, 4.

12. Santesso, *Careful Longing*, 15.

13. On this point, see Chase and Shaw, "Dimensions of Nostalgia," 6.

14. Stuart Tannock, "Nostalgia Critique," *Cultural Studies* 9 (1995): 453–64.

15. Susan Stewart, *On Longing: Narratives of the Miniature, the Gigantic, the Souvenir, the Collection* (Durham, NC: Duke University Press, 1993), 23.

16. Karl Marx, "The Eighteenth Brumaire of Louis Bonaparte, in *Karl Marx: Surveys from Exile; Political Writings*, vol. 2 (New York: Penguin, 1973), 149.

17. Frederic Jameson, *Postmodernism; or, The Logic of Late Capitalism* (Durham, NC: Duke University Press, 2003), 296; Richard Sennett, *The Fall of Public Man* (New York: Alfred Knopf, 1977), 259.

18. Sean Scanlan, "Introduction: Nostalgia," *Iowa Journal of Cultural Studies* 5 (2009), http://www.uiowa.edu/~ijcs/nostalgia/nostint.htm.

19. Christopher Lasch, "The Politics of Nostalgia," *Harper's Magazine*, November 1984, 67.

20. Timothy Barney, "When We Was Red: *Good Bye Lenin!* and Nostalgia for the 'Everyday GDR,'" *Communication and Critical/Cultural Studies* 6 (2009): 132–33.

21. Ibid., 133.

22. Bonnett, *Left in the Past*, 3, 8.

23. Numerous rhetorical scholars have engaged the contours of nostalgia, including Greg Dickinson, "Memories for Sale: Nostalgia and the Construction of Identity in Old Pasadena," *Quarterly Journal of Speech* 83 (1997): 1–27; Shawn J. Parry-Giles and Trevor Parry-Giles, "Collective Memory, Political Nostalgia, and the Rhetorical Presidency: Bill Clinton's Commemoration of the March on Washington, August 28, 1998," *Quarterly Journal of Speech* 86 (2000): 417–37; and Ron Von Burg and Paul E. Johnson, "Yearning for a Past That Never Was: Baseball, Steroids, and the Anxiety of the American Dream," *Critical Studies in Media Communication* 26 (2009): 351–71.

24. See, for example, the essays appearing in my *Framing Public Memory* (Tuscaloosa: University of Alabama Press, 2004).

25. Bonnett, *Left in the Past*, 44.

26. Marouf Hasian, "Nostalgic Longings, Memories of the 'Good War,' and Cinematic Representations in *Saving Private Ryan*," *Critical Studies in Media Communication* 18 (2001): 341.

27. Jennifer Ladino, "Longing for Wonderland: Nostalgia for Nature in Post-Frontier America," *Iowa Journal of Cultural Studies* 5 (2004), accessed September 5, 2010, http://www.uiowa.edu/~ijcs/nostalgia/ladino.htm.

28. Christine Spengler, *Screening Nostalgia: Populuxe Props and Technicolor Aesthetics in Contemporary American Film* (New York: Berghahn Books, 2009), 62.

29. Daniel Marcus, *Happy Days and Wonder Years: The Fifties and the Sixties in Contemporary Cultural Politics* (New Brunswick, NJ: Rutgers University Press, 2004), 41.

30. Bonnett, *Left in the Past*, 10.

31. Boym, *Future of Nostalgia*, 41.

32. Bonnett, *Left in the Past*, 10.

33. Ibid., 31.

34. Boym, *Future of Nostalgia*, 43.

35. Charles J. G. Griffin, "Jedidiah Morse and the Bavarian Illuminati: An Essay in the Rhetoric of Conspiracy," *Communication Studies* 39 (1988): 293–303.

36. G. Thomas Goodnight and John Poulakos, "Conspiracy Rhetoric: From Pragmatism to Fantasy in Public Discourse," *Western Journal of Speech Communication* 45 (1981): 307.

37. Boym, *Future of Nostalgia*, 42.

38. Jacques Lacan, *The Ethics of Psychoanalysis, 1959–1960: The Seminar of Jacques Lacan, Book VII*, ed. Jacques-Alain Miller, trans. Dennis Porter (New York: W. W. Norton & Company, 1997); Joshua Gunn, "Father Trouble: Staging Sovereignty in Spielberg's *War of the Worlds*," *Critical Studies in Media Communication* 25 (2008): 10.

39. Lacan, *Ethics of Psychoanalysis*, 308.

40. Gunn, "Father Trouble," 19.

41. Given the consistent use of father figures in Moore's films, a more sophisticated student of Lacanian psychoanalysis undoubtedly could provide a nuanced and powerful reading of the filmmaker's work.

42. Kimberly K. Smith, "Mere Nostalgia: Notes on a Progressive Paratheory," *Rhetoric and Public Affairs* 3 (2000): 523.

43. Alexandra Juhasz and Jesse Lerner, introduction to *F Is for Phony: Fake Documentary and Truth's Undoing*, edited by Alexandra Juhasz and Jesse Lerner (Minneapolis: University of Minnesota Press, 2006), 15.

Bibliography

Contributors

Index

Bibliography

Acland, Charles R. "Moore Than This: Fahrenheit 9/11, Screen Numbers, and Political Community." *Environment & Planning: Society & Space* 22 (2004): 901–6.

———. *Youth, Murder, Spectacle: The Cultural Politics of "Youth in Crisis."* Boulder, CO: Westview Press, 1995.

Agnew, John. "Foolish Leader or Failing Hegemony? The Insight and Confusion of Fahrenheit 9/11." *Environment & Planning: Society & Space* 22 (2004): 927–29.

Ahmed, Sara. *The Cultural Politics of Emotion.* New York: Routledge, 2004.

Al-Arian, Abdullah A. "Michael Moore's 'Fahrenheit 9/11': A Searing Portrait of Bush's America." *Washington Report on Middle East Affairs* 23, no. 7 (2004): 48–49.

Alexander, Jeffrey C. "Toward a Theory of Cultural Trauma." In *Cultural Trauma and Collective Identity*, edited by Jeffrey C. Alexander, Ron Eyerman, Bernhard Giesen, Neil J. Smelser and Piotr Sztompka, 1–30. Berkeley: University of California Press, 2004.

Alexander, William. *Film on the Left: American Documentary Film from 1931 to 1942.* Princeton, NJ: Princeton University Press, 1981.

Altieri, Charles. *The Particulars of Rapture: An Aesthetics of the Affects.* Ithaca, NY: Cornell University Press, 2003.

Anderson, Carolyn, and Thomas W. Benson. *Documentary Dilemmas: Frederick Wiseman's "Titicut Follies."* Carbondale: Southern Illinois University Press, 1991.

Anderson, James. "Saving the World from American Hegemony." *Environment & Planning: Society & Space* 22 (2004): 911–14.

Ansen, David. "Michael Moore's Cure for What Ails Us." Review of *Sicko*. *Newsweek*, June 22, 2007. http://www.newsweek.com/david-ansen-reviews -sicko-102123/.

Aristotle. *Poetics*. Translated by Ingram Bywater. New York: Random House, 1954.

Armstrong, David. "Everyman Makes Waves." Review of *Roger & Me*. *San Francisco Examiner*, January 12, 1990, C90.

Arnold, Carroll C. "Reflections on American Public Discourse." *Central States Speech Journal* 28 (1977): 73–85.

Aufderheide, Patricia. "The Changing Documentary Marketplace." *Cineaste* 30, no. 3 (2005): 24–28.

———. *Documentary Film: A Very Short Introduction*. New York: Oxford University Press, 2007.

———. "Your Country, My Country: How Films about the Iraq War Construct Publics." *Framework: The Journal of Cinema and Media* 48, no. 2 (2007): 56–65.

Barilli, Renato. *A Course on Aesthetics*. Translated by Karen E. Pinkus. Minneapolis: University of Minnesota Press, 1993.

Barney, Timothy. "When We Was Red: *Good Bye Lenin!* and Nostalgia for the 'Everyday GDR.'" *Communication and Critical/Cultural Studies* 6 (2009): 132–51.

Barnouw, Eric. *Documentary: A History of the Non-fiction Film*. 3rd ed. New York: Oxford University Press, 1993.

Barry, Ann Marie Seward. *Visual Intelligence: Perception, Image, and Manipulation in Visual Communication*. Albany: State University of New York Press, 1997.

Barsam, Richard Meran. *Nonfiction Film: A Critical History*. Bloomington: Indiana University Press, 1992.

Barthes, Roland. *Image–Music–Text*. Translated by Stephen Heath. New York: Hill and Wang, 1977.

Bazin, Andre. "Ontology of the Photographic Image." In *What Is Cinema?*, edited by Hugh Gray, 9–16. Berkeley: University of California Press, 1967.

Beattie, Keith. *Documentary Screens: Non-Fiction Film and Television*. London: Palgrave, 2004.

Behrens, Lawrence. "The Argument in Film: Applying Rhetorical Theory to Film Criticism." *Journal of University Film and Video Association* 31 (1979): 3–11.

Benson, Thomas W. "Another Shooting in Cowtown." *Quarterly Journal of Speech* 67 (1981): 347–406.

———. "*Joe*: An Essay in the Rhetorical Criticism of Film." *Journal of Popular Culture* 8 (1974): 608–18.

——. "Looking for the Public in the Popular: Collective Memory and the Hollywood Blacklist." In *The Terministic Screen: Rhetorical Perspectives on Film*, edited by David Blakesley, 129–45. Carbondale: Southern Illinois University Press, 2003.

——. "Respecting the Reader." *Quarterly Journal of Speech* 72 (1986): 197–204.

——. "The Rhetorical Structure of Frederick Wiseman's *High School*." *Communication Monographs* 47 (1980): 233–61.

——. "The Rhetorical Structure of Frederick Wiseman's *Primate*." *Quarterly Journal of Speech* 71 (1985): 204–17.

——. "The Senses of Rhetoric: A Topical System for Critics." *Central States Speech Journal* 29 (1978): 237–50.

——. "Thinking through Film: Hollywood Remembers the Blacklist." In *Rhetoric and Community*, edited by J. Michael Hogan, 218–55. Columbia: University of South Carolina Press, 1998.

Benson, Thomas W., and Carolyn Anderson. *Reality Fictions: The Films of Frederick Wiseman*. 2nd ed. Carbondale: Southern Illinois University Press, 2002.

——. "The Rhetorical Structure of Frederick Wiseman's *Model*." *Journal of Film & Video* 36, no. 4 (1984): 30–40.

——. "The Ultimate Technology: Frederick Wiseman's *Missile*." In *Communication and the Culture of Technology*, edited by Martin J. Medhurst, Alberto Gonzalez, and Tarla Rai Peterson, 257–83. Pullman: Washington State University Press, 1990.

Benson, Thomas W., and Brian J. Snee. "New Political Documentary: Rhetoric, Propaganda, and Civic Prospect." In *The Rhetoric of the New Political Documentary*, edited by Thomas W. Benson and Brian J. Snee, 1–23. Carbondale: Southern Illinois University Press, 2008.

——, eds. *The Rhetoric of the New Political Documentary*. Carbondale: Southern Illinois University Press, 2008.

Berardinelli, James. Review of *Sicko*. *ReelViews*, June 22, 2007. http://www.reelviews.net/php_review_template.php?identifier=480.

Bercovitch, Sacvan. *The American Jeremiad*. Madison: University of Wisconsin Press, 1978.

Berg, Chris. "Big Government: A Love Story." *Institute of Public Affairs Review* 61, no. 3 (2009): 19.

Bernstein, Matthew. "Documentaphobia and Mixed Modes: Michael Moore's *Roger and Me*." In *Documenting the Documentary: Close Readings of Documentary Film and Video*, edited by Barry Keith Grant and Jeannette Sloniowski, 397–415. Detroit: Wayne State University Press, 1998.

———, ed. *Michael Moore: Filmmaker, Newsmaker, Cultural Icon.* Ann Arbor: University of Michigan Press, 2010.

———. "Roger and Me: Documentaphobia and Mixed Modes." *Journal of Film & Video* 46, no. 1 (1994): 3–18.

Bernstein, Richard. "'Roger and Me': Redefining the Limits." Review of *Roger & Me. New York Times*, February 1, 1990.

Bettig, Ronald V., and Jeanne Lynn Hall. "Outfoxing the Myth of the Liberal Media." In *The Rhetoric of the New Political Documentary*, edited by Thomas W. Benson and Brian J. Snee, 173–201. Carbondale: Southern Illinois University Press, 2008.

Biancolli, Amy. "A Fiercely Effective Call to Arms." Review of *Sicko. Houston Chronicle*, June 29, 2007. http://www.chron.com/entertainment/movies /article/Sicko-re-release-1555210.php.

———. "Moore's Stirring 'Story.'" Review of *Capitalism: A Love Story. San Francisco Chronicle*, October 2, 2009.

Blakesley, David, ed. *The Terministic Screen: Rhetorical Perspectives on Film.* Carbondale: Southern Illinois University Press, 2003.

Blitzer, Wolf. *The Situation Room.* CNN, July 9, 2007. http://transcripts.cnn .com/TRANSCRIPTS/0707/09/sitroom.03.html.

Boltanski, Luc, and Eve Chiapello. *The New Spirit of Capitalism.* Translated by Gregory Elliott. New York: Verso, 2007.

Bonnett, Alastair. *Left in the Past: Radicalism and the Politics of Nostalgia.* New York: Continuum, 2010.

Bonnstetter, Beth E., and Brian L. Ott. "(Re)Writing Mary Sue: *Écriture Féminine* and the Performance of Subjectivity." *Text and Performance Quarterly* 31, no. 4 (2011): 342–67.

Borda, Jennifer L. "Documentary Dialectics or Dogmatism? *Fahrenhype 9/11, Celsius 41.11,* and the New Politics of Documentary Film." In *The Rhetoric of New Political Documentary*, edited by Thomas W. Benson and Brian J. Snee, 54–77. Carbondale: Southern Illinois University Press, 2008.

———. "Feminist Critique and Cinematic Counterhistory in the Documentary *With Babies and Banners," Women's Studies in Communication* 28, no. 2 (2005): 157–82.

———. "Negotiating Feminist Politics in the Third Wave: Labor Struggles and Solidarity in *Live Nude Girls Unite!" Communication Quarterly* 57, no. 2 (2009): 117–35.

———. "Portrait of a Woman Artist: The Rhetorical Construction of *Camille Claudel* as a Tragic Feminist Heroine," *Feminist Media Studies* 9, no. 2 (2009): 227–42.

———. *Women Labor Activists in the Movies: Nine Depictions of Workplace Organizers, 1954–2005.* Jefferson, NC: McFarland, 2011.

———. "Working-Class Women, Protofeminist Performance, and Resistant Ruptures in the Movie Musical *The Pajama Game*," *Text and Performance Quarterly* 30, no. 3 (2010): 227–46.

Bormann, Ernest. "Fetching Good out of Evil: A Rhetorical Use of Calamity." *Quarterly Journal of Speech* 63 (1977): 130–39.

Box Office Mojo. "Documentary: 1982–Present." Internet Movie Data Base. Accessed October 20, 2014. http://www.boxofficemojo.com/genres/chart/?id=documentary.htm.

———. "Documentary–Political: 1982–Present." Internet Movie Database. Accessed August 16, 2011. http://boxofficemojo.com/genres/chart/?id=politicaldoc.htm.

———. "Sicko." Internet Movie Database. Accessed August 16, 2011. http://boxofficemojo.com/movies/?id=sicko.htm.

Boym, Svetlana. *The Future of Nostalgia.* New York: Basic Books, 2001.

Brady, Emily, and Arto Haapala. "Melancholy as an Aesthetic Emotion." *Contemporary Aesthetics* 1 (2003). http://hdl.handle.net/2027/spo.7523862.0001.006.

Bratsis, Peter. "The Construction of Corruption, or Rules of Separation and Illusions of Purity in Bourgeois Societies." *Social Text* 21, no. 4 (2003): 9–33.

Briley, Ron. "Fahrenheit 9/11: Michael Moore Heats It Up." *Film & History* 35, no. 2 (2005): 11–12.

Brown, Megan. *The Cultural Work of Corporations.* New York: Palgrave Macmillan, 2009.

Bruzzi, Stella. *New Documentary.* 2nd ed. New York: Routledge, 2006.

Buckley, Cara Louise, and Brian L. Ott. "Fashion(able/ing) Selves: Consumption, Identity, and *Sex and the City*." In *It's Not TV: Watching HBO in the Post-Television Era*, edited by Marc Leverette, Brian L. Ott, and Cara Louise Buckley, 209–26. New York: Routledge, 2008.

Burke, Edmund. *A Philosophical Enquiry into the Origin of Our Ideas of the Sublime and Beautiful.* New York: Harper & Brothers, 1844.

Burke, Kenneth. *Attitudes toward History.* 3rd ed. Berkeley: University of California Press, 1984.

———. *A Grammar of Motives.* Berkeley: University of California Press, 1969.

———. "Four Master Tropes." In *A Grammar of Motives*, 503–17. Berkeley: University of California Press, 1969.

————. *The Rhetoric of Motives*. Berkeley: University of California Press, 1969.

Burr, Ty. "Moore at His Feverish Best in Hilarious, Sobering 'Sicko.'" Review of *Sicko*. *Boston Globe*, June 29, 2007. http://www.boston.com/ae/movies/ articles/2007/06/29/moore_at_his_feverish_best_in_hilarious_sobering _sicko/.

Butler, Judith. *Precarious Life: The Power of Mourning and Violence*. New York: Verso, 2004.

Callenbach, Ernest. "*Sicko*: Ernest Callenbach Applauds a Witty Documentary Broadside." Review of *Sicko*. *Film Quarterly* 61, no. 2 (2007): 18–20.

Carlson, A. Cheree. "Limitations on the Comic Frame: Some Witty American Women of the Nineteenth Century." *Quarterly Journal of Speech* 74 (1988): 310–22.

Carr, Jay. "Michael Moore on the Attack Again." *Boston Globe*, April 10, 1998.

Chaloupka, William. "What's the Matter with Us? The Meaning of Post-11/2 Politics." *Theory & Event* 8, no. 2 (2005).

Chanan, Michael. *The Politics of Documentary*. London: British Film Institute, 2007.

Charity, Tom. "'Sicko' a Tonic, Even with Flaws." Review of *Sicko*. *CNN*, June 29, 2007, http://edition.cnn.com/2007/SHOWBIZ/Movies/06/28 /review.sicko/index.html?iref=newssearch.

Chase, Malcolm, and Christopher Shaw. "The Dimensions of Nostalgia." In *The Imagined Past*, edited by Malcolm Chase and Christopher Shaw, 1–17. Manchester, UK: Manchester University Press, 1989.

Chomsky, Noam. *Profit over People: Neoliberalism and Global Order*. New York: Seven Stories Press, 1999.

Christensen, Christian. "The Politics of a Political Film: Thoughts on *Fahrenheit 9/11*." *Screen Education* 37 (2004): 20–24.

Clore, Gerald, and Stanley Colcombe. "The Parallel Worlds of Affective Concepts and Feelings." In *The Psychology of Evaluation: Affective Processes in Cognition and Emotion*, edited by Jochen Musch and Karl Christoph Klauer, 335–69. Mahwah: Lawrence Erlbaum Associates, 2003.

"CNN's Response to Michael Moore." *CNN*, July 15, 2007. http://articles. cnn.com/2007-07-15/entertainment/moore.gupta_1_sicko-michael -moore-cnn-programs?_s=PM:SHOWBIZ.

Coffman, Elizabeth. "Documentary and Collaboration: Placing the Camera in the Community." *Journal of Film and Video* 61, no. 1 (2009): 62–78.

Cohan, Carley, and Gary Crowdus. "Reflections on *Roger & Me*, Michael Moore, and His Critics." *Cineaste* 17, no. 4 (1990): 25–30.

Cooper, Rand Richards. "At War." *Commonweal*, August 13, 2004.

————. "Realpolitik." *Commonweal*, November 22, 2002, 18.

Corliss, Mary. "A First Look at *Fahrenheit 9/11*." Review of *Fahrenheit 9/11*. *Time*, May 17, 2004. http://www.time.com/time/arts/article/0,8599,638819,00 .html#ixzz0y775XCdW.

Corliss, Richard. "What's Michael Moore Doing This Election?" Michael Moore website. Accessed June 15, 2010. http://www.michaelmoore .com/words/mike-in-the-news/whats-michael-moore-doing-this -election.

Corner, John, ed. Preface to *Documentary and the Mass Media*, vii–xiv. Baltimore: Edward Arnold, 1986.

Corrigan, Timothy. *The Essay Film: From Montaigne, after Marker*. New York: Oxford University Press, 2011.

Cowie, Elizabeth. *Recording Reality: Desiring the Real*. Minneapolis: University of Minnesota Press, 2011.

Curiel, Jonathan. "Moore Captures US Zeitgeist/'Bowling for Columbine' Explains Violence." Review of *Bowling for Columbine*. *San Francisco Chronicle*, October 18, 2002. http://www.sfgate.com/entertainment/article /Moore-captures-U-S-zeitgeist-Bowling-for-2761485.php.

Cushman, John. "Nike Pledges to End Child Labor and Apply US Rules Abroad." *New York Times*, May 13, 1998.

Dargis, Manohla. "Greed Is Good? He Begs to Differ." *New York Times*, September 23, 2009.

Darsey, James. "The Legend of Eugene Debs: Prophetic *Ethos* as Radical Argument." *Quarterly Journal of Speech* 74 (1988): 434–52.

———. *The Prophetic Tradition and Radical Rhetoric in America*. New York: New York University Press, 1997.

Dear, Michael. "*Fahrenheit 9/11*: The Temperature at Which Regimes Burn?" *Environment & Planning: Society & Space* 22 (2004): 924–26.

Deming, Mark. "Michael Moore: Full Biography." *New York Times*. Accessed July 27, 2011. http://movies.nytimes.com/person/103383/Michael-Moore /biography.

Denby, David. "Do No Harm: 'Sicko' and 'Evening.'" Review of *Sicko*. *New Yorker*, July 2, 2007. http://www.newyorker.com/magazine/2007/07/02 /do-no-harm.

———. "George and Me." Review of *Fahrenheit 9/11*. *New Yorker*, June 28, 2004. http://www.newyorker.com/archive/2004/06/28/.040628crci_cinema ?currentPage=2#ixzz0y72CEIor.

Dickinson, Greg. "Memories for Sale: Nostalgia and the Construction of Identity in Old Pasadena." *Quarterly Journal of Speech* 83 (1997): 1–27.

Disch, Lisa Jane. "Minnesota and the 'Populism' of Political Opposition." *Theory & Event* 3, no. 2 (1999).

Doel, Marcus A. "A Comedy of Terrors." *Environment & Planning: Society & Space* 22 (2004): 915–18.

Doherty, Thomas. "Review of *Michael Moore's "Fahrenheit 9/11": How One Film Divided a Nation*, by Robert Brent Toplin." *Historical Journal of Film, Radio & Television* 27, no. 3 (2007): 413–15.

Donato, Raffaele, and Martin Scorsese. "Docufictions: An Interview with Martin Scorsese on Documentary Film." *Film History: An International Journal* 19, no. 2 (2007): 199–207.

Duncan, Hugh Dalziel. *Communication and Social Order.* New York: Oxford University Press, 1962.

Ebert, Roger. "Attacks on 'Roger & Me' Completely Miss Point of Film." Roger Ebert's Journal, *Chicago Sun Tribune*, February 11, 1990. http://rogerebert.suntimes.com/apps/pbcs.dll/article?AID=/19900211/COMMENTARY/22010306.

———. Review of *Roger & Me. Dog Eat Dog Films*, December 1989. Accessed February 2, 2011. http://dogeatdog.michaelmoore.com/ebert.html.

Economou, Rose. "Documentaries Raise Questions Journalists Should Ask Themselves." *Nieman Reports* 58, no. 3 (2004): 81.

Edelstein, Alan. "Camera Obscura: Making and Breaking Images in Taliban-Era Afghanistan." *Transition* 13, no. 3 (2008): 120–37.

Ehrenreich, Barbara. *Bright-Sided: How Positive Thinking Is Undermining America.* New York: Picador, 2010.

Elliott, David. "Burning Point." Review of *Fahrenheit 9/11. San Diego Union-Tribune*, June 24, 2004.

Ellis, Jack C., and Betsy A. McLane. *A New History of Documentary Film.* New York: Continuum, 2005.

Eng, David L. "Melancholia in the Late Twentieth Century." *Signs* 25 (2000): 1275–81.

Fabj, Valeria. "Intolerance, Forgiveness, and Promise in the Rhetoric of Conversion: Italian Women Defy the Mafia." *Quarterly Journal of Speech* 84 (1998): 190–208.

Fawcett, Marlowe. "Fear and Goading." Review of *Bowling for Columbine. Times Literary Supplement*, December 13, 2002, 20.

Feagin, Susan L. "Time and Timing." In *Passionate Views: Film, Cognition, and Emotion*, edited by Carl Plantinga and Greg M. Smith, 168–79. Baltimore: Johns Hopkins University Press, 1999.

Fierman, Daniel. "Ready for Moore?" *Entertainment Weekly*, May 25, 2007. http://www.ew.com/ew/article/0,,20040352,00.html.

Finn, Patrick. Review of *Bowling for Columbine. Film & History* 33, no. 1 (2003): 65–66.

Fischer, Lucy. "Documentary Film and the Discourse of Historical/Hysterical Narrative." In *Documenting the Documentary: Close Readings of Documentary Film and Video*, edited by Barry Keith Grant and Jeannette Sloniowski, 333–43. Detroit: Wayne State University Press, 1998.

Fish, Stanley. "Neoliberalism and Higher Education." *Opinionator* (blog). *New York Times*, March 8, 2009. http://opinionator.blogs.nytimes.com/2009/03/08/neoliberalism-and-higher-education/.

Fisher, Walter. "Reaffirmation and Subversion of the American Dream." *Quarterly Journal of Speech* 59 (1973): 160–67.

Fleischmann, Aloys. "The Rhetorical Function of Comedy in Michael Moore's *Fahrenheit 9/11*." *Mosaic: A Journal for the Interdisciplinary Study of Literature* 40 (2007): 69–85.

Fraser, Laura. "In 'Roger & Me,' Michael Moore Plays Fast and Loose with the Facts." *San Francisco Guardian*, January 17, 1990.

Frentz, Thomas S. "Mass Media as Rhetorical Narration." The Van Zelst Lecture in Communication, Northwestern University School of Speech, Evanston, IL, May 1984.

———. "The Rhetoric of 'Rocky': Part II." *Western Journal of Speech Communication* 42 (1978): 231–40.

Frentz, Thomas S., and Thomas B. Farrell. "Conversion of America's Consciousness: The Rhetoric of *The Exorcist*." *Quarterly Journal of Speech* 61, no. 1 (1975): 40–47.

Frentz, Thomas S., and Janice Hocker Rushing. "Integrating Ideology and Archetype in Rhetorical Criticism, Part II: A Case Study of *Jaws*." *Quarterly Journal of Speech* 79, no. 1 (1993): 61–81.

———. "The Frankenstein Myth in Contemporary Cinema." In *Critical Questions: Invention, Creativity, and the Criticism of Discourse and Media*, edited by William Nothstine, Carol Blair, and Gary Copeland, 155–82. New York: St. Martin's Press, 1993.

———. "'Mother's Not Herself Today': Myth and Spectacle in *The Matrix*," *Critical Studies in Media Communication* 19 (March 2002): 64–86.

———. "The Technological Shadow in *The Manchurian Candidate*." In *Communication and the Culture of Technology*, edited by Martin J. Medhurst, Alberto Gonzalez, and Tarla Rai Peterson, 239–56. Pullman: Washington State University Press, 1990.

Freud, Sigmund. "Mourning and Melancholia." In *The Freud Reader*, edited by Peter Gay, 584–88. New York: W. W. Norton & Company, 1989.

Gadamer, Hans-Georg. *Truth and Method*. Translated by Garrett Barden and John Cumming. New York: Continuum, 1975.

Gaines, Jane M. "Political Mimesis." In *Collecting Visible Evidence*, edited by Jane M. Gaines and Michael Renov, 84–102 (Minneapolis: University of Minnesota Press, 1999).

Gaines, Jane M., and Michael Renov, eds. *Collecting Visible Evidence*. Minneapolis: University of Minnesota Press, 1999.

Galloway, Dayna, Kenneth B. McAlpine, and Paul Harris. "From Michael Moore to JFK Reloaded: Towards a Working Model of Interactive Documentary." *Journal of Media Practice* 8, no. 3 (2007): 325–39.

Gates, Anita. "How the Other Half Lives." *New York Times*, December 29, 1996. Accessed July 27, 2011. http://www.nytimes.com/1996/12/29/books /how-the-other-half-lives.html?src=pm.

Germain, David. "Michael Moore: I May Quit Documentaries." *Huffington Post*, September 15, 2009. http://www.huffingtonpost.com/2009/09/15 /michael-moore-i-may-quit-_n_286854.html.

Golden, James L., Goodwin F. Berquist, and William Coleman. "Secular and Religious Conversion." In *The Rhetoric of Western Thought*, 4th ed., edited by James L. Golden, Goodwin F. Berquist, and William Coleman, 565–86. Dubuque, IA: Kendall-Hunt, 1989.

Goodnight, G. Thomas. "*The Passion of the Christ* Meets *Fahrenheit 9/11*: A Study in Celebrity Advocacy." *American Behavioral Scientist* 49 (2005): 410–35.

Goodnight, G. Thomas, and John Poulakos. "Conspiracy Rhetoric: From Pragmatism to Fantasy in Public Discourse." *Western Journal of Speech Communication* 45 (1981): 299–316.

Grant, Barry Keith, and Jeannette Sloniowski, eds. *Documenting the Documentary: Close Readings of Documentary Film and Video*. Detroit: Wayne State University Press, 1998.

Greene, Doyle. *The American Worker on Film: A Critical History, 1909–1999*. Jefferson, NC: McFarland, 2010.

Grierson, John. "The Documentary Idea." In *Nonfiction Film Theory and Criticism*, edited by Richard Meran Barsam, 84–94. New York: E. P. Dutton, 1976. Originally published as an essay in 1942.

Griffin, Charles J. G. "Jedidiah Morse and the Bavarian Illuminati: An Essay in the Rhetoric of Conspiracy." *Communication Studies* 39 (1988): 293–303.

———. "The Rhetoric of Form in Conversion Narratives." *Quarterly Journal of Speech* 76 (1990): 152–63.

Grindon, Leger. "Q & A: Poetics of the Documentary Film Interview." *Velvet Light Trap* 60 (2007): 4–12.

Gunn, Joshua. "Father Trouble: Staging Sovereignty in Spielberg's *War of the Worlds*." *Critical Studies in Media Communication* 25 (2008): 1–27.

———. "Maranatha." *Quarterly Journal of Speech* 98, no. 4 (2012): 359–85.

Gunn, Joshua, and Thomas Frentz. "Alchemical Rhetoric in *The Da Vinci Code.*" *Western Communication Journal* 72, no. 2 (2008): 1–25.

———. "Fighting for Father: *Fight Club* as Cinematic Psychosis." *Western Journal of Communication* 74 (May–June 2010): 269–91.

Gunn, Joshua, and Jenny Edbauer Rice. "About Face/Stuttering Discipline." *Communication and Critical/Cultural Studies* 6, no. 2 (2009): 215–19. doi:10.1080/14791420902868029.

Hafen, Susan. "Patriots in the Classroom: Performing Positionalities Post 9/11." *Communication & Critical/Cultural Studies* 6, no. 1 (2009): 61–83.

Hamill, Denis. "Moore's Message Delivered." Review of *Fahrenheit 9/11.* *New York Daily News*, June 29, 2004.

Hamm, Theodore. *The New Blue Media.* New York: New Press, 2008.

Hariman, Robert. *Political Style: The Artistry of Power.* Chicago: University of Chicago Press, 1995.

———. "Speaking of Evil." *Rhetoric & Public Affairs* 6, no. 3 (2003): 511–17.

Harman, Chris. "Theorizing Neoliberalism." *International Socialism* 117 (Winter 2008). http://www.isj.org.uk/index.php4?id=399&issue=117.

Harrington, John. *The Rhetoric of Film.* New York: Holt, Rinehart and Winston, 1973.

Harvey, David. *A Brief History of Neoliberalism.* New York: Oxford University Press, 2007.

Hasian, Marouf. "Nostalgic Longings, Memories of the "Good War," and Cinematic Representations in *Saving Private Ryan.*" *Critical Studies in Media Communication* 18 (2001): 338–58.

Hass, Janis. "*Sicko* Strikes a Chord." *Canadian Medical Association Journal* 177, no. 4 (2007): 379.

"Healthy, but Sore." *Taiwan Review* 58, no. 2 (2008): 1.

Higgins, Lynn A. "Documentary in an Age of Terror." *South Central Review* 22, no. 2 (2005): 20–38.

Hill, Charles A., and Marguerite Helmers, eds. *Defining Visual Rhetorics.* Mahwah, NJ: Lawrence Erlbaum, 2004.

Hinson, Hal. Review of *Roger & Me. Washington Post*, January 12, 1990. http://www.washingtonpost.com/wp-srv/style/longterm/movies/videos/rogermerhinson_a0a906.htm.

Hoberman, J. Review of *Roger & Me. Village Voice*, October 3, 1989. http://cinefiles.bampfa.berkeley.edu/cinefiles/DocDetail?docId=45719.

———. "They Aim to Please." Review of *Bowling for Columbine. Village Voice*, October 8, 2002. http://www.villagevoice.com/2002-10-08/film/they-aim-to-please/.

Holbert, R. Lance, and Glenn J. Hansen. "*Fahrenheit 9-11*, Need for Closure and the Priming of Affective Ambivalence: An Assessment of Intra-Affective Structures by Party Identification." *Human Communication Research* 32, no. 2 (2006): 109–29.

———. "Stepping beyond Message Specificity in the Study of Emotion as Mediator and Inter-Emotion Associations across Attitude Objects: *Fahrenheit 9/11*, Anger, and Debate Superiority." *Media Psychology* 11 (2008): 98–118.

Holbert, R. Lance, Glenn J. Hansen, Scott E. Caplan, and Steve Mortensen. "An Analysis of the Relative Influences of *Fahrenheit 9/11* and Presidential Debate Viewing on Shifting Confidence in President George W. Bush." *Communication Research Reports* 23, no. 3 (2006): 209–16.

———. "Presidential Debate Viewing and Michael Moore's *Fahrenheit 9/11*: A Study of Affect-as-Transfer and Passionate Reasoning." *Media Psychology* 9, no. 3 (2007): 673–94.

Holt, Patricia. "Moore Banging on Corporate Doors Again." *San Francisco Chronicle*, September 2, 1996. http://www.dogeatdogfilms.com /dtsfchrn.html.

Hornaday, Ann. "Moore's Passion Yields Dividends in 'Capitalism.'" *Washington Post*, October 2, 2009.

———. "'My, That's a Big One': Masculinity and Monstrosity in *Dirty Harry*." In *Monsters In and Among Us*, edited by Caroline J. S. Picart and Cecil Greek, 65–90. Madison, NJ: Farleigh Dickinson University Press, 2007.

Houck, Davis W. "Earl's Loins; or, Inventing Tiger Woods." In *A Companion to Sport*, edited by David L. Andrews and Ben Carrington, 564–81. Malden, MA: Wiley-Blackwell, 2013.

Houck, Davis W., and Caroline J. S. Picart. "Opening the Text: Reading Gender, Christianity, and American Intervention in Deliverance." In *The Terministic Screen: Rhetorical Perspectives on Film and Film Theory*, edited by David Blakesley, 163–89. Carbondale: Southern Illinois University Press, 2003.

Howell, Peter. "Prescription for Trouble." Review of *Sicko*. *Toronto Star*, June 29, 2007. http://www.thestar.com/news/2007/06/29/prescription _for_trouble.html/.

Hunter, Stephen. "'Sicko': Michael Moore's Anemic Checkup." Review of *Sicko*. *Washington Post*, June 29, 2007. http://www.washingtonpost.com /wp-dyn/content/article/2007/06/28/AR2007062802280.html/.

Hutcheon, Linda. *Irony's Edge*. New York: Routledge, 1995.

Isikoff, Michael, and Mark Hosenball. "Terror Watch: More Distortions from Michael Moore." Review of *Fahrenheit 9/11*. *Newsweek*, June 29, 2004.

http://www.newsweek.com/2004/06/29/terror-watch-more-distortions
-from-michael-moore.html.

Jacobson, Harlan. "Michael & Me." *Film Comment* 25, no. 6 (1989): 16–26.

Jameson, Frederic. *Postmodernism; or, The Logic of Late Capitalism.* Durham,
NC: Duke University Press, 2003.

Jamieson, Kathleen Hall, and Joseph N. Cappella. *Echo Chamber: Rush
Limbaugh and the Conservative Media Establishment.* New York: Oxford
University Press, 2008.

Jendrysik, Mark S. "The Modern Jeremiad: Bloom, Bennett, and Bork on
American Decline." *Journal of Popular Culture* 36, no. 2 (2002): 361–83.

Johannesen, Richard L. "Ronald Reagan's Economic Jeremiad." *Central States
Speech Journal* 37, no. 2 (1986): 79–89.

Johnson, Thomas C., and Edward Schiappa. "An Exploratory Study of the
Relationships between Televised Sports Viewing Habits and Conformity
to Masculine Norms." *Journal of Sports Media* 5 (2010): 53–78.

Juhasz, Alexandra, and Jesse Lerner, eds. *F Is for Phony: Fake Documentary
and Truth's Undoing.* Minneapolis: University of Minnesota Press, 2006.

Kael, Pauline. "Melodrama/Cartoon/Mess." Review of *Roger & Me. New
Yorker,* January 8, 1990.

Kaltenbach, Chris. "French Hail Their New Hero: Step Aside, Jerry
Lewis—Cannes Goes Wild for Michael Moore and His Film, 'Bowling for Columbine.'" Review of *Bowling for Columbine. Baltimore
Sun,* June 2, 2002. http://articles.baltimoresun.com/2002-06-02
/entertainment/0206010199_1_michael-moore-cannes-jerry-lewis.

Kaplan, E. Ann. *Trauma Culture: The Politics of Terror and Loss in Media and
Literature.* New Brunswick, NJ: Rutgers University Press, 2005.

Kehr, David. "'Roger & Me' Treads on Shaky Ground with Filmmaking Style."
Review of *Roger & Me. Chicago Tribune,* January 12, 1990.

Kelleher, Ed. Review of *Roger & Me." Film Journal International,* January 1990.
http://cinefiles.bampfa.berkeley.edu/cinefiles/DocDetail?docId=45740.

Kelly, Richard. Review of *Bowling for Columbine. Sight & Sound* 12, no. 11
(2002): 40.

Kennedy, Barbara M. *Deleuze and Cinema: The Aesthetics of Sensation.* Edinburgh, Scotland: Edinburgh University Press, 2000.

Kennedy, George A. *Aristotle on Rhetoric: A Theory of Civic Discourse.* 2nd
ed. New York: Oxford University Press, 2007.

Kennedy, Lisa. "'Sicko' Isn't Strong Enough for Health Care Ailment." Review of *Sicko. Denver Post,* June 28, 2007. http://www.denverpost.com
/movies/ci_6245558.

King, Larry. *Larry King Live. CNN*, July 10, 2007. http://transcripts.cnn.com /TRANSCRIPTS/0707/10/lkl.01.html.

Klawans, Stuart. Review of *Roger & Me. Nation*, January 1, 2009. http://www .thenation.com/article/roger-and-me.

Klein, Naomi. *Shock Doctrine: The Rise of Disaster Capitalism*. New York: Picador, 2007.

Knutsen, B., and E. Pettersen. "The Arts of Michael Moore and American Soft Power." *Tamara Journal for Critical Organization Inquiry* 7, no. 3–4 (2009): 107.

Kozloff, Sarah. *Invisible Storytellers: Voice-over Narration in American Fiction Film*. Berkeley: University of California Press, 1988.

Kristeva, Julia. "On the Melancholic Imaginary." *New Formations* 3 (1987): 5–18.

Labash, Matt. "Michael Moore, One-Trick Phony." *Weekly Standard*. June 8, 1998.

Lacan, Jacques. *The Ethics of Psychoanalysis, 1959–1960: The Seminar of Jacques Lacan, Book VII*. Edited by Jacques-Alain Miller. Translated by Dennis Porter. New York: W. W. Norton & Company, 1997.

Ladino, Jennifer. "Longing for Wonderland: Nostalgia for Nature in Post-Frontier America." *Iowa Journal of Cultural Studies* 5 (2004): 88–109. http: //www.uiowa.edu/~ijcs/nostalgia/ladino.htm.

Lang, Berel. "The Limits of Irony." *New Literary History* 27, no. 3 (1996): 571–88.

Lanham, Richard A. *A Handlist of Rhetorical Terms: A Guide for Students of English Literature*. Berkeley: University of California Press, 1968.

Larkin, Ralph. "The Columbine Legacy: Rampage Shootings as Political Acts." *American Behavioral Scientist* 52, no. 9 (2009): 1309–26.

Larner, Jesse. *Forgive Us Our Spins: Michael Moore and the Future of the Left*. Hoboken, NJ: J. Wiley & Sons, 2006.

LaSalle, Mick. "Need a Doctor? That's Too Bad." Review of *Sicko. San Francisco Chronicle*, June 29, 2009. http://www.sfgate.com/movies/article /Need-a-doctor-That-s-too-bad-2554436.php/.

Lasch, Christopher. "The Politics of Nostalgia." *Harper's Magazine*, November 1984, 65–70.

Lawrence, Regina G. "*Fahrenheit 9/11*." *Political Communication* 22, no. 2 (2005): 253–55.

Leonard, Elizabeth Weeks. "Teaching Health Law." *Journal of Law, Medicine & Ethics* 37, no. 1 (2009): 139.

Leverette, Marc, Brian L. Ott, and Cara Louise Buckley, eds. *It's Not TV: Watching HBO in the Post-Television Era*. New York: Routledge, 2008.

Levine, George, ed. *Aesthetics and Ideology*. New Brunswick, NJ: Rutgers University Press, 1994.

Levy, Ronald N. "You: Ready for Michael Moore?" *Public Relations Quarterly* 52, no. 1 (2007): 27–29.

Leydon, Joe. Review of *Captain Mike across America*. *Variety*, September 8, 2007. http://www.variety.com/review/VE1117934650.html?categoryid=31&cs=1&p=0.

Lowenthal, David. "Nostalgia Tells It like It Wasn't." In *The Imagined Past*, edited by Christopher Shaw and Malcolm Chase, 18–32. Manchester, UK: Manchester University Press, 1989.

Lundberg, Christian. "Enjoying God's Death: *The Passion of the Christ* and the Practices of an Evangelical Public." *Quarterly Journal of Speech* 95 (2009): 387–411.

Mackey-Kallis, Susan. "Talking Heads Rock the House: Robert Greenwald's *Uncovered: The War on Iraq*." In *The Rhetoric of the New Political Documentary*, edited by Thomas W. Benson and Brian J. Snee, 153–72. Carbondale: Southern Illinois University Press, 2008.

Mann, Bonnie. "How America Justifies Its War: A Modern/Postmodern Aesthetics of Masculinity and Sovereignty." *Hypatia* 21, no. 4 (2006): 147–63.

Marcus, Daniel. *Happy Days and Wonder Years: The Fifties and the Sixties in Contemporary Cultural Politics*. New Brunswick, NJ: Rutgers University Press, 2004.

Marx, Karl. "The Eighteenth Brumaire of Louis Bonaparte." In *Karl Marx: Surveys from Exile; Political Writings*, vol. 2, 143–249. New York: Penguin, 1973.

McCreadie, Marsha. *Documentary Superstars: How Today's Filmmakers Are Reinventing the Form*. New York: Allworth Press, 2008.

McCune, William. "Innovative Employee Communication." *Public Relations Quarterly* 36, no. 1 (1991): 7.

McGreal, Chris. "'Capitalism Is Evil . . . You Have to Eliminate It.'" *Guardian*, January 29, 2010.

McLane, Betsy A. *A New History of Documentary*. 2nd ed. New York: Continuum, 2012.

Medhurst, Martin J., and Thomas W. Benson. "*The City*: The Rhetoric of Rhythm." *Communication Monographs* 48 (1981): 54–72.

———, eds. *Rhetorical Dimensions in Media*. Dubuque, IA: Kendall/Hunt, 1984.

"Michael Moore Is a Slimeball." *News24.com*, October 14, 2004. http://www.news24.com/Content/World/Archives/USElections2004/1076/a0d9868a795f470dbb94a783694f8103/14-10-2004-10-26/Michael_Moore_is_a_slimeball (site discontinued).

Micheli, Raphaël. "Emotions as Objects of Argumentative Constructions." *Argumentation* 24, no. 1 (2010): 1–17.

Miller, Elizabeth. "Building Participation in the Outreach for the Documentary *The Water Front*." *Journal of Canadian Studies* 43, no. 1 (2009): 59–86.

Mintz, Steven. "Michael Moore and the Re-birth of the Documentary." *Film & History* 35, no. 2 (2005): 10–11.

Misiak, Anna. "Not a Stupid White Man: The Democratic Context of Michael Moore's Documentaries." *Journal of Popular Film and Television* 33, no. 3 (2005): 160–68.

Mondello, Bob. Review of *Sicko*. NPR, June 22, 2007. http://www.npr.org /templates/story/story.php?storyId=11285928.

Moore, Dinty. *The Emperor's Virtual Clothes*. Chapel Hill, NC: Algonquin Books, 1995.

"Moore Fires Oscar Anti-war Salvo." *BBC News*, March 23, 2003. http://news .bbc.co.uk/2/hi/entertainment/2879857.stm#speech.

Moore, Michael. "America Is NOT Broke." *MichaelMoore.com*, March 5, 2011. http: //www.michaelmoore.com/words/mike-friends-blog/america-is-not-broke.

———. "CNN Throws in Towel, Admits to Two Errors, and States That All 'Sicko' Facts Are True to Their Source (or Something like That) . . ." *MichaelMoore.com*, July 17, 2007. http://www.michaelmoore.com/words /mikes-letter/cnn-throws-in-towel-admits-to-two-errors-and-states-that-all -sicko-facts-are-true-to-their-source-or-something-like-that.

———. *Downsize This! Random Threats from an Unarmed American*. New York: Harper, 1997.

———. *The Official "Fahrenheit 9/11" Reader*. New York: Simon & Schuster, 2004.

———. *Here Comes Trouble: Stories from My Life*. New York: Grand Central Publishing, 2011.

———. "Putting It on the Line." *Journal of Aesthetic Education* 41, no. 1 (2007): 62–73.

———. *Sicko*. DVD. New York: Weinstein Company, 2007.

———. *Slacker Uprising*. DVD. Culver City, CA: Brave New Films, 2008.

Morgenstern, Joe. "Pixar Cooks with Joy, Inventiveness in 'Ratatouille,' a Comic Tour De Force; 'Sicko' Is Political Theater with Some Blind Spots." Review of *Sicko*. *Wall Street Journal*, June 29, 2007. http://online.wsj.com /news/articles/SB118307125242752135.

Mulshine, Paul. "A Stupid White Man and a Smart One." *Newark Star Ledger*, March 30, 2003.

Murfin, Ross, and Supryia M. Ray. *The Bedford Glossary of Critical and Literary Terms*. Boston: Bedford Books, 1997.

Bibliography

Murphy, Andrew R. "Longing, Nostalgia, and Golden Age Politics: The American Jeremiad and the Power of the Past." *Perspectives on Politics* 7, no. 1 (2009): 125–41.

Murphy, John M. "'A Time of Shame and Sorrow': Robert F. Kennedy and the American Jeremiad." *Quarterly Journal of Speech* 76 (1990): 401–14.

Muschert, Glenn W. "Frame-Changing in the Media Coverage of a School Shooting: The Rise of Columbine as a National Concern." *Social Science Journal* 46 (2009): 164–70.

Musser, Charles. "Film Truth in the Age of George W. Bush." *Framework: The Journal of Cinema and Media* 48, no. 2 (2007): 9–35.

———. "Truth and Rhetoric in Michael Moore's *Fahrenheit 9/11*." In *Michael Moore: Filmmaker, Newsmaker, Cultural Icon*, edited by Matthew H. Bernstein, 167–201. Ann Arbor: University of Michigan Press, 2010.

Neal, Arthur G. *National Trauma and Collective Memory: Extraordinary Events in the American Experience*. 2nd ed. New York: M. E. Sharpe, 2005.

Ness, Richard R. "Prelude to Moore: A Comparison of Rhetorical Techniques in Frank Capra's *Why We Fight* Series and Michael Moore's *Fahrenheit 9/11*." In *Michael Moore: Filmmaker, Newsmaker, Cultural Icon*, edited by Matthew H. Bernstein, 149–66. Ann Arbor: University of Michigan Press, 2010.

Nesselson, Lisa. Review of *Bowling for Columbine*. *Variety*, May 16, 2002. https://variety.com/2002/film/reviews/bowling-for-columbine-1200549676/.

Newman, Bruce. Review of *Sicko*. *San Jose Mercury News*, June 28, 2007. http://www.mercurynews.com/movies/ci_6252211.

Nichols, Bill. "History, Myth, and Narrative in Documentary." *Film Quarterly* 41 (Fall 1987): 9–20.

———. *Introduction to Documentary*. Bloomington: Indiana University Press, 2001.

———. "Questions of Magnitude." In *Documentary and the Mass Media*, edited by John Corner, 107–24. Baltimore: Edward Arnold, 1986.

———. *Representing Reality: Issues and Concepts in Documentary*. Bloomington: Indiana University Press, 1991.

———. "The Voice of Documentary." In *Movies and Methods*, vol. 2, edited by Bill Nichols, 258–73. Berkeley: University of California Press, 1985.

———. "What Current Documentaries Do and Can't Do." *Velvet Light Trap* 60 (2007): 85–86.

Normand, Carrey. "Agit-Doc." *Canadian Medical Association Journal* 171, no. 6 (2004): 617.

Nussbaum, Martha. *Political Emotions: Why Love Matters for Justice.* Cambridge, MA: Belknap Press of Harvard University Press, 2013.

Oberacker, Jon Scott. "The People and Me: Michael Moore and the Politics of Political Documentary." PhD diss., University of Massachusetts, 2009. http://scholarworks.umass.edu/cgi/viewcontent.cgi?article=1061&context=open_access_dissertations.

———. "The Reel Deal: Michael Moore, Political Documentary and the Discourse of Celebrity." *Celebrity Studies* 1, no. 2 (2010): 170–88.

Ordoñez-Jasis, Rosarion, and Pablo Jasis. "*Bowling for Columbine*: Critically Interrogating the Industry of Fear." *Social Justice* 30 (2003): 127–33.

O'Reilly, Bill. "Rank Propaganda." Review of *Fahrenheit 9/11. Chicago Sun-Times,* June 29, 2004.

Orgeron, Marsha, and Devin Orgeron. "Familial Pursuits, Editorial Acts: Documentaries after the Age of Home Video." *Velvet Light Trap* 60 (2007): 47–62.

Orvell, Miles. *After the Machine: Visual Arts and the Erasing of Cultural Boundaries.* Jackson: University Press of Mississippi, 1995.

———. "Documentary Film and the Power of Interrogation." *Film Quarterly* 48, no. 2 (1994): 10.

———. "Documentary Film and the Power of Interrogation: *American Dream* and *Roger & Me.*" In *Michael Moore: Filmmaker, Newsmaker, Cultural Icon,* edited by Matthew H. Bernstein, 127–40. Ann Arbor: University of Michigan Press, 2010.

Osborn, Michael. "Rhetorical Depiction." In *Form, Genre, and the Study of Political Discourse,* edited by Herbert W. Simons and Aram A. Aghazarian, 79–107. Columbia: University of South Carolina Press, 1986.

O'Shaughnessy, Nicholas J., and Stephan C. Henneberg. "The Selling of the President 2004: A Marketing Perspective." *Journal of Public Affairs* 7 (2007): 249–68.

Ott, Brian L. "'I'm Bart Simpson, Who the Hell Are You?' A Study in Postmodern Identity (Re)Construction." *Journal of Popular Culture* 37, no. 1 (2003): 56–82.

———. "Memorializing the Holocaust: *Schindler's List* and Public Memory." *Review of Education/Pedagogy/Cultural Studies* 18, no. 4 (1996): 443–57. doi:10.1080/1071441960180409.

———. "'Oh My God, They Digitized Kenny!' Travels in the *South Park* Cybercommunity v4.0." In *Prime Time Animation: Television Animation and American Culture,* edited by Carol A. Stabile and Mark Harrison, 220–42. New York: Routledge, 2003.

———. "The Pleasures of *South Park* (An Experiment in Media Erotics)." In *Taking "South Park" Seriously*, edited by Jeffrey Andrew Weinstock, 39–58. Albany: State University of New York Press, 2008.

———. "(Re)Framing Fear: Equipment for Living in a Post-9/11 World." In *Cylons in America: Critical Studies in "Battlestar Galactica,"* edited by Tiffany Potter and C. W. Marshall, 13–26. New York: Continuum, 2008.

———. "(Re)Locating Pleasure in Media Studies: Toward an Erotics of Reading." *Communication and Critical/Cultural Studies* 1, no. 2 (2004): 194–212.

———. *The Small Screen: How Television Equips Us to Live in the Information Age.* Malden, MA: Wiley-Blackwell, 2007.

———. "Television as Lover, Part I: Writing Dirty Theory." *Cultural Studies <=> Critical Methodologies* 7, no. 1 (2007): 26–47. doi:10.1177/1532708606288650.

———. "Television as Lover, Part II: Doing Auto[Erotic]Ethnography." *Cultural Studies <=> Critical Methodologies* 7, no. 3 (2007): 294–307. doi:10.1177/1532708606290843.

———. "Unnecessary Roughness: ESPN's Construction of Hypermasculine Citizenship in the Penn State Sex Abuse Scandal." *Cultural Studies <=> Critical Methodologies* 12, no. 4 (2012): 332–34.

———. "The Visceral Politics of *V for Vendetta*: On Political Affect in Cinema." *Critical Studies in Media Communication* 27, no. 1 (2010): 32–47. doi:10.1080/15295030903554359.

Ott, Brian L., and Eric Aoki. "The Colonization and Commodification of Racial Identities: Stereotyping and Exoticizing Cultural Difference in *Rush Hour*." In *Pop Perspectives: Readings to Critique Contemporary Culture*, edited by Laura Gray-Rosendale, 513–20. New York: McGraw-Hill, 2007.

———. "Counter-imagination as Interpretive Practice: Futuristic Fantasy and *The Fifth Element*." *Women's Studies in Communication* 27, no. 2 (2004): 149–76.

———. "The Politics of Negotiating Public Tragedy: Media Framing of the Matthew Shepard Murder." *Rhetoric and Public Affairs* 5, no. 3 (2002): 483–505.

———. "Popular Imagination and Identity Politics: Reading the Future in *Star Trek: The Next Generation*." *Western Journal of Communication* 65, no. 4 (2001): 392–415.

Ott, Brian L., and Beth Bonnstetter. "'We're at Now, Now': *Spaceballs* as Parodic Tourism." *Southern Journal of Communication* 72, no. 4 (2007): 309–27.

Ott, Brian L., and Carl Burgchardt. "On Critical-Rhetorical Pedagogy: Dialoging with *Schindler's List*." *Western Journal of Communication* 77, no. 1 (2013): 14–33.

Ott, Brian L., and Greg Dickinson. "Visual Rhetoric and/as Critical Pedagogy." In *The SAGE Handbook of Rhetorical Studies*, edited by Andrea Lunsford, 391–405. Thousand Oaks, CA: Sage, 2009.

Ott, Brian L., and Diane Marie Keeling. "Cinema and Choric Connection: *Lost in Translation* as Sensual Experience." *Quarterly Journal of Speech* 97, no. 4 (2011): 363–86.

———. "Transborder Politics: The Embodied Call of Conscience in *Traffic*." In *Border Rhetorics: Charting Enactments of Citizenship and Identity on the US-Mexico Frontier*, edited by D. Robert DeChaine, 181–96. Tuscaloosa: University of Alabama Press, 2012.

Ott, Brian L., and Gordana Lazić. "The Pedagogy and Politics of Art in Postmodernity: Cognitive Mapping and *The Bothersome Man*." *Quarterly Journal of Speech* 99, no. 3 (2013): 259–82.

Ott, Brian L., and Robert L. Mack. *Critical Media Studies: An Introduction*. 2nd ed. Malden, MA: Wiley-Blackwell, 2014.

Ott, Brian L., and Cameron Walter. "Intertextuality: Interpretive Practice and Textual Strategy." *Critical Studies in Media Communication* 17, no. 4 (2000): 429–46.

Parry-Giles, Shawn J., and Trevor Parry-Giles. "Collective Memory, Political Nostalgia, and the Rhetorical Presidency: Bill Clinton's Commemoration of the March on Washington, August 28, 1998." *Quarterly Journal of Speech* 86 (2000): 417–37.

———. "Virtual Realism and the Limits of Commodified Dissent in *Fahrenheit 9/11*." In *The Rhetoric of the New Political Documentary*, edited by Thomas W. Benson and Brian J. Snee, 24–53. Carbondale: Southern Illinois University Press, 2008.

Patterson, Alex. "Putting a Face on the Enemy." Review of *Roger & Me. Village Voice*, September 26, 1989.

Pepi, Leistyna. "Exposing the Ruling Class in the United States Using Television and Documentary Film." *Radical Teacher* 85 (2009): 12–15.

Pereboom, Maarten, and John E. O'Connor. "Michael Moore: Cinematic Historian or Propagandist? A Historians Film Committee Panel Presented at the 2005 American Historical Association Meeting." *Film & History* 35, no. 2 (2005): 7–16.

Peters, Tom. *Thriving on Chaos: Handbook for a Management Revolution*. New York: HarperCollins, 1988.

Phillips, K. R., ed. *Framing Public Memory*. Tuscaloosa: University of Alabama Press, 2004.

Plantinga, Carl. *Rhetoric and Representation in Nonfiction Film.* New York: Cambridge University Press, 1997.

———. "Roger and History and Irony and Me." *Michigan Academician* 24, no. 3 (1992): 511–20.

Poindexter, Mark. "Art Objects: The Works of Michael Moore and Peter Watkins." *Journal of Popular Culture* 44, no. 6 (2011): 1268–88.

Potter, Wendell. *Deadly Spin: An Insurance Company Insider Speaks Out on How Corporate PR Is Killing Health Care and Deceiving Americans.* New York: Bloomsbury Press, 2010.

———. Interview by Amy Goodman. *Democracy Now,* November 17, 2010. http://www.democracynow.org/2010/11/17/push_michael_moore_off_a_cliff.

Poulakos, John, and Steve Whitson. "Rhetoric Denuded and Redressed: Figs and Figures." *Quarterly Journal of Speech* 81 (1995): 378–85.

Prelli, Lawrence J., ed. *Rhetorics of Display.* Columbia: University of South Carolina Press, 2006.

Puig, Claudia. "'Capitalism' Markets in Impassioned Outrage." Review of *Capitalism: A Love Story. USA Today,* September 24, 2009.

———. "Moore Wields a Sharp Scalpel in Ambitious 'Sicko.'" Review of *Sicko. USA Today,* June 22, 2007. http://usatoday30.usatoday.com/life/movies/reviews/2007-06-21-sicko_N.htm.

Quinn, Arthur. *Figures of Speech: 60 Ways to Turn a Phrase.* Salt Lake City: G. M. Smith, 1982.

Rabinowitz, Paula. "Sentimental Contracts: Dreams and Documents of American Labor." In *Feminism and Documentary,* edited by Diane Waldman and Janet Walker, 43–63 (Minneapolis: University of Minnesota Press, 1999). *They Must Be Represented: The Politics of Documentary.* New York: Verso, 1994.

Rainer, Peter. "Film Maker Michael Moore Takes on Roger Smith and His Giant Corporation in Cutting Satire." Review of *Roger & Me. Los Angeles Times,* December 20, 1989. Reprinted at *Dog Eat Dog Films,* http://dogeatdog.michaelmoore.com/rainer.html, accessed February 2, 2011.

Rapoport, Roger. *Citizen Moore: The Life and Times of an American Iconoclast.* Berkeley, CA: RDR Books, 2007.

Rascaroli, Laura. "The Essay Film: Problems, Definitions, Textual Commitments." *Framework: The Journal of Cinema and Media* 49, no. 2 (2008): 24–47.

Reinhardt, Uwe. "Getting America to Take the Shame." *British Medical Journal* 335, no. 7611 (2007): 128.

Renov, Michael. *The Subject of Documentary*. Minneapolis: University of Minnesota Press, 2004.

———. *Theorizing Documentary*. AFI Film Readers. New York: Routledge, 1993.

Rich, B. Ruby. "Documentary Disciplines: An Introduction." *Cinema Journal* 46, no. 1 (2006): 108–15.

Richards, Jonathan F. "Sicko: Documentary." Review of *Sicko*. *Film-Freak.be*, July 15, 2007. http://www.filmfreak.be/index.php?module =filmfreak&func=viewpub&tid=9&pid=424&title=Sicko.

Rickey, Carrie. "Fire Starter: Filmmaker Michael Moore Lobs Grenades at President Bush with 'Fahrenheit 911,' Accusing Him of Putting War Contractors before US Soldiers." Review of *Fahrenheit 9/11*. *Philadelphia Inquirer*, June 20, 2004.

Ritter, Kurt W. "American Political Rhetoric and the Jeremiad Tradition: Presidential Nomination Acceptance Addresses, 1960–1976." *Central States Speech Journal* 31 (1980): 153–71.

Rizzo, Sergio. "Why Less Is Still Moore." *Film Quarterly* 59, no. 2 (2005): 32–39.

Rollins, Peter C. "AHA for 2005: Seattle, January 6–9, 2005." *Film & History* 34, no. 2 (2004): 4–5.

Roscoe, Jane, and Craig Hight. *Faking It: Mock-Documentary and the Subversion of Factuality*. Manchester, UK: Manchester University Press, 2001.

Rosenbaum, Jonathan. "Nihilism for the Masses [ROGER & ME]." On Rosenbaum's website, February 2, 1990. http://www.jonathanrosenbaum.net /1990/02/nihilism-for-the-masses/.

Rosenberg, Sharon. "Neither Forgotten nor Fully Remembered: Tracing an Ambivalent Public Memory on the 10th Anniversary of the Montréal Massacre." *Feminist Theory* 4, no. 1 (2003): 5–27.

Ross, Christine. *The Aesthetics of Disengagement: Contemporary Art and Depression*. Minneapolis: University of Minnesota Press, 2006.

Rosteck, Thomas. "The Intertextuality of the Man from Hope: Bill Clinton as Person? Bill Clinton as Persona? Bill Clinton as Star?" In *On Stump, State and Stage: Bill Clinton and Political Communication*, edited by Stephen A. Smith, 223–48. Fayetteville: University of Arkansas Press.

———. *"See It Now" Confronts McCarthyism: Television Documentary and the Politics of Representation*. Tuscaloosa: University of Alabama Press, 1994.

———. "Synecdoche and Audience in *See It Now*'s 'The Case of Milo Radulovich.'" *Southern Communication Journal* 57 (1992): 229–40.

Rosteck, Thomas, and Thomas S. Frentz, "Myth and Multiple Readings in Environmental Rhetoric: The Case of *An Inconvenient Truth*." *Quarterly Journal of Speech*. 95, no. 1 (2009): 1–20.

Rothman, William. *Documentary Film Classics*. Cambridge, UK: Cambridge University Press, 1997.

Rotten Tomatoes. Reviews of *Sicko*. Accessed August 16, 2011. http://www.rottentomatoes.com/m/sicko/.

Rowe, Chip. "A Funny, Subversive '60 Minutes.'" *American Journalism Review* 17, no. 6 (1995): 13.

Rushing, Janice Hocker, and Thomas S. Frentz. "'The Deer Hunter': Rhetoric of the Warrior." *Quarterly Journal of Speech* 66 (1980): 392–406.

———. "The Frankenstein Myth in Contemporary Cinema." *Critical Studies in Mass Communication* 6 (1989): 61–80.

———. "Integrating Ideology and Archetype in Rhetorical Criticism." *Quarterly Journal of Speech* 77 (1991): 385–406.

———. *Projecting the Shadow: The Cyborg Hero in American Film*. Chicago: University of Chicago Press, 1995.

———. "The Rhetoric of 'Rocky': A Social Value Model of Criticism." *Western Journal of Speech Communication* 42 (1978): 63–72.

———. "Singing over the Bones: James Cameron's *Titanic*." *Critical Studies in Mass Communication* 17 (March 2000): 1–27.

Santesso, Aaron. *A Careful Longing: The Poetics and Problems of Nostalgia*. Newark: University of Delaware Press, 2006.

Sarris, Andrew. "License to Ill." Review of *Sicko*. *New York Observer*, July 17, 2007. http://observer.com/2007/07/license-to-ill/.

Scanlan, Sean. "Introduction: Nostalgia." *Iowa Journal of Cultural Studies* 5 (2009): 3–9. http://www.uiowa.edu/~ijcs/nostalgia/nostint.htm.

Schiappa, Edward. *Beyond Representational Correctness: Rethinking Criticism of Popular Media*. Albany: State University of New York Press, 2008.

———. *Defining Reality: Definitions and the Politics of Meaning*. Carbondale: Southern Illinois University Press, 2003.

Schiappa, Edward, Mike Allen, and Peter Gregg. "Parasocial Relationships and Television: A Meta-analysis of the Effects." In *Mass Media Effects: Advances Through Meta-analysis*, edited by Ray Preiss, Barbara Gayle, Nancy Burrell, Mike Allen, and Jennings Bryant, 301–14. Mahwah, NJ: Lawrence Erlbaum, 2007.

Schiappa, Edward, Peter B. Gregg, and Dean E. Hewes. "Can a Television Series Change Attitudes about Death? A Study of College Students and *Six Feet Under*." *Death Studies* 28 (2004): 459–74.

———. "Can One TV Show Make a Difference? *Will & Grace* and the Parasocial Contact Hypothesis." *Journal of Homosexuality* 51 (2006): 15–37.

——. "The Parasocial Contact Hypothesis." *Communication Monographs* 72 (2005): 95–118.

Schiappa, Edward, and Emanuelle Wessels. "Listening to Audiences: A Brief Rationale & History of Audience Research in Popular Media Studies." *International Journal of Listening* 21 (2007): 14–23.

Schultz, Emily. *Michael Moore: A Biography*. Toronto: ECW Press, 2005.

Schwarzbaum, Lisa. Review of *Sicko*. *Entertainment Weekly*, June 29, 2007. http://www.ew.com/ew/article/0,,20044198,00.html/.

Scott, A. O. "Unruly Scorn Leaves Room for Restraint, but Not a Lot." Review of *Fahrenheit 9/11*. *New York Times*, June 23, 2004.

Scott, Bijana. "Picturing Irony: The Subversive Power of Photography." *Visual Communication* 3, no. 1 (2004): 31–59.

Secor, Anna J. "*Fahrenheit 9/11*: War, Fantasy, and Society." *Environment & Planning: Society & Space* 22 (2004): 919–23.

Sennett, Richard. *The Culture of the New Capitalism*. New Haven, CT: Yale University Press, 2006.

——. *The Fall of Public Man*. New York: Alfred Knopf, 1977.

Sharrett, Christopher, and William Luhr. Review of *Bowling for Columbine*. *Cineaste* 28, no. 2 (2003): 36–38.

Sicher, Efraim, and Natalia Skradol. "A World Neither Brave nor New: Reading Dystopian Fiction after 9/11." *Partial Answers: Journal of Literature and the History of Ideas* 4, no. 1 (2006): 151–79.

Silverstone, Roger. *The Message of Television: Myth and Narrative in Contemporary Culture*. London: Heinemann, 1981.

"Small and Large Acts of Resistance—Ann Sparanese." *Library Journal*, March 15, 2003. Accessed July 28, 2011. http://www.libraryjournal.com /article/CA281662.html.

Smith, Kimberly K. "Mere Nostalgia: Notes on a Progressive Paratheory." *Rhetoric and Public Affairs* 3 (2000): 505–27.

Snee, Brian J. "Free Guns and Speech Control: The Structural and Thematic Rhetoric of *Bowling for Columbine*." In *Visual Communication: Perception, Rhetoric, and Technology*, edited by Diane S. Hope, 193–209. Cresskill, NJ: Hampton Press, 2006.

Sontag, Susan. *Regarding the Pain of Others*. New York: Farrar, Straus and Giroux, 2003.

Spence, Louise, and Vinicius Navarro. *Crafting Truth: Documentary Form and Meaning*. New Brunswick, NJ: Rutgers University Press, 2011.

Spencer, J. William, and Glenn W. Muschert. "The Contested Meaning of the Crosses at Columbine." *American Behavioral Scientist* 52 (2009): 1371–86.

Spengler, Christine. *Screening Nostalgia: Populuxe Props and Technicolor Aesthetics in Contemporary American Film.* New York: Berghahn Books, 2009.

Sragow, Michael. "Roger and the Demagogue." Review of *Roger & Me. San Francisco Examiner,* January 12, 1990.

Stam, Robert, and Ella Shohat. "Variations on an Anti-American Theme." *CR: The New Centennial Review* 5, no. 1 (2005): 141–78.

Steele, Brent J. "Irony, Emotions and Critical Distance." *Millennium: Journal of International Studies* 39, no. 1 (2010): 89–107.

Sterritt, David. "George W. and Me." Review of *Fahrenheit 9/11. Christian Science Monitor,* June 25, 2004.

Stevens, Dana. "Sick Joke: Michael Moore Gathers Our Rage at America's Health-Care System." Review of *Sicko. Slate,* June 29, 2007. http://www.unz.org/Pub/Slate-2007jun-00312.

Stewart, Susan. *On Longing: Narratives of the Miniature, the Gigantic, the Souvenir, the Collection.* Durham, NC: Duke University Press, 1993.

Stromer-Galley, Jennifer, and Edward Schiappa. "The Argumentative Burdens of Audience Conjectures: Audience Research in Popular Culture Criticism." *Communication Theory* 8 (1998): 27–62.

Stroud, Natalie Jomini. *Niche News: The Politics of News Choice.* Oxford, UK: Oxford University Press, 2011.

Stuckey, Mary E. "Review of *Michael Moore's "Fahrenheit 9/11": How One Film Divided a Nation.*" *Journal of American History* 93, no. 4 (2007): 1327.

Tanner, Michael. "*Sicko*: Michael Moore's Latest Fantasy." *IPA Review* 59, no. 2 (2007): 21.

Tannock, Stuart. "Nostalgia Critique." *Cultural Studies* 9 (1995): 453–64.

Tavcar, Larry. "Public Relations on the Screen: 17 Films to See." *Public Relations Quarterly* 38, no. 3 (1993): 21–23.

Terry, Valerie, and Edward Schiappa. "Disclosing Anti-feminism in Michael Crichton's Post-feminist *Disclosure.*" *Journal of Communication Inquiry* 23 (1999): 69–89.

Tetzlaff, David. "Dystopia Now: *Fahrenheit 9/11*'s Red Pill." In *Michael Moore: Filmmaker, Newsmaker, Cultural Icon,* edited by Matthew H. Bernstein, 202–21. Ann Arbor: University of Michigan Press, 2010.

Tibbetts, John C. "An Interview with Michael Moore." *Film & History* 34, no. 2 (2004): 86–88.

Tobias, Scott. Review of *Slacker Uprising. A.V. Club.* Accessed June 15, 2010. http://www.avclub.com/articles/slacker-uprising,2763/.

Tonn, Mari Boor. "The Rhetorical Personae of Mary Harris 'Mother' Jones: Industrial Labor's Maternal Prophet." PhD diss., University of Kansas, 1987.

Toplin, Robert Brent. "Fahrenheit 9/11." *Journal of American History* 91, no. 3 (2004): 1146.

———. "The Long Battle over *Fahrenheit 9/11*: A Matter of Politics, Not Aesthetics." *Film & History* 35, no. 2 (2005): 8–10.

———. *Michael Moore's "Fahrenheit 9/11": How One Film Divided a Nation.* Lawrence: University Press of Kansas, 2006.

Trilling, Lionel. *The Liberal Imagination.* 1950. Reprint, New York: New York Review of Books, 2008.

Trudeau, Garry. "Sneakers in Tinseltown." *Time*, April 20, 1998.

Turan, Kenneth. "Moore Fun and Commentary in 'Big One.'" Review of *The Big One*. *Los Angeles Times*, April 10, 1998.

Tyler, Josh. Review of *Slacker Uprising. Cinema Blend*, 2008. Accessed June 15, 2010. http://www.cinemablend.com/dvds/Slacker-Uprising-3375.html.

Uchitelle, Louis. *The Disposable American: Layoffs and Their Consequences.* New York: Vintage, 2007.

Urban, Hugh B. "The Secrets of the Kingdom: Spiritual Discourse and Material Interests in the Bush Administration." *Discourse* 27, no. 1 (2005): 141–65.

Vogels, Jonathan B. *The Direct Cinema of David and Albert Maysles.* Carbondale: Southern Illinois University Press, 2005.

Von Burg, Ron, and Paul E. Johnson. "Yearning for a Past That Never Was: Baseball, Steroids, and the Anxiety of the American Dream." *Critical Studies in Media Communication* 26 (2009): 351–71.

Waak, Erika. "*Bowling for Columbine*: Are We a Nation of Gun Nuts or Are We Just Nuts?" Review of *Bowling for Columbine. Humanist* 63, no. 2 (2003): 41.

Walker, Janet. "Moving Testimonies: Documentary, 'Truth,' and Reconciliation." *Velvet Light Trap* 60 (2007): 87–88.

Walker, Jesse. "Let the Viewer Decide." *Reason*, December 2007. http://reason.com/archives/2007/11/16/let-the-viewer-decide.

Walters, Ben. Review of *Slacker Uprising. Guardian*, September 23, 2008. http://www.guardian.co.uk/film/2008/sep/23/review.slackeruprising.

Wanner, Kevin J. "'Lord Help Us': Religion in Michael Moore's *Fahrenheit 9/11*." *Method & Theory in the Study of Religion* 18 (2006): 166–78.

Warren, Charles, ed. *Beyond Document: Essays on Nonfiction Film.* Hanover, NH: University Press of New England, 1996.

Waugh, Thomas. *The Right to Play Oneself: Looking Back on Documentary Film.* Minneapolis: University of Minnesota Press, 2011.

———, ed. *"Show Us Life": Toward a History and Aesthetics of the Committed Documentary.* Metuchen, NJ: Scarecrow Press, 1984.

Weber, Cynthia. "*Fahrenheit 9/11*: The Temperature Where Morality Burns." *Journal of American Studies* 40, no. 1 (2006): 113–31.

Wehmeyer, Jim. "Critical Media Studies and the North American Media Literacy Movement." *Cinema Journal* 39, no. 4 (2000): 94–101.

Weinberger, Seth. "The Corporation, Directed and Produced." *Political Communication* 23, no. 2 (2006): 250–52.

White, Hayden. *Metahistory: The Historical Imagination in Nineteenth-Century Europe*. Baltimore: Johns Hopkins University Press, 1973.

———. "The Value of Narrativity in the Representation of Reality." In *On Narrative*, edited by W. J. T. Mitchell, 1–23. Chicago: University of Chicago Press, 1981.

White, Jerry. "Documentaries and Scenarios." *Velvet Light Trap* 60 (2007): 88–90.

Wigley, Shelley, and Michael Pfau. "Arguing with Emotion: A Closer Look at Affect and the Inoculation Process." *Communication Research Reports* 27, no. 3 (2010): 217–29. doi:10.1080/08824091003737901.

Williams, Joe. "'Fahrenheit 9/11' Goes to War against Bush." Review of *Fahrenheit 9/11*. *St. Louis Post-Dispatch*, June 25, 2004.

Williams, Linda. "Mirrors without Memories: Truth, History, and the New Documentary." *Film Quarterly* 46, no. 3 (1993): 9–21.

Wilshire, Peter. "Presentation and Representation in Michael Moore's *Bowling for Columbine*." *Australian Screen Education* 35 (Winter 2004): 91–95.

Winstead, Antoinette. "Review of *Michael Moore's "Fahrenheit 9/11": How One Film Divided a Nation*, by Robert Brent Toplin." *Film & History* 37, no. 1 (2007): 92.

Winston, Brian. *Claiming the Real II: Documentary; Grierson and Beyond*. 2nd ed. London: British Film Institute, 2008.

———. *Lies, Damn Lies, and Documentaries*. London: British Film Institute, 2000.

Wood, James A. "An Application of Rhetorical Theory to Filmic Persuasion." PhD diss., Cornell University, 1967. ProQuest (AAT 6800681).

Woodward, Kathleen. *Statistical Panic: Cultural Politics and Poetics of the Emotions*. Durham, NC: Duke University Press, 2009.

Zacharek, Stephanie. Review of *Sicko*. *Salon*, June 22, 2007. http://www.salon.com/2007/06/22/sicko/.

Zimmerman, Patricia Rodden. *States of Emergency: Documentaries, Wars, Democracies*. Minneapolis: University of Minnesota Press, 2000.

Contributors

Thomas W. Benson is the Edwin Erle Sparks Professor of Rhetoric at Pennsylvania State University. He is a former editor of the *Quarterly Journal of Speech*, *Communication Quarterly*, and *Review of Communication*, and the winner of the Distinguished Scholar Award of the National Communication Association. He is the author or editor of several books, including *Reality Fictions: The Films of Frederick Wiseman* (with Carolyn Anderson); *American Rhetoric in the New Deal Era, 1932–1945*; *Writing JFK: Presidential Rhetoric and the Press in the Bay of Pigs Crisis*; and *The Rhetoric of the New Political Documentary* (with Brian Snee).

Jennifer L. Borda is an associate professor of communication at the University of New Hampshire. Her research emphasizes the intersection of rhetorical scholarship, feminist studies, and media criticism. Her scholarship has appeared in various journals, including *Text and Performance Quarterly*, *Communication Quarterly*, *Feminist Media Studies*, and *Women's Studies in Communication*. She is the author of *Women Labor Activists in the Movies: Nine Depictions of Workplace Organizers, 1954–2005*.

Joseph Delbert Davenport is the director of digital media for Flip Learning and has developed documentaries, advocacy films, and educational videos. An Emmy-winning illustrator, animator, writer, and filmmaker, he has produced and edited documentaries for public television, short films about conservation, videos for Florida nonprofits, and Flip Learning's digital assets.

Thomas S. Frentz is a professor of communication at the University of Arkansas, Fayetteville. His research covers a range of issues in rhetorical studies, including the rhetoric of fiction and nonfiction film. In addition to authoring thirty scholarly articles, he is the author or coauthor of three books, including *Projecting the Shadow: The Cyborg Hero in American Film*.

Peter B. Gregg is a senior lecturer at the University of Minnesota. His research interests include media influence and the history of television. His research has appeared in *Communication Monographs, Journal of Popular Culture, Journal of Homosexuality*, and *Death Studies*. He is a cocreator of the online series *Forsythia*.

Christine Harold is an associate professor in the Department of Communication at the University of Washington, Seattle. Her work focuses on the relationship among commercial culture, rhetoric, and the possibilities for political engagement within contemporary capitalism. Her book *OurSpace: Resisting the Corporate Control of Culture* examines culture jamming as a response to corporate power. Harold's current research considers the environmental and ethical implications of the design, manufacture, and consumption of commercial products.

Daniel Ladislau Horvath is a lecturer at California State University, Stanislaus. His research interests lie at the intersection of rhetoric and continental philosophy. His work has appeared in *Sex Roles*.

Davis W. Houck is a professor in the School of Communication at Florida State University. He has authored several books on the American civil rights movement, including *Emmett Till and the Mississippi Press* (with Matthew A. Grindy) and *Women and the Civil Rights Movement, 1954–1965* (with David E. Dixon). His earlier scholarship focused on American presidential rhetoric and includes *Rhetoric as Currency: Hoover, Roosevelt, and the Great Depression*, which won the 2002 Marie Hochmuth Nichols Prize for the best book in American public address.

Brian L. Ott is a professor of rhetoric and media studies at the University of Colorado, Denver. He studies the rhetoric of film, television, and museums. His articles have appeared in numerous journals, including *Critical Studies in Media Communication, Rhetoric and Public Affairs*, and the *Quarterly Journal of Speech*. He is the author of *The Small Screen: How Television Equips Us to Live in the Information Age* and a coeditor of *It's Not TV: Watching HBO in the Post-Television Era* and *Places of Public Memory: The Rhetoric of Museums and Memorials*.

Kendall R. Phillips is a professor of communication and rhetorical studies and the associate dean for research and graduate studies in the College of Visual and Performing Arts at Syracuse University. His research addresses rhetoric, public discourse, and popular film and culture, and it has appeared in numerous rhetoric and film journals. He is the author of *Projected Fears: Horror Films and American Culture* and *Controversial Cinema: The Films That Outraged America*, as well as the editor of *Framing Public Memory*.

Thomas Rosteck is an associate professor of communication at the University of Arkansas, Fayetteville. His research has been published in the *Quarterly Journal of Speech, Southern Communication Journal, Journal of Communication Studies*, and *Western Journal of Communication*. He is the author of *"See It Now" Confronts McCarthyism: Television Documentary and the Politics of Representation*.

Edward Schiappa is a professor and the head of comparative media studies and writing at the Massachusetts Institute of Technology, where he holds the John E. Burchard Chair of Humanities. He conducts research in argumentation, media influence, and rhetorical theory. Schiappa's numerous books include *Beyond Representational Correctness: Rethinking Criticism of Popular Media* and *Defining Reality: Definitions and the Politics of Meaning*. His research has appeared in such journals as *Philosophy and Rhetoric, Quarterly Journal of Speech, Rhetoric Review, Argumentation, Communication Monographs*, and *Communication Theory*.

Susan A. Sci is an assistant professor of communication and the director of communication-intensive courses at Regis University in Denver. Her research spans four general areas of interest: rhetoric, media, affect, and argumentation. More specifically, her work focuses on the rhetorical and affective dimensions of memes, video games, and social controversy. Her work has been published in *Culture, Theory and Critique* and the *Northwest Journal of Communication*.

Brian J. Snee is an associate professor and the chair of the Department of Communication Studies at Manhattanville College. His research is in the rhetoric of film and media and has appeared in such journals as *Communication Quarterly, Literature/Film Quarterly*, and the *Journal of Media and Religion*. He is a coeditor of *The Rhetoric of the New Political Documentary*.

Index

Italicized page numbers indicate figures.